M000209011

Cover Artist: Mr. John Clopton

International Standard Book Number
#0-9648181-1-6

Manufactured in the United States of America
(Self-Help/Spirituality/Black Studies $14.95)

First Printing, November 1996
Second Printing, June 1997
Third Printing, April 1998
Fourth Printing, December 1998

Published By:
Nia Communications/Press
P.O. Box 724742 • Atlanta, GA • 31139-1742

Toll-Free Order Line 1-888-244-5770
w h o l e s a l e   &   r e t a i l   b o o k s e l l e r s

Nia Comm./Press
" c o m m u n i c a t i n g   w i t h   a   p u r p o s e "

Other Books By Author
Currently in Print

---

1. **"There are only Two Religions in the Whole World"**
   Religious Confusion vs. The Black Spiritual Rise
   Akil (80 pgs. Nia Comm./Press $7.95)

2. 12-Lessons To Restore The Image,
   The Character, & The Responsibility of:
   "The Goddess Blackwoman"
   Akil (170 pgs. Nia Comm./Press $12.95)

3. **"From Niggas to Gods Pt. 1"**
   Akil (250 pgs. Nia Comm./Press $12.95)

Nia Comm./Press
" c o m m u n i c a t i n g   w i t h   a   p u r p o s e "

50 Other Relevant Books

Incomplete Listing

1. **Stolen Legacy**
   George G.M. James

2. **African Orgin of Biological Psychiatry**
   Dr. Richard King

3. **Our Saviour Has Arrived**
   Hon. Elijah Muhammad

4. **African Heritage Study Bible**
   The James C. Winston Publishing Co.

5. **Holy Quran**
   A. Yusef Ali Translation
   & Mulana Muhammad Ali Translation

6. **Message to The Blackman**
   Hon. Elijah Muhammad

7. **God, The Blackman & Truth**
   (Rahbee) Ben Ammi

8. **The I Ching**
   Wilhelm/Baynes Translation

9. **Selections From The Husia:**
   (Sacred Wisdom of Ancient Egypt)
   Maulana Karenga Translation

10. **Tapping The Power Within**
    Iyanla Van Zant

11. **The Destruction of Black Civilization**
    Chancellor Williams III

12. **The Iceman Inheritance**
    Michael Bradley

13. **Slavery: The African American Psychic Trauma**
    Sultan Abdul Latif & Naimah Latif

14. **The Browder Files**
    Anthony T. Browder

15. The **Fall of America**
    Hon. Elijah Muhammad

16. **100 Years of Lynching**
    Ralph Ginzberg

10 Relevant Training Sources to Follow-Up the chapter:
"The Changing of The Gods! pt. 2"

1. **Choosing Your Future** (Tape Series)
   Les Brown-The Motivator
   Les Brown Unlimited 1-800-733-4226 for catalog

2. **Lead the Field** (Tape Series)
   Earl Nightingale
   Nightingale-Conant 1-800-525-9000 for catalog

3. **Psychology of Achievement** (Tape Series)
   Brian Tracy
   Nigtingale-Conant 1-800-525-9000 for catalog

4. **Black Labor/White Wealth** (Book)
   Claude Anderson

5. **Think & Grow Rich: A Black Choice** (Book)
   Dennis Kimbro & Napoleon Hill

6. **Why Should White Guys Have all the Fun?** (Book)
   Reginald Lewis & Blair Walker

7. **The Richest Man in Babylon** (Book)
   George S. Clason

8. **Inc. Magazine** (Periodical)

9. **Entreprenuer Magazine** (Periodical)

10. **Self-Employed Professional Magaazine** (Periodical)

A Few Relevant Lectures:

1. **Ancient Egypt:** New Perspective of an African Civilization
   Anthony T. Browder
   Institute of Karmic Guidance 301-853-2465 for catolog

2. **Developing Black Self Love**
   Dr. Naim Akbar
   Mind Productions 904-222-1764 for catalog

3. **Goals for Black Men**
   Dr. Naim Akbar
   Mind Productions 904-222-1764 for catalog

4. **Who is God?**
   Min. Louis Farrakhan (Chicago 1991)
   Final Call Books & Tapes 773-602-1230 for listing

5. **Historic Saviour's Day 1997**
   Min. Louis Farrakhan (Chicago)
   Final Call Books & Tapes 773-602-1230

6. **Address to the Association of Black Psychologists**
   Min. Louis Farrakhan (Chicago 1996)
   Final Call Books & Tapes 773-602-1230

7. **The Theology of Time** (Lecture Series)
   Hon. Elijah Muhammad
   Final Call Books & Tapes 773-602-1230

8. **The Murder of Malcolm X: 25 Years Later**
   Min. Louis Farrakhan (at Malcolm X College)
   Final Call Books & Tapes 773-602-1230
   Tape Connection 202-667-7887 for catalog listing

9. **An Interview with The Arab Press**
   Min. Louis Farrakhan (Chicago 1995)
   Final Call Books & Tapes 773-602-1230
   Tape Connection 202-667-7887 for catalog listing

10. **Brief History of the Nation of Islam**
    Abdul Akbar Muhammad
    Final Call Books & Tapes 773-602-1230
    Tape Connection 202-667-7887 for catalog listing

National Black Book Distributors

Easteren U.S.
- African World Books 410-383-2006 Baltimore, MD
- A&B Book Distributors 718-783-7808 Brooklyn, NY
- Afro-Mission Book Dist. 215-731-1680 Philadelphia, PA
- D&J Distributors 718-949-5400 Laurelton, NY

Midwesteren U.S.
- Lushena Book Distributors 773-975-9945 Chicago, IL

Westeren U.S.
- Culture Plus Book Dist. 1-800-982-3762 Inglewood, CA

International
- Pepukayi Book Distribution 011-44-181-0205 London, U.K.

Thanks to the many Brothers & Sisters whom have given up much love, in appreciation of this message, **"From Niggas To Gods Pt. 1."**

May Peace & Blessings
Be Upon You All.

(brief excerpts from a few letters)

"...(A Brother/Teacher) recently allowed me to experience the book, *'From Niggas to Gods Pt. 1.'* You've given the Spirit of Truth a clear, resounding, penetrating, far reaching voice. In producing these writings, you have fashioned an effective tool that can pierce the crust of ignorance that covers the collective Black mind."

-Brother from
The Midwest

"I am writing in regards to your book, *'From Niggas to Gods Pt. 1.'* Your book is well needed in the Black community. It provides enlightenment that we all need, as a Black nation. I really enjoyed it and can't wait for Part II."

-Brother from
The Midwest

"Much peace, love and respect to you sir. I enjoyed reading your book *'From Niggas to Gods Pt. 1.'* I thank you for writing a book of that nature. It enlightened my mind and helped me with my quest, to wake up to reality since I've been incarcerated. I also began to find out about myself and what I like to do in life other than chillin' with the fellas and getting in trouble. I believe that it's time for me to put away my foolish and childish ways. When I get back into society I'm going to make it a must to become a better man than I was before."

-Brother from
The Midwest

"This book is the perfect guide to prepare an African-American with full knowledge of self."

-Brother from
The West Coast

"I've read *'From Niggas to Gods'*, a very positive book...this book really opened my eyes."

-Sister from
The Southwest

"I found the book *'From Niggas to Gods'* to be real good information on self." -Brother from
The Mideast

"I purchased from *'Niggas to Gods Pt. 1'* and it is good that someone can interpret our Master's Teachings to the much needed youth." -Brother from
The Southeast

"I want to extend my sincere gratitude to you for writing the dynamic, *'From Niggas to Gods'*. It is our duty as upright, righteous Blackmen in the wilderness of North America to re-educate our young brothers and sisters of the knowledge of self. Continue to awaken the sleeping giant (black people)."

-Brother from
The East Coast

"The book, *'From Niggas to Gods'* really made an impact on my life and now I have vision. Thank you and keep on teaching."

-Brother from
The South

"This book is simply perfect. It is easy to read. Easy to understand. And, of course, the information is just "MIND-STAGGERING!"

-Brother from
The East Coast

All Praise Be To The Most High
Make way for The Creams of The Planet.
"God Crushed to The Earth, shall Rise Again!!!"

The Struggle continues...

Dedication

Tupac Shakur:
It didn't have to be that way.
Much Tears. Rest in Peace 9/96

From

Niggas

to Gods

Vol. II

Escaping "Niggativity"
& Becoming God

Table of Contents

An Opening Word

Becoming God Pt. I

Becoming God I I

Becoming God III

Gratitude

An Opening Word

"Fishing for the Righteous, in this Lake of Fire". Yes, the Struggle continues. It has just begun...but it "has begun". It is time to clean-up the self.

Humanity is in great pain. This life is something. It is hard. It is painful...more so to some than to others; but none of us are strangers to this pain. Yet, these words are extended, that we may overcome that pain. I think that there are many of us who are tired of living like we do, and are ready to move on to something real in life. Here is our chance.

The wise know that these pages have been delivered to us. In them, you will find warning, scolding, instruction, encouragement, and direction. Truth does all of these things.

A brother recently said, that he saw "From Niggas to Gods Pt. 1" as a "de-programmer". He is right. His description is very correct. We are here to "deprogram" one destructive attitude, and "reprogram" the productive attitude.

In this here "Volume II", we label this process "Escaping Niggativity & Becoming God". The purposes of these pages, are to completely destroy one attitude, and usher in another. For every given day that you walk this earth, it is your "attitude" that will determine your direction and destination. And where are you Blackman and Woman?

What many of us are not aware of though, is the direct link of much of our present pain, to the past traumatic brutalities suffered by our people since being placed in America.

Our experiences here have been especially brutal; first assaultive to our bodies, now more assaultive to our minds. We are even destroyed to the fact of not realizing our destruction; a victim unconscious to his/her victimization. But, that's allright. That is why we are here reading these pages today. That is why we are here. We are here for a personal liberation...a liberation from this ill self-oppression. We are here. And, we are strong.

I, myself, am not a Master of these teachings; yet for mastery I am determined to strive. A compilation of essays sporadically inspired between 1993-1996; this is "Escaping Niggativity & Becoming God!"...a cupful of Truth/Medicine to heal the trauma.

Welcome...and Congratulations. You hold the beginning processes in your hand. You are more courageous than most. And you are worthy, of the due respect. *"Many can make war with the demons of another man, but who can make war with the demon of self?"*

Most have run, from where you choose to stand. You have agreed to walk over The burning sands of truth. Peace. I'll see you on the other side.

The Aims & Purposes of The Devil?

(...to murder your Life Away!)

Let's explain this thing. The aims and purposes of the devil is to murder your life; rob you of the quality of your life; deceive you out of your destiny. What is your destiny? Your destiny is to meet with Your God. I don't mean "meet" with your God in a regular sense, I mean to meet with the highest potentials, capabilities, talents, and abilities that you were born with from your mother's Womb. You were born with these things, resources in you, this greatness in you, but somewhere in between the original womb and where you are right now in your life, you were indirectly attacked by the outstretched hands/powers and influences of the devil.

I'm not talking about any formless spirits and spooks, I'm talking about spirits (energy and mind-states) that dwell in, live in, move in, and animate human beings. God and Devil. Two mentalities. Two minds that emanate influence. One desires to lift you up, the other desires to crush you down from life.

How does the devil carry out his aim & purpose of

murdering your life and destiny? He does this by killing off the productive activities of your mind. He tries to tie your thinking into a confusing chaotic knot. He discourages and decreases your power of will to do anything of good for yourself, family, and kind. His aim is to "dis-tract" you from any and all things that would make you a sane, healthy, effective, productive, and righteously civilized human being. He wants to "dis-tract" you. Take you off of the "tract", "track", or "path" that would lead you unto the successes of your own life. This is his Aim. This is his Purpose.

You know when you are doing what you are supposed to be doing in life. You know what habits and what lifestyles will lead you unto a better condition of your life and future. Yes, you do. And you also know that as soon as you even just think about thinking about doing something right and productive for your life, here comes your devil! Am I lying? No. Here comes your devil trying to "dis-tract" you off of the right path that would lead you unto good fortune and productive results in your life. That devil may even come in the form of so-called friends, family, or your own inner conscience. The Anti-Christs!

But know...know that all of these people that come to attack you with their "Niggativity", have been trained, conditioned, and taught to do this by an outside force...an outside force, that has now poured itself up into the brains of your friends, family, and your ownself. This force originally comes from "those who have always" sought to pull a Black Mind down. If you don't know who that is, then you need to go back and study "From Niggas to Gods Pt. 1".

Modern day slavery calls for modern day techniques of oppression. Instead of those persons who act as your enemy, whipping your flesh open, with lash after lash,, there is a "new" way. Now, the technique is to whip your brains to death with stupidity, ignorance, and dumbness. I mean the technological science to literally make a damned fool out you, by bombarding you with a steady diet of "Niggativity" pushed into your mind! He is on you. A "damned" Fool, is a "condemned" fool; condemned into STOOPIDISM! His aim is to either keep you Drunken with Your Own Emotions, or infested with Insignificant Ignorance! I know you see this.

Got "niggas" trained like circus monkeys! Damn! Shame! You know? Look at us! Look at us! Man, you don't function according to your own will! Can't you see? You ain't running nothing up in here son! Don't you see the science being laid on your brains? You think you the Big Ass Man, but them devils is programming your script like little puppets for they exploitation pleasure. You ain't got nothing to show for your life but a stuck-out chest thinking you did something to confirm your Manhood. But have yet to learn what True Manhood is. Brains being played son, I'm telling you. Lyrics continue.

"Niggativity" Explained!

(Aims & Purposes of The devil Pt. 2.)

Modern day slave making techniques of "oppression"? Back in the days of juvenile early developing stages of slavery, the slavemaster stopped whipping the Black Slaves himself personally. He had advanced his slave mastering techniques to the level where he could train another Black Man to beat his own brother, at his command! You know? Hell, he probably had a Black Man so trained to even beat his own Mother, if she thought about running up off that plantation. You know?

Well, as we approach the year 2000, such is the same today, just in a more advanced way. Ain't that be a damned shame? This devil say, instead of hanging niggas myself, I'm gonna teach niggas to hang themselves! And this he did. He say, instead of me spending all of my day trying to destroy nigga's lives, I'll just teach them niggas to sabotage and destroy their own lives!!!

He says... *"Come here nigga! Listen to me! Here, I want you to take this whip, boy! I'm tired of whipping on you! Boy, I got more important things to do...I got a whole world to colonize without them even knowing I'm colonizing them. Now, that takes time, work, and skill. So listen, I want you to take this whip, and everytime you even just think about doing something positive, or doing something to set yourself free, or doing something to make your life better, or doing something...doing something that you know I wouldn't like...I want you to take this here whip and whip your own ass with it. You here me boy! I mean whip it hard too! Just whip it real good like you know I would want you to! And if you see anybody else that's thinking about doing something I would not like, I want you to whip on them too! You hear me boy? You hear me boy???"*

Now, this whip that he handed us for the purposes of beating ourselves down and our people down, is a mind-set called "NIGGATIVITY" (Nigga-tivity). That is a self-destructive style or form of thoughts and actions. It is a niggative thought pattern that produces a niggative behavior. And we whooping our asses with it everyday. See?

See, the devil got some aims and purposes for your life, because you ain't pushed out no aims and purposes for your own life! If you don't move, you will be moved.

Hell, the devil say, if you ain't' gonna use your brains for nothing, then I will! If you ain't gonna drive the force and direction of your life, I'll drive it for you! I'll drive you crazy! I'll drive you to the grave! I'll drive you to jail! I'll drive you to drugs! I'll drive you insane! But nigga, if you stupid enough to let me drive your life, I'll drive you straight to Hell!!!

Cipher that word, true. Now we enter "From Niggas to Gods Vol. II".

A Warning To The Black Youth!
"You are being made Public Enemy #1"

Niggas must be "Killable" before they are "Killed"!

(The Assassination of God)

"...most Black people in AmeriKKKa today have been psychologically duped into believing that they actually operate according to their own will. These misled perceptions can not be further from the actual truth. You are, indeed, in-thought, and in-fact, still a slave."

From Niggas to Gods pt. 1
(chap. 1, pg. 1)

We shall drill this point. Look into your mind for a second. Look at everything you think. Look at everything you do. Look at every word you say. Look at it. Look at it. Don't you know that somebody is making you "do what you do", "think what you think", and "say what you say"? I said, somebody is making you "do what you do", "think what you think", and "say what you say". You are not in control, even though you think you are.

Look at the words you choose to use, the way that you choose to act, behave, or move. Look at what you do. Do you really think that you made these choices alone? Don't you know that someone else is controlling, influencing, and moving all of that? Don't you know that someone else is moving you? You are not in control.

When someone else can control what you choose to choose, you are not free. You are the worst kind of slave; a slave who thinks he is free.

Pay much attention. You are not in control. You, yes... "you" are being moved and manipulated like a puppet on a string. "You". Look at the word "man"-ipulated. There are string-attachments coming from the control of one "man's" hand, directly out and into the control center of another man's brains. One man is "man"-ipulating another man. You the puppet, and he's the puppet-master. The slavemaster. One mind, controlling another.

Now, "what man" is this, that stimulates your every thought, therefore pre-plans and predicts your every action? "What man" is in control of "your" mind? "Where" is this man? "Who" is this man? How is this man doing this? I don't see anybody? Well, let's find out who and how this is.

You might not see the visible hand of this man, pulling your strings, but he is there. When a man can **stimulate** your **every thought,** he **therefore** "**pre-plans**" and "**predicts**" your every action. Pay attention, this science is real.

"All persons are a direct reflection of their atmosphere." Once again, "All persons are a direct reflection of their atmosphere". This means that all persons, will "unconsciously" reflect and imitate their atmosphere...imitate the things that they see in their atmosphere...and even become what they see in their atmosphere...become their atmosphere.

Now, if all persons imitate, become, and reflect what they see in their atmosphere, then this means that the one who "creates" the atmosphere, also "creates" the person-ality of the persons in that atmosphere. The one who "creates" the atmosphere, "creates" the thinking, the actions, and the movements of the people who are immersed in that atmosphere. Do you understand this???

Now, the question you want to ask is... "Who is it that creates and controls 'your' atmosphere?" Who is the Lord of Your World??? Look around you. You might not see your interior decorator face to face, but I am telling you that somebody has been hanging pictures on the interior walls of Your Mind! Somebody has been pumping images, pictures, sounds, or in other words pumping "thoughts", into your Brains!! Your Mind is not your Own! Nope! You are Manufactured, son. You are mortal-Man-Made product!

Wait...slow down. Hold it. Okay so, you are being manipulated, yes you are...but the manipulation itself, is not the bad part, no. That is not the bad part. What is the bad part, is "who" you are allowing yourself to be manipulated by. That is what is bad. That is what is bad.

See, as "men", or rather, "as minds" on the planet, we all will be guided by the force of "other minds" that are "more developed" than our own. That is natural, and as it should be.

When we are born, we are first guided by our "Mother's mind", then we move on to "other minds" that will guide us on to "higher" or "more specific" realms of mind development. All throughout life, there are minds wiser than us, that guide us, as we also guide those other minds that have not developed to the · level of even our own minds. Natural.

So, manipulation is not bad within itself, but the question that you want to scream at yourself is, "who", "who", "who" do you allow to manipulate, or guide you?!? "Who" do you allow to influence your thoughts, your actions, and your direction in Life? · "Who?" Are you being moved by a "Righteous Mind (Man)", or an "Evil Wicked Mind (Man)"? You are automatically going to be moved by "some-mind", but "whose mind"?

Are you guided by those who have your best interest at heart, or by those who are "Your Enemy"? By those who "Hate You"? By those who "Don't give a Damn About You"?! By those who would rather "See You Dead"?!? Your Enemy!!! Who is really running your show?

Do you want an answer? All that you have to do is look at your atmosphere! Atmosphere is the pictures, images, sounds, therefore the thoughts that surround and encircle You! Who painted the Imagery on the walls and ceilings that encase the thinking of your own Brains??? Did you put it there? Was it someone who gives a damn about your life, that put it there? What do you see all around you?

If all that you see around you are the images and sounds of The Stupidity of Death, then "who" painted it there? Who painted it there, that your own mind may only be able to reflect the images that it did not even choose to affix it's naively impressionable gaze upon??? Who is in control of the Mind, of the so-called "Nigga"? Your enemy is. "Who?" Your enemy is. "Who?" Your enemy is!

"Nigga" is a manufactured state of mind, "nigga"...handcrafted by your enemy. "Niggas", made and manufactured in the U.S.A. from the finest raw materials imported directly from Africa. They call it "human resources".

So now that you are no longer resourceful to the economics of America, you are "human waste"...no longer an asset, but a liability. So, what is done with un-reformed, un-resourceful, un-recycled waste? It is dumped and destroyed.

But, before you are thrown away Blackman and Blackwoman, your enemy must make it appear to the world that you are indeed nothing but "garbage". This is how you are being "Made", "Manufactured", and "Prepared" for "Murder".

"Your" murder! Prepped for the kill. "You". Yes, your enemy must first make you "killable", before he kills you, in front of The Whole World. This is the plan at hand. Better pay good attention to this with some focused serious thought.

Your enemy seeks to manufacture you into a "Nigga". "You". "You", Blackman. "You", as an individual person... "You" must be made into a "No-good-Nigga" before the eyes of the World. Why? Because, a "No-good-Sub-Human-Beast" is despicable, hateable, contemptible, and most of all "killable".

"You", must be made "killable", before you are "killed", that it may be a "justifyable-homicide", before the eyes of the World. "You" must be "made" and "manufactured" into that which nobody would mind seeing killed! "You" must be made to be "useless to yourself" and "useless to society". This is happening right now.

"<u>You</u>" must be made to appear ignorant, stupid, and inferior to all humanity. "<u>You</u>" must be made to look like a threat to all society. "<u>You</u>" must look like the lowest Scum and Scourge of the Earth! Then, and only then, will even your own Mother call for your death. "<u>You</u>" are being set-up. You are being made this way. Prepared for Death. Marked for Execution. <u>Every</u> Blackman is Public Enemy #1...guilty by association.

Amerikkka is finished with her slaves, and she never intended on letting them go free, for fear that they would one day rise and retaliate. She has no more use for her slaves, and she never wanted them to be used again, by any other nation, and definitely not to be used by, nor useful to them own selves.

Her slaves are no longer a usable resource, but rather a problematic burden to her. She is finished with your Black Bodies. She now wants to dump her human waste...you and all of your family into a Mass Grave of Death, as if you never existed. But how can she dump you or kill you, without the whole world retaliating against her...therefore losing her delicate political control over the whole world??? How can she do this, without looking like the Devil Savage Beast that she is, and always has been? She will craft "you" to appear as the devil savage beast instead.

She will take you like clay between her fingers, and make you into a savage-nigga-beast! She will make, shape, manipulate, and manufacture your wasted mind into an uncivilized, wild, ignorant, violent, murderous, threatening, animalistic, Savage Beast of a human being!!! Then! Then, she will feel justified to catch you, kill you, or cage You! Catch that Beast! Kill that Beast! Cage that Beast!

America has courageously saved the world from the Savage Nigga Beast! She wants the world to applaud your murder! And Damn!..is you falling for the trap or what? I said...is you falling for the trap or what, Blackman? The "set-up", before "the murder". Extermination of the Black Male. The Assassination of God.

Remember, the formula for a public assassination is always this. The Character Assassination always precedes the Physical assassination. Never forget that.

•••

Blackman. Blackwoman. Your enemy got you, right where he wants you. He wants you "ignorant". He wants you "wild". He wants you "worthless" to yourself, and anybody else. He wants you "stupid". He wants you "uncivilized". He wants you "savage". He wants you "killable", so that he can kill you! And that's right where he has you! Now, what in this hell are you going to do about it???????????

Is you gon' raise this fool up off you or what? Huh? In order to do that, you must raise "his" foolishness up off you! Is you gon' raise-up into that which is "Respectable", or continue to get "punked" and "pimped" into his plans to kill your life away??? What you gon' do? What in this hell is you gonna do?

(Stop-Think)

Bible: Exodus chap. 1, verses 8-16

8 Now there arose up a new king over Egypt, which knew not Joseph.

9 And he said unto his people, Behold, the people of the children of Israel are more and mightier than we:

10 Come on, let us deal wisely with them; lest they multiply, and it come to pass, that, when there falleth out any war, they join also unto our enemies, and fight against us, and so get them up out of the land.

16 And he said, When ye do the office of a mid-wife to the Hebrew women, and see them upon the stools; if it be a son, then ye shall kill him: but if it be a daughter, then she shall live.

The Science of:
Manufacturing The Criminal Black Mind!

He got you swingin from his puppet strings. Haven't you ever wondered how all of this "Nigga-tivity" got so widespread across the country, so fast? Huh?

Haven't you ever wondered why, all of a sudden, everybody from L.A. to New York, and from Minnesota to Mississippi, want to all of a sudden be a hardcore gansta-ass "nigga"??? Just, all of a sudden? So fast? Have you ever thought about this? Why is that? Well, let us see.

There is nothing that "just happens" on it's own. Every "effect" has a "cause". Everything that happens, has been orchestrated by some mind, somewhere. Everything that moves has been set in motion by some mind, somewhere. There is a cause and effect to all things! Now, who caused you to be a "Nigga", and proud to be one???

Who "caused", this "effect"!? And, whose hand originally set this "Nigga-tivity" into motion, to the point that it now perpetuates it's own motion, and cycles of "Niggativity"!?! That should be Very Clear by now.

But you still don't see this do you? There is no one trying to murder you...Right? ...nobody but your own kind, right? Nobody is manipulating you...Right? Well, I understand. Yes, I understand. If you don't see it in front of you, then you don't believe it is there, right? Just keep looking.

You may be a disbeliever, but there are unseen sciences that go on all around us everyday that are not apparent to the casual eye. There just may be an "unseen cause" to the "effects that you see" all around you. Follow this.

Of course, gravity is "unseen", but you "see the effects" of gravity. You "didn't see" your Mother and Father come together, but "you" are the effect of that occurrence. You calculate the components of the "unseen" by the sum of what is "seen".

So listen...if you "see" criminality infesting itself all throughout the Black community, what is the "unseen" cause? What is the math and science here? Let us see.

(Pause-Think)

The Science of Manufacturing The Criminal Black Mind? A "Nigga-Mind" must be created...grafted from the "Original Black Mind", stage by stage. He takes influence of your young black brains, as early as he can, and places them on the road to destruction. The road that he paved for you.

He's just like God, he's a scientist too. Your enemy is a scientist too. One scientist trying to bring you to life, the other one trying to march you to death. It's true.

He experiments on you. The Ghettos is the laboratory. You are the laboratory rat. After the riots and the fires burned down the ghettos in the late 1960's, there was widespread doom, despair, destruction, and depression, mentally a well as economically. Perfect place for an experiment. He experiments on you. The Ghettos is the laboratory.

Listen closely to what your enemy says:

Okay, these niggas are mad, angry, hungry, and depressed. What are we going to do? We don't need any more riots. That is bad for business, international business. We need something to distract them until we can completely destroy them later on.

I've got a plan, but first let me see if it will work. Let me experiment my plan in the laboratory first, using my lab-rats. Okay.

Now, let us begin. Bring those two rats over here. Let's start by making one rat so hungry, that he becomes very angry. Okay. Now let's give this "angry-hungry-rat" a deadly-weapon, and let's give this "other-rat" a big piece of cheese. Now, let's put them in a small box together, and see what happens.

Oh no! Look! The "angry-rat" just stabbed the "other-rat" and took the cheese! And now the "other-rat" is vowing "revenge"! Gosh, did you see that? Hey, this is fun!

Now, let's give the "other-rat" that had the cheese, a bigger, more deadly weapon than what the "angry-rat" has, and see what happens.

Look! The "other-rat" is beginning to violently attack the "angry-rat" in revenge! Oh no, the "other-rat" just killed the "angry-rat" cold! What a shame.

Here, let's start all over with a "new rat" in the box (a new "nigga" on the block), and do it again. I like these little projects! After we finish learning from these rats, we gonna put our lil' niggras in some "projects" too! I can't wait to try this same experiment on our stupid lil' niggas.

Come on let's do it!

Step #1   Take all the "angry niggas", and give'em the most deadly weapons we can find!

Step #2   Take all of them "depressed niggas", and hook them on some "crack", or whatever type of drug that we can cook-up that's cheap to buy.   You know these niggas ain't got no money.

Step #3   Take them "jobless niggas", and show them how to sell the "crack" to them "depressed niggas", they'll make all the money.

Step #4   Then we will make them "angry niggas" with the guns, jealous of them "crack-selling-niggas" with all the money.

Step #5   Now, put all these niggas in a box together, on one side of town, and close the lid.

We'll only open up the box maybe once a week to take out the dead-niggas (dead-rats), and throw in some more for the slaughter, along with some new "fresh crack rocks", "new ammunition", and "more deadly weapons".

We should come back in about 10-15 years, and all these dumb stupid niggas will be laid-over dead for sure.   It worked in the first projects.   Hell, it will work in these projects too!   "Niggas in the ghetto", is just like "rats in a box".

Now, look at us, 10 years later. Fussin! Cussin! Shootin! Killin! Robbin! Stealin! And Dope-Dealin! Niggas is right on the Execution Schedule. Shot-up! Cracked-up! or Locked-up!

A Discussion with Your Devil (continued)

Question: Mr. Devil, could you explain to the Blackman, how you managed to destroy the life of today's Blackman to such a devastating degree, and not even get your hands dirty?

Answer: Sure. Yeah, well...in different ghettos around the country, we had been experimenting with different tactics, methods, and means of creating "Niggativity", before we perfected our science.

We observed that our experiment was going so successfully and so quickly in the ghettos of Los Angeles, that we decided to make an attempt at spreading this more potent type of "Niggativity disease" (nigga-mentality), all over the country. We spread it as far as we could!

How did we do it? How did we get you to buy into this "Niggativity"? Oh, it was easy. We just advertised! We just advertised, like we do with any other product we want you to buy.

We "baited you", "hooked you", and "swallowed your life whole". We wanted you to buy into our product. We wanted you to become a consumer of the "Nigga Mentality" and "Nigga Lifestyle", so that nothing productive would result of your little life. We wanted to make you the most despicable type of Nigga we could. And we did.

So, like I said, since our experiment was progressing so well in L.A. laboratories, we decided to take a sampling of the germ and spread it around. We did this by taking a few movie cameras down into the project, filmed a few murders...a few of those "drive-by shootings"...paid one of our Movie Directors some money, wrote a script, and made a movie about gang-"Colors". Remember that? Yeah, that was us. We did that.

Yeah, you know, we just took a few dollars and distributed the movie out to as many Ghetto Theaters that we could find, so that we could train the rest of our ghetto-niggas around the country, on the best ways to use the Guns and the Crack that we gave them. Simple.

We wanted other cities to pick up the Murder Pace, so we used our L.A. Niggas as our model. Yeah, we figured that the other niggas around the country would get jealous of how much exposure we were given the L.A. niggas, and start trying to catch up. You know how dumb our niggas are. They fell for it.

It was working so well, that we decided to get some more money and make some more movies for our dumb niggas to imitate! These niggas loved it! Then, our niggas started wanting to make more of these movies themselves, so we said "go right ahead!". Well hell, they were better at it than we were!

We even found out that some of our "criminal minded niggas", that we had manufactured in our experiment, knew how to do that jungle-drumming rap-music noise. You know them African Jungle Niggas hear a drum, and lose they damn mind, so we used this too! It worked great! It worked most of all!

We got tired of all of them damned Black Radical Militant Malcolm-X ass niggas rapping about Revolution, so we decided to drown them out, stop making money off of them, and give our money to our new project! We gave our new rappin gangsta niggas widespread exposure to every ghetto we could find! And now we making mega-money off of them! It's working so well.

T.V.! Radio! C.D.'s! Tapes! Movies! Videos! It was all Advertisement! We came at their brains from every direction! From their Left-Side, Right-Side, Front-Side, and their Back-

Side! We wanted to create the "Nigga Atmosphere"! "Nigga Thinking"! "Nigga Acting"! "Nigga Talking"! "Nigga Clothing"! "Nigga Attitude"! "Nigga Behavior"! A whole "Nigga Culture"! A whole "Nigga Atmosphere"!!! And we did it! Really they did it...we just got them started.

You know niggas imitate their atmosphere, so we just manufactured an atmosphere for our niggas to imitate...we manufactured a Nigga. Dropped the lab-rats in a box, closed the top, and sat back and watched. And now this "Niggativity" is from Coast to Coast and from Border to Border, non-stop. Designed, Planned, and Executed. Designed, Planned, and Executed. Designed, Planned, and Executed. Yes...I am god over my world.

The Final Stage is to use our media to convince the world of how despicable, dangerous, and destructive these niggas are, then we will kill them. "Killable"...then "Killed". That will be real soon. The niggas are doing it all on their own now. It is just a matter of time. They will never figure it out. Mission Accomplished. It was simple.

The Manufacturing of the Criminal Mind. "Niggas"...handcrafted in the U.S.A, by the devil himself.

The Recapturing of The Slave!

(The Devil wants You!)

Question: Mr. Devil, you had something else you wanted to say?

Answer: *Yes, very briefly though...you know I am very busy these days. Ummm...oh yes. I wanted to say, just like we must make The Blackman "killable" before we kill him today, we must make him "cageable", before we "cage" him today. We are thinking about a "Plan B" for our negroes too.*

We are going to save a few, and put them into our cages. We will re-capture them for our new slavery, that we call "The Prison Labor System".

See, if I take my money, build me a "Prison House" somewhere out in the country, then pay the inner city police to capture me some no-good street-dwelling criminal-minded animal niggas, lock them niggas up in a chain-gang or something, and make them work for me all day long for little or no pay, I can contract out my Prison Labor to The Corporations of the International Market! I can get filthy rich again!! Just like my Devil Daddy did, when he had his niggas in slavery!!! He had a "Plantation Farm", I have a "Prison Farm"! God Bless America! I love it!

Corporate America doesn't want to pay their workers decent wages anymore, that's why they are downsizing. So, we will get their products manufactured for little of nothing...

that is except the money that they put in my pockets. I'll give the prisoners 90 cents to a dollar an hour, so that they can afford to buy some stamps to write their Mammas, before I find a way to lock they asses up too.

Hey, these negroes say they need some jobs? I'll give it to them. Your criminal record is the only resume I'll need. I'll be like...a CEO/Warden! Life is great!

All you niggas that need a job? Apply at your local Police Department. We are taking applications 24-hrs a day. If you don't have transportation...transportation will be provided for you. You don't have to call us...we'll come get "you".

Escaping Niggativity:
"Hurling Truth at The Brains of Falsehood"

Do "Niggas"
Deserve
To Be Free???

So you say you wants to be free? Free? Free? You wants to be free? Blackfolks say they wants to be free. We know we oppressed, suppressed, and chronically depressed. And so now we wants to be free...you, me, I, and we. We wants to be free. Okay. Okay. Yeah, you wants to be free, but so what. So what? Sooooooo what???

Blackman & Blackwoman...why do "you" think, that "you" should be let free? Why? "For what"? For "what reason" should you be let free? Let free "for what"? Huh? Let free to "do what"? Huh? Think deeply about this thing. Give this your attention.

You want to be free? Let me ask you the all important earth shattering question. What you gonna do if you was let "free"? What do you plan to do with some freedom???? Huh?

What "do you plan",..."do you plan",..."do you plan",..."do you plan"...what "do you plan" to do if somebody was to "let you free"? Huh? Can you answer that? Do you have any "plans" for this freedom that you desire so badly? Hmmm? Talk to me, we want to hear your answers?

See, everybody wants to be "free", but don't know what they want to be "free" for...or what they would do with some "freedom" once they got it. Huh? Have you ever thought that this just may be the exact primary reason why we don't have this "freedom" today! Huh? Now, what's that all about? What's that all about? Huh?

What the hell we gonna do with some "freedom"? To tell you the straight honest truth, we ain't did too much of damn thing with the little freedom that we have gained! Is that right? I said, is that right?!! Yes, that is absolutely right! Oh yes, we are going to get straight up into your chest today, to the heart of the matter! We need to think right here and right now.

"Freedom"! "Freedom"! "Freedom" is what we say we want! We talking all about this freedom! But who? Who? Who said that we even "deserved" to be free, anyway? Who has said that? What makes you think that you even "deserve" to be free Blackman? What makes you think that one should even consider letting you go free Blackwoman? Free? For what? To do what? What you gon' do? Please. Huh?

See, it used to be this european-caucasian that had you all "locked-up", "chained-up", "strung-up" and "tied-up"! But you...you...you...you need to know who it is, that really got you all chained-up! You need to know that, today. You should be ready to handle that type of knowledge today. The real deal.

You might think that this whiteman is your "gate-keeper" but it's time for you to start thinking a little deeper, a little clearer, and a little wiser today. Come on, let's think together.

Yes, your caucasian may have been the ones who physically chained and locked you up allright, but you have to be courageous enough to ask yourself "who" gave him the chains, and "who" gave him the locks? Just, think about that down in your heart.

And after contemplating those two questions, you need to start trying to find out "who" it is that has the key, to those locks and those chains? "Who"...because this lil' whiteman ain't working for himself. Can't be. How could a man, banished from the light of civilization, walk out of a dark cave, and all of a sudden conquer the Whole Known World? He now exerts his Supremacy, his Mastery, over every "known" being on this planet, walking out of a cave??? And he did this on his own?

No, no, no...see, this man is working by the permission of another Man. I said, this man is working by the "permission" of another Man. It's time to talk about this.

Who is at the Root of our Oppression?

The man that "you see", is working by the permissive will of another man that you "don't see". This man, the one who gives you hell, is working by the permissive will of Your Own God. Let's repeat that.

We said, this man, the one who gives you hell, is working by the permissive will of Your Own God. What??? Yes, Your OWN GOD. Your Own God, The Master of This Universe, and Orchestrater of all it's affairs...Your True and Living God...The Overseer and Ruler of All that is Animated before your eyes...Your Own God...the Master God...Your God. The one that you are made in the image and likeness of...Your God.

The enemy, your enemy, exerts his will by the permission of this Master God. There is really only "One" power in this Universe. Any devil that functions, is "allowed" to function. It is Your Own God today, that is the One who has "you" all locked up in the many forms of bondage that plague you today, Blackman and Blackwoman! Your enemy is just a pawn on a chessboard. God is locking you up today! This is serious to your life.

Can you imagine that? It is Your Own God who is "locking up your movements" today, who is "withholding your blessings" today, who is "<u>letting you trip over your own feet</u>" today, and who is "<u>allowing you to be held down by the 'fearful grip' of your own hands</u>" today! Your Own God is holding you down today...nobody but you and yours. You and Yours.

But, "why" would Our Own God do this to us? "Why?" "Why?" "Why, God?" "Why", would "You" keep us from "being free"??? Why? Why, would you do such a horrible thing?

And then The God says: *"Question me not, until you first question yourself! Instead of you asking me 'why' I have not granted you complete freedom, you tell Me, 'why' I should?!? Who said that you have made yourself deserving of any freedom, Blackman?"*

Hmmm. Okay? Wait. That is surely something for us to think about. I said, that is surely something for us to think about! I'm telling you, beloved. We have got a lot of little, smutty, pestilent, arrogant nerve. He asked, have we even made ourselves deserving of any freedom!?! He said, do you even "deserve" My Freedom, Blackman? Are you even worthy of my freedom Blackwoman? That is a serious question. Listen.

Let the truth be told to the people. This ain't no little, weak, punkly God that we are dealing with today. This God ain't trying to love every-damn-body, talking-bout some "We are The World!" Boy, This God will kill you where you stand! Evil is His Enemy! And His Enemy, is all of those who willfully align themselves with Evil and Evil Doings! Negroes, do you understand this??? This is Real! Real! Real God!

Your God Says: *Why in this hell should I, The God, let this Blackman be free today?!? Huh? I said, "why"? Let you free for what?!!?*

Let you free to be a wild and shameless 'Nigga'??!!

Huh? Let you free to be a damned Crack-Head??? Huh? Let you free to be a damned Pimp-Daddy?? Huh?

Let you free to be a scrupleless Dope-Seller??? Let you free to be a voluntary Slave-Minded, Inferior-Acting, Bowing & Scratching, Tap-Dancing House-Nigga, for your whiteman, when I AM YOUR GOD??? Am I supposed to let you free to be a Damnnnnnned Foooooooool!!!! Huh? Is that what I am supposed to do? You Insult Me, and you Disgust Me.

Since when in this hell do 'Niggas', I said 'Niggas', not True Blackmen & True Blackwomen', but since when do 'Niggas' think that they 'deserve' to be free??? Look at you! Look at you! Look at you!!! You are not of 'Me'! I can't see you! You must be out of your mind??

Look at your condition! You little cheap, dirty, back-stabbing, stealing, lying, cheating, jealous, envious, arrogant, petty, small-minded, filthy-hearted people!!! You are no son of mine! You are no daughter of mine! I will never claim you in this foul condition! You are not of 'Me'! You have become the dirt beneath my feet!

Oh, you hurt me to My Heart, Blackman and Blackwoman. You hurt me to My Heart.

I give your enemy freedom to do his evil, because I created him for evil, but my own Sons and Daughters are not created for such vile, sickening disgust!!! Do you hear 'Me'???? DO-YOU-HEAR-ME???

Do you think that I should let you free, as the Blood Soaked Murderers of your own community, your own families??? Do you think that I should let you free, as the Sickening Perverted Rapists of your own daughters, your own Mothers, and your own wives?? Do you think that I should let you free, as a Cold-Hearted, Criminal-Minded, Immoraly-Uncivilized, Savage-Acting Animalistic Beastial Devil????!!!!!

HELL NO!!! I WILL KILL YOU FIRST!!! I WILL CHOKE

YOU TOO DEATH WITH THE FOUL STINCH OF YOUR OWN DISGUSTING STATE OF EXISTENCE!!!

I will NEVER let you free in your foolishness! 'Niggas' ain't never ever gonna be free!!! Never!! 'Niggas' ain't never, ever, never, ever, never, ever, never, ever gonna be free as a bunch of 'Niggas'!!!! I said, HELL NO!!! NO! NO! NO! I Will Kill You Myself!!! Oh, you hurt me so. You hurt me so.

I want to justly destroy your enemies for their evil. I do not want to destroy you. I have come to justly raise you up out of your niggardly condition, into an up-right, respectfully civilized Nation of Blackmen & Blackwomen again.

Yet, if you reject Me, and reject My Guidance. I will kill you at the appointed time, along with your enemy. If you do not have sense enough to want Me, I will no longer have mercy enough to want you."

(Stop-Think...and then stop and think again.)

Do "Niggas" Deserve To Be Free?

(The Question Continued pt. 2)

The Righteous God Power of Your Mind

Let us continue. It is clear. The God will not let us go "free", to spread our "Niggativity" all over this planet. That will not happen. No. That is clear.

There was already a man made to spread "beastiality" and "uncivilized savagery" all around the planet, and that purpose has already been served. We have had the reign and tyranny of one devil, and we don't need another. That is not the nature of "your" creation.

You, the sons of God, the daughters of Allah, your Purpose to this Planet is different. **The creator, bringer and giver of Divine Technology, Divine Science, Divine Mathematics, Divine Law, Divine Government, and Divine Fine Arts to the World...that is who you are!** That is your legacy to the Earth. That is <u>your</u> purpose to the Earth today.

And of course, if you are not going to live your life to serve your "own" purpose, then your life will never truly be successful. You will continuously stay locked up in that "Dead Type of Mentality" and that "Dead Type of Life" until you die off physically, slowly killing your own self. Either you carry out your Purpose and Duty on the planet, or you are Dismissed and Discharged off the Planet. That is The Law.

All rebellious devils are receiving their orders to leave the Planet today, because their purpose has already been served. Either they leave voluntarily, or The Universe will do it by Force...by a Deadly Force of Nature...even This Earth is naturally standing up for herself today against the criminals and their crimes committed against her.

She justifiably requites their assault with an avenged Natural Disaster after Natural Disaster...and she is Direct and Precise with the Skill of Her Aim. Look around. There is no hiding place from Justified Retribution. It is The Law above all laws. Cause and Effect, what goes around...has come around, You will Reap what You Sow. The Law.

A Fool can Never Be Free

In this, a brand new day of Creation, we just plain will not be "free" to be that same fool that we have been, foolishly inflicting our foolishness upon yourself, others and the environment around us. No sir, no ma'am, that experiment is over.

The Law has come down on all of us, if we just take a closer look at what is really going on. We are not actually "free" to do "foolishness" now, because it is always impossible for a "fool" to be "free".

This is impossible, because a "fool" is constantly being entrapped by the "self-created circumstances" of his "own foolishness". Stop, think.

To be really, really, really truthful, we are functioning as our Own Oppressor...oppressed by the "Negativity" of our own "Niggativity". Stop, think.

Example: This happens when we are locked up in the jail of our own **"Rebellious Behavior"**...encased by the boundaries of our own **"Destructive Thinking Patterns"**...held down by the weight and heaviness of our own **"Diseased Heart"**...intoxicated and drunken by the fearful false pride of our own **"Arrogant Vanity"**...and constantly plagued by the repercussions of our own **"Ugly Attitude"** and **"Foul Personality"**! Stuck in this "Niggativity"...in this "Niggative" cycle. This is our condition.

And this condition gets even worse because, deep down inside, "you" hate the reality that you see about "you". True. True. True! This is the Truth! Wait, you've got to listen to this one closely. This is rough territory that we must cover, to get to where we are going. Hold tight.

Self-Hatred leads to Self-Execution

You have so much power. I know that you may not really know it, but that same God that just spoke to you earlier in the first part of this chapter, is rooted deeply within You. He is programed into you deep up under all the filth that this world has dumped on top of you. The God is in there. He is in the core of your pure nature.

Whenever "He" is dissatisfied with you, "you" are unconsciously dissatisfied with your own self, deep down inside. Think. Your own unconscious dissatisfaction turns into self-hatred and causes you to behave in self-defeating behaviors and lifestyles. Think. Yes, you have more God in you than you know. You can bless you, or you can damn you. That is a lot of power in your hands.

Listen beloved brother and sister, we suffer immensely from this Self-Hatred. If "you"-hate-the-reality-that-you-see-about-"you", it will be this exact same Self-Hatred that keeps you from the "life you desire"...the "freedom you desire". It is deadly. I am saying that this psychological cycle is what is creating the Self-Destructive condition in the Black Community.

This Self-Hatred leads to your Self-Execution, or your Subliminal Self-Destruction. All of this goes on in the world of your mind.

This is how it goes. "You" will see "you" everyday, and you dislike or hate what you see in you...so then you <u>judge</u> you, then you <u>sentence</u> you to death, then you <u>kill</u> you. All of this goes on in your mind. You are your own Judge, Jury, and Executioner. And so you die.. and so we die everyday...guilty as charged. Killing ourselves through our Deathly Lifestyle. Self-Inflicted Execution. Think about that. Okay, you have the point.

But, instead of just sitting there hating what you see, why not choose to take that actions that will change what you see? Instead of hating, judging, and eventually killing yourself through the penalization of a Self-Execution, why don't "you" choose to reform "you" through a true "System of Corrections"? Why would you refuse to "Rehabilitate" you? Why would you refuse to "Correct" your ways? Why would you refuse that?

Why would you refuse to "<u>Reform</u>" yourself into something or someone that you "**Could Accept**", someone that you "**Could Respect**", someone that you "**Could Love**" and someone that you "**Could See as Worthy**" of freedom and life itself? God. You are not purposely trying to destroy your own life are you?

Deep, deep deep in your heart, you know that greatness is your nature! That's exactly why you are dissatisfied! Deep in the truth of your heart you know that you are not all that you "could" , "would", and "should" be...or rather not even trying to be, not even "trying" to be! <u>You know this</u>. If you really believed that you were nothing but a little devil, it wouldn't bother you! But since you know you slipping less than your nature, it plagues you! Yes it does, because you are The Righteous by Nature.

You know right from wrong. You never will love you in a broken down degenerate trifling, moral-less, non-productive, non-purposeful type of state. You might sit there tolerating the odor of your condition, and get used to it, but you still will not love nor respect you. That is against the nature that God Created you in.

We can't say this enough! **You will not "love" you, Blackman and Blackwoman, until you make yourself worthy of your own love, of your own self!!!!** And it is that "Love for Self", that "Respect for Self" that is the absolute real F-R-E-E-D-O-M!!! To achieve <u>this freedom</u> gives you the peace of mind, and the power of spirit to achieve anything and everything else in the world!!! Believe that!

You may not know it, but that is true! It is just true! You start doing the things you respect in other people, and watch what happens...start being a real Blackman and Blackwoman, watch what happens! You will begin to respect yourself, and feel good about yourself automatically! Automatically! You just watch.

You have to change "<u>now</u>" in order to save your life! <u>You</u> will not let <u>your ownself</u> free without a change! It doesn't matter if you are still aware of this or not, but you have an automatic built-in mechanism of Divine Judgement. If you are evil, your own psyche will begin to self-destruct against your own existence. You put this in your own system before birth. All of this is written into your Nature from trillions of years ago, when you originated with The Originator. Did you know that you are the withholder of your own blessings and the administer of your own punishment? Did you know that in your own hands is the balance of Heaven and Hell? Can you handle that...that power? It is not beyond your scope.

"Niggas" can not love themselves as "Niggas"

No one hates "Niggas more than "Niggas" hate themselves as "Niggas", because "Niggas" know that they are not "Niggas" at all, because "Niggas" are convinced that they are "God"!!! ABSOLUTELY CONVINCED!!!

This is exactly why "Niggas" kill "Niggas" every day and every night! It's an "Indirect Suicide"...but it is suicide all the same. "Niggas" know that they don't deserve to be "free" as they are, so we sentence ourselves to death everyday. Everyday. It's Automatic. Riding around the ghettos looking for an image of yourself to attack. True.

See, you are the nature of The Supreme Being, and we have just discussed of how Your God is your gate-keeper, from freedom. And you agree that Your God is justified, because you would do the same thing. You instituted the law. What would you do if you were The Master God today?

What would you do if you had a wild and crazy bunch of untamed destructive animal-acting beasts in your house? You would do the exact same thing...withhold freedom!

You would do exactly what you already do! You would chain and lock that destructive beast up! You would not let that beast run free throughout your house to tear it up! This is what you do when you get a wild acting untamed Dog in your house...you chain that beast up until it exemplifies and displays that it can act like it got some sense in it's head without tearing up your house! Is that right?

The beast has to prove itself worthy enough to deserve the freedom to roam around your house freely. Right? Right. That is the program. That is the system. Freedom is earned. That is the law that "you" laid down. This is "your law".

According to "your" law we have no choice but to grow-up into a civilized Blackman and Blackwoman before This God is going to let us go free to do anything in life of value and worth. You will let you free when you feel you deserve it. Your mind is powerful!

The Master God ain't gonna get "Niggas" up out of the Ghetto, until "Niggas" clean the ghetto up out of them! Otherwise we would make a ghetto out of wherever we went, turning any "neighborhood" into a "niggahood". That is the sad truth.

●●●

Now, as for the chapter title **"Do 'Niggas' deserve to be Free?"** Well, according to your law, you say that "Niggas" **don't** deserve to be free...but as "Civilized Blackmen and Civilized Blackwomen" we **definitely** deserve all the freedom in the World! I agree with you. I agree with you.

"Civilized Black Men and Women" is what we truly are...and **"Niggas"** is what the enemy is trying to train us to be so that we will be unworthy of The God and his Freedom of a Successful Life.

Now, are we gonna let this fool take our life??? Hell no! Be Yourself! Don't be "Nigga". Be "God"...and be "Free".

Peace.

Mission Statement: What are we doing? We are "Escaping Niggativity" to "Become God".

Problem: Our people are entrapped within the vices of their oppressors, making them unworthy of the Successful Life. Ignorantly, we are now <u>choosing</u> to live in filth...forfeiting any chance of a future.

Solutions: Become "aware" of our condition. Become "ashamed" of our condition. Then, become "angry" at our condition. Take that emotional energy and aggressively "change" our condition...saving our lives.

How do I do that? Acquiring a sense of shame. Setting righteous principles and moral standards in your life that you refuse to break. Be too proud, and too esteemed to live as an uncivilized beast. You are not as your enemy. Separate your lifestyle from the lifestyle of your oppressor.

Live a life centered on principles, that will make you a deserving recipient of freedom...Self-Love & Self Respect.

What's The Purpose of Your Black Life???

Look at you.

"Look at Who?"

Look at you. What you doing?

"Nothing."

Why?

"Cause it ain't nothing to do. I'm just hanging out with the fellas...my clique, my crew, my clan...you know? The fellas."

Just hanging with the fellas? That's it??? So, that's all you do everyday...hang with the fellas? That's all your life about?

"What'chu mean?"

I mean is that all there is to your life..just hanging out with the fellas wasting time?

"Naw nigga, you know I gots to sneak-up on me some hoes now and then...aww yeah, believe that there...see?."

Damn, so that's all your life about...hangin and acting a fool with the fellas during the day, and trying to sex some promiscuous prostituting mentally dead woman at night? Is that all that there is to your Black Life? Is that it? Damn, that's sad...that is really sad. And you are not even ashamed of yourself, are you? Sad.

Come on Blackman, you can do better than that. Do you mean to say, that all that you do every hour of the day, basically, adds up to nothing? You ain't doing nothing?...ain't trying to be nothing? Wait, wait, wait, you can't be telling me that? Come on Blackman, you can't be telling me that. Noooooooooooo...you can't be saying that?

I mean...what are you living for? What are you alive for? What are you here for? What are you breathing up oxygen for? What are you taking up space on the Planet for? How old are you? How long have you been here? Answer...Answer...Answer! Talk to me dear brother, or dear sister.

For what reason, do you even open your eyes to wake-up every morning? For what reason did you wake-up "this" morning? Do you have an answer to that question? Why are you here? I mean, do you wake-up every morning just to do "nothing"? (Stop-Think)

I know that you couldn't have been living all of these years just to be "nothing"? Right? Don't you know that "you are what you do"? And if you do "nothing", you be "nothing"? "You know a Man by his works, his deeds, and his actions, or the lack thereof". (Stop-Think)

Listen. Were you pushed out of your Mother's womb just to be absolutely "nothing"? Damn! I'm trying to talk to you. Well, just what the hell are you here for!!!??? What is the Purpose of Your Precious Black Life???!!! Huh? You have got to think about this. You have no choice! We are going to talk about this thing up in here today. THIS-IS-YOUR-LIFE!

Beloved Blackman, Beautiful Blackwoman...listen. I'm telling you, I'm telling you, I'm telling you that "every" little-bity individual thing in this entire Universe has a Reasoned Purpose for it's existence! Everything! And ain't nothing created by accident! Nothing! No, not even "you". Not even "you". So, what is "your" Reasoned Purpose for Existing???

Huh? Don't get mad, I'm just asking you questions, cause we gonna think, think, think.

See, "you" ain't no accident either! Your Creation is no accident! Are you listening? You and your life are no "accident", but you "tripping", "stumbling", and "falling" all throughout life, because somebody else taught you that your life don't mean a damn thing to nobody, not even your own self. Somebody taught you that your life ain't "worth nothing", and so now that is how you spend it; "worthlessly" like it's nothing. Just wasting away.

You are being Robbed of Your Destiny

See, somebody else got access to your brains. Somebody else immediately got access to them brains as soon as you hit the planet, and they have been working to make a fool out of you from the day of your birth. And by six years old, your brain, heart, and mind, was already crippled to the original form by which it came. Re-shaped, re-molded out of it's Original Creation.

There was somebody already here on the Earth waiting for you to be born, so that they could stand between You and Your Ordained Life Destiny. I hope that you are listening. You were born directly into their hands of sin, and eventually shaped into the mind of their inequity. This happened to us all.

"We" think like "they" have taught us to think. Our enemy taught us that we were nothing no more than no-good, nappy-headed, non-thinking niggas...and we believed our enemy.

It is true. Here is this Blackman and Blackwoman of Ancestral Genius who created all of the sciences that facilitated and continues to facilitate the advancement of this modern world, asleep to the reality of who you are, trying to pretend like you really are nothing no more than a lazy, no-good, nappy-headed, non-thinking nigga, allowing your enemy to be your Maker, your Creator, your Lord, your God.

Yes, he did make and shape you into the image and likeness that you are currently in, and he is your overseeing lord and god, that controls and manipulates you and your life to make sure that you never amount to anything more than a insignificant human being with no positive contribution to life in anyway. He wants no competition...and so you are no competition. (Stop-Think)

●●●

You may not directly see it, but it is true. Someone is robbing you of your life, your existence, your identity, your destiny. But yet, the only thieving hands that you see reaching in to steal your life away are your own hands, because he has now trained you to rob yourself. (Stop-Think)

If you don't believe that you are being robbed of your life and your destiny, just take a look at the reality of your present day life. **Do you really think that you were born to live like you live?** That is a serious question. Let me just talk straight to you for a minute.

Why did your Creator take the "time" and "mind" to put you into your Father's seed, plant you into your Mother's womb, grow you and evolve you stage after stage for nine long months!!?? Why??

Why did your Creator decide to create "<u>you</u>" specifically as an individual? What is so special about "<u>you</u>"? Huh? "Why <u>You</u>"? Why are you on this Earth at this particular time in history? Huh? "Why <u>You</u>"?

Why did your Creator "specifically" give you a "particular genetic coding" and "particular personal bio-chemical mixture" to specifically make-up your individual one character and personality? What are "you" for? Why "you"? Who are "you"? What are "You" for? "You"? "You"?? "You"??? "You"?????

Did your Creator take the time and the Concentrated Mind to Intricately and Masterfully and Skillfully, take each little Sub-Atomic Particle of material matter to weave together the Millions, Billions, and Trillions of fibers that it takes to make up Your Entire Being, just so that you could come to the planet to do nothing with Your Black Life at all???????!!!!!!!! Do you think that God is a Fool just because you trying to act like one? No! No! No! No! No!

Your Creator put more work, time, and effort into Your Life, than you are putting into your own! It is obvious that Your Creator thinks more of You and Your Life, than You think of yourself and Your Own Life! Get a clue! Don't you see how special you are. If you were not needed by this world, you would not have been created into this world.

Listen. HE created everything in this Universe for an intelligent "reason", "purpose", and "function"! Now, what's your "function" to the World, the Universe? Talk to Me!!

What is "Your Function" Blackman??? Are you here to function as a pimp-daddy, ho-macking, drug-selling, street-dwelling buck-wild-ass nigga acting a damn fool for the rest of your life??? Is that what your function is to this Universe??? Sir, is that all you have to offer to life??? Is that all that there is to you? Is that all the substance that there is to you? Huh? Is that what you were born for? You better think hard about that there.

And what about You Blackwoman? What about you? What in this hell are You Here For? If Everything in this Universe is created and put here for a "Reason", "Purpose", and "Function", is it your function in life to be laying up on your back every damn day and night as a little cheap, sex-starved, rump-shaking, baby-making, check-cashing, prostitutionalized public-hoar for anything and everybody that will lay down with your silly self???!!! Huh? Have you lost your damned mind today? Damn right you lost your mind, cause you know we crazy as hell today! You know we crazy! Beloved, Beautiful Blackwoman, what has happened to you??? My God!

Every time I cut on the T.V. today, you got your little naked black-behind wigglin in the face of the Entire World, as a disgrace to you and your people!!! Yes, I'm talking to "You"! You need to stop trying to roll your lil' neck, and try to put some clothes on your lil' naked-behind.

Go sit down somewhere and think about how crazy you have become. You know you just a damn shame. Standing up before the World showing the shame of your nakedness and the shame of your ignorance at the same time. Damn, we some sick folks. We some sick folks. And it hurts so bad. It hurts so, so, so bad.

We all just as crazy as hell today. This Blackman thinks he's a damn gangsta-pimp, and this Blackwoman thinks she's a damn party-freaking prostitute. Pimping and Hoing your way through life. Imagine that? The Original God of The Universe wants to be a cheap nickel and dime Hoodlum, while The Original Mother of Civilization wants to be a cheap nickel and dime Hoar. God, we some sick folks. Somebody help us please. Please help.

Hell, if that degraded state of existence is all that we were born onto this planet to be, we might as well slit our throats right now. You know what I mean? If we been here struggling all of these years just to act a damn fool for the rest of our lives, then this life just ain't worth living "like that". It just ain't worth it. I mean, what are we here for?

Are you Alive, but Dead?

I have not been trying to insult you or hurt your feelings, and I hope that you have not taken me as such. But rather, I am trying to love and care about the quality of your life. I'm trying to get us to think today. We can not lay here in this grave, satisfied with this death! And we are so numb, dumb, and dead that we think that everything is fine, and that we are alive and well!

But, how do you figure you are alive and well "with life", if you are not carrying out any purpose and function "in life"??? Answer me that. Read that question again, and again, and again.

When some-thing or some mechanical appliance ceases to carry out the productive and purposeful function for which it was originally created, it is then considered to be "unnecessary junk", "useless clutter", "dead waste", "dead trash", "dead" and "unnecessary" to the purposes and functions of life itself...just dead!!!...junk!...waste!...trash! Think. Think. Think!

This is why I keep asking you "What is the Productive Purpose of Your Precious Black Life?"!!! What mechanical function are you carrying out in Your life? What are you doing with the energy of your mind and body?

Important Questions: How are you spending your valuable time? What are you doing from day to day?...night to night? Look closely at what it is that you are doing during your "life"-"time"...the time in which your life is made up of. Is it your life's destiny to do what you <u>have been doing</u> and <u>are currently doing</u> with your life today? You better think about this one real good.

Reflect for a second. How do we really spend the days of our lives? What have we been doing for the past 24 hours?...48 hours? What did we do "yesterday"? What did we do the "day before"? What were we doing "last week"? Huh? Come on?

Were you doing anything of any significance? What "goal" were you trying to meet for your life? What purpose were you trying to fulfill in your life? Are we "living", or "just alive"?

See, these are the type of questions that give us a clear look at the truest reality of our own lives. This let's us know whether we are fulfilling our destinies, or just wasting our lives away frivolously. These are the types of questions that can give us the opportunity to <u>save our own lives</u>, before we completely blow it! Now, let's work on this problem.

Will the Real Lunatic, please Stand Up?

See, we can't be sitting up here doing all of this crying and complaining about life, if we ain't even doing a damn thing to change the condition of our lives or improve the value of our own selves! No, we gots to come real today! Doing all of this crying and whining, but ain't doing nothing about it...just laying back whining. What is that? Insanity. Insanity! Insanity!!!

I once heard a wise person say something like, "Insanity is, doing the same things over and over in your life, while at the same time expecting the outcome of your life to just all of a sudden mysteriously change." Do we fit this definition for

"Insanity" or what? Yes, most of us deserve a personal full-page color photo in the dictionary right next to the word "Insanity". We fit the definition perfectly. Really, we all need to take a group photo.

We do the "exact same" activities, fall into the "exact same" habits, make the "exact same" mistakes, afraid to reach out and try "something new or different" for our lives, and then have the nerve to get frustrated because our lives still ain't getting nowhere! This is pretty crazy.

That's just like a man driving his car round and round and round the same block over and over again...and then he's wondering why he ain't getting nowhere and why the scenery is always the same. That's pretty crazy...isn't it? Don't you think that there is a little something wrong with a man that exhibits behavior like that? Don't you think that this is questionable behavior?

So now, if this gentleman who drives his car around in circles everyday, but he gets angrily frustrated because he can't seem to get anywhere, ...if this man can be considered a bit "loony", how "loony" are we considered, when we <u>drive our lives around in the same little repetitive circles</u> getting frustrated and mad because our lives don't seem to be getting anywhere??? Will the real lunatic please stand up? Allright, you can sit back down now. Here, I'll take my seat as well.

●●●

Listen. Are you doing absolutely "Nothing in Your Life", but expecting to get "Something out of Your Life"? What are you...some type of magician or something? You waiting on some "magic-poof" or something? You gonna be waiting a long time.

Do you really think that you can just sit back and "Give

Nothing" to life and expect to "Get Something" back from life in return? I hope not, cause it just don't work that way partner, so you might as well just snap up out that daze.

"If you don't like what you reaping, take a look at what you sowing, cause you sowing what you reaping and you reaping what you sowing". If you don't like what you are getting out of life, take a look at what you are putting into life! That's what I'm saying.

If you start changing what you put into life, you will start seeing a change in what your are getting out of this life. Cause and Effect. That's just The Law of Sanity. That's all it is. It's just sane thinking...that's all. Now look, let's get serious.

Question #1: What do you want out of Life?

You Answer:

Question #2: Well, what are you doing, to get what you want out of Life?

You Answer:

Question #3: What have you been doing for the past week, month, and year, that is setting you up to receive what you want out of Your Life in the future?

You Answer:

Question #4: Okay, so now...as a responsible and an intelligent Man or Woman, what do you now "plan" to do differently, to get what you say you want out of life for your future?

You Answer:

Question #5: How?

You Answer:

Question #6: When?

You Answer:

These are some hard questions. But don't run from them, look them straight in the eye and state your answer. Write it down. And if you don't have an answer, have the courage enough to go out and make real changes in your life, so that the next time you read this, you will have some real answers. Can you do that? Do you have the courage to do that? Why not? What else you got to do?

What do you have on your schedule that keeps you so busy that you don't have time to do something with your life??? How can you be "too busy" to "get busy"!?! Huh?? What you doing? What are you really doing? Nothing.

You tell me how in the hell is watching videos all the day long gonna help you achieve success in your Life? Huh? You tell me how in the hell is hangin with them fellas gonna bring you a successful change in your life? Huh? You tell me how in the hell is turning up that 40oz. of malt liquor and puffin on that phillie-blunt gonna bring you some Success in your Life!!!??? Huh?!?! Huh?!!! You'll be a Successful Fool! Yes, sir. Very Successful. Probably the best!

I'm just asking questions...so answer me? "Nigga" you God and all that...you got all the answers, so just answer that one there sir. Huh? **Where are you going to be in your life, 5 years, 10 years, 15 years form now...if you keep on doing what you been doing? Where are your friends and associates going to be in that time, doing what they are doing?** Better wake-up God.

I'm just asking questions. This is "all love" for you, that's why I'm talking to you straight! Ain't nobody gonna love you like me fool, so take that frown off your face. This is love. I'm concerned about your future and your well being! Your future and well-being is tied in to my future and my well-being.

I can't truly be satisfied and happy if you are not

satisfied and happy. And you ain't never gonna be satisfied and happy with yourself until you start productively succeeding with your life. And you ain't gonna become successful in your life by being silly all throughout your life. It just ain't gonna happen! It just ain't gonna happen like that!

You know that lifestyle ain't gonna bring you nothing but that same condition of life you complaining about. Insanity is doing the same stupid things over and over, but expecting a different outcome. True? True. What's the Purpose of "Your" Black Life? "You". (Stop-Think)

A Second Chance at Life.

Can you imagine yourself...laying on your deathbed at the end of your life...thinking to yourself what you "would've", "could've", and "should've" done with your life? Imagine that.

Can you imagine laying on your deathbed, reflecting back over the years thinking about how miserable and unhappy you "really were" deep down inside...and feeling sorry and regretful because you never really took the courage and the time to go out in the pursuit of that happiness you could of had, if you would have just tried...just tried...just really tried? But I just laid around for decades waiting, wishing, and hoping for a good life to come my way...to come my way.

Can you imagine laying on your deathbed wishing that you had the chance to do it all over again? "Hell" must be at the end of life, when God shows you all that you "would've", "could've", and "should've" been, if only you had got up and did something with your Life. Hell must be that...and that must be hell.

But, all praises be to Allah, we have another chance at life...a second chance to live this thing right.

So, how are you going to live your life this time, brother? How are you going to live your life this time, sister? How old are you right now? How old will you be in five years? What kind of person, and where do you want to be at the age in your life?

Start now! Decide what the purpose of your life will be. And live on that Purpose. Live on a directed Purpose, lest your whole life be in vain. Resurrect!

Peace, and Much Love.

Mission Statement: What are we doing? We are "Escaping Niggativity" to "Become God".

Problem: We are satisfied with living in a state of death. We are being deceived out of our destiny and blessings of life, being made to believe that our lives our worth "nothing", so we live it as "nothing".

Solutions: Become "aware" of your condition. Become "ashamed" of your condition. Then, become "angry" at your condition. Take that emotional energy and aggressively "change" your condition...saving your life.

How do I do that? You do that with what is called a "determined idea".

(Read the forthcoming chapter entitled "The Changing of the Gods pt. 2 for more details)

Is You just All Punked Out, or What?

Hold up. Hold up. Wait, wait, wait. I thought that you was supposed to be all "<u>this and this</u>" and "<u>that and that</u>"? Wha's-up? I thought that you said you was "all that" and then some? What happened Blackman?

If you supposed to be "all this" and "all that", then why ain't you doing "all this" and "all that"? I thought you was "The Man" and all that?...that is, if you really even know what a "Man" is?

Blackman. Look at us! We just layin around in them ghettos whimpering and cryin like lil' "weak ass punks"...sittin around "bitchin" all day long, but quick to call somebody else a "bitch"...now ain't that a...? You know what I'm talking about? I mean...you know? Wha's-up with all that?

Everytime I turn around, you whining and cryin about "I ain't got no money!", "I ain't got no loot!", "I ain't got no ends!", "I ain't got no job!", "I ain't got nothing!"...."I ain't got this!", "I ain't got that!", "I can't do this!", or "I can't do that!"

Damn!!! This is how we sound as Black "Men"?? Sound like a bunch of "bitchin-bitches"?...whining and crying?...ain't got nothing positive to say about nothing!...everything come out

of our mouth is "Niggative!" "Niggative!" "Niggative!"
"Niggative!" Oh, Blackman, we in some bad shape here.
I ain't got this...I ain't got that. Just complaining and
complaining and complaining, but if somebody asks you "why"
you ain't got no money, "why" you ain't got no job, "why" you
ain't got this or that, then you say;

- *"because...I can't get no job"*.

- Well, "why" can't you get no job?

- *"Because they won't give me no job."*

- Well "why" won't "they" give you no job?

- *"Cause...cause I'm Black...I'm a Blackman living in
this whiteman's world...you know what I'm saying?...see, so all
a nigga like me can do is sell drugs, take shorts, rob, steal, or
kill or some other street hustle to get mines! You know what
I'm saying?"*

Yeah....I know exactly what you saying. You saying you
just a Big Punk. Oh yes sir, that's all you saying. You saying
that, in other words, since a whiteman won't "give" me a job,
and take care of my Big Overgrown black-ass like he supposed
to take care of his slaves, I'm gonna sit here "whining and
crying", while I'm broke, hungry, and homeless. Right?
And if he still won't give me nothing, then I'm going to
throw a "temper tantrum" and go Buck Wild in the streets
everyday causing Mass Criminal Chaos in my neighborhood
until I get some attention!!!
This Criminal Chaos ain't nothing but a Big Overgrown
Ass Rebellious Temper Tantrum! Just like a little child! Just

like a little child!

Imagine a little child begging his Daddy for a "cookie" and the Daddy says, "no". Then the child gets angry and starts going buck-wild running and screaming through the house tearing up the house because Daddy won't give him a cookie!!! "Daddy"! "Daddy"! "Daddy"! I want a "cookie"! "Cookie"! "Cookie"!

Well, Big Bad-Ass Blackman!!! Look at you, me, and us. Look at it! I'll be damned, partner!

I'll be damned if you don't look like a big Black Beard-Growing Baby, running around the ghetto in a pair of sagging diapers...fussin, cussin, shootin, killin, robbin, and stealin!!!...having a Full Blown Temper-Tantrum, tearing-up the neighborhood cause your "Daddy" (the whiteman), won't give you a lil' nasty piece of crumb from "his" funky cookie!!! Dammmmn!!! Trip off of that! Trip off that. Trips...off...that.

Niggas want so much damn "respect", but won't do what's necessary to earn "true respect". That's real. Want the respect of a "Man", but won't be what a true "Man" is.

Straight talk. Here you are 20 yrs. old, 30 yrs. old, 50 yrs. old and up, crying and whining about what your "Daddy" (the whiteman) ain't gave you! Ain't gave you? It's no wonder that our women are disgusted and ashamed of us.

I thought that you was a "BLACK-MAN"?...not a little "black-boy" crying to your "white-daddy"? Hell, I didn't know your "Daddy" was white? You must have been adopted cause you show don't look like him, even though you running-up behind him pullin on his pants-leg beggin for a quarter just like his lil' "boy". That's right! Don't get mad at me for telling the truth! This is all LOVE! If I hated you, I'd let you continue playing the fool!

Deep, deep, deep, deep down inside, you still think you just his little nigga-boy, don't you? Huh? Once a slave, always a slave? But...I thought...I thought...I thought you said...I thought you was "The Man" and all that? But, I see you still a "boy"...still a baby. Overgrown, whimpering, whining, baby.

Oh no sir, and I don't wanna hear all of this *"But, but, it's the whiteman's world, that's why I ain't got nothing."*

Just wait the hell a minute up in here...now what do you mean when you say "it's the whiteman's world"? Who in the hell died and made him God? Hmmm? (You did.)

Since when did this "land-stealing", "country-colonizing", "corrupt-criminal-minded", caucasian, pronounce himself to be Lord of the Worlds!!?? Ain't nobody God up in here but you fool! Huh? What you got to say to that?

I just know that you are not telling me what I think you are trying to tell me?

Do you mean to tell me that the only way that I can have peace and prosperity in my life, is by the permission of The Almighty Whiteman???...only if the whiteman "let me"?

Do you mean to say that the only way I can make money to support my family is by the permission of The Almighty Whiteman???...only if the whiteman "let me"?

Do you mean to say that the only way that I can have happiness, success, sustenance, and meaning to my life is by the permission of the Almighty Whiteman???...only if he "let me"? Do you mean to say that the only way that I can have a life is by the permission of the Almighty Whiteman??? Is This What You Are Saying To Me??? Huh? Huh? Speak-Up!

Well, if this is what you are saying to me, then TO HELL with what you talking about, son!!! To the ABSOLUTE CENTER OF HELL with what you trying to say to me!!!

Boy, I can't hear you stressing that mess you trying to con-test up in my face!!! Talking bout...'if the whiteman let me'...like that lil' hell-raising rebel is my "Daddy" or something? That fool ain't my "Daddy"! My Father's name is God-Allah-Amen-Ra-Jehovah-Jah-Krishna-Christ! ...or whatever you want to call his righteous name!!! "All-ah" means, "All" of his Righteous Names put together in One!!! Do you understand me???

That is My Father! And none other has produced me! None! He is The Supreme Ruler of This Here Universe, Lord of this Lord, King of this King, resonating from the core of the Infinitely Intelligent Black Eternal Mind that guides the Evolution of All Life, and all it's realms of activity, from a Head-Quarters that You See Not!!! Ohhhhh, the Blackman is not understanding me!

See...and I just am not talking about no free-floating formless spook flying around in the clouds! Get Real! I'm talking about The Internal Infinite Power moving flesh, bone, and blood from that secret place! This is The Father I'm talking about. The Real Deal. True and Living God. Sleeping Son of God, I'm talking about Your Real Father.

This is the only Father that has the True Power to grant you and I the sustenance of life out of This Earth, because He is the only one that gave us the Substance of Life in the first place. He has the power to take the sustenance out of one man's wicked hand, to put it into another man's righteous hand.

Yet, we runnin-up behind this caucasian man begging him to give us a better quality of life, as if he is The Life-Giver? What in the hell is wrong with us? Did he give You Life? I said, "Did he give You Life?", Blackman! We are the Source that gave him Life!

Sleeping Son of God, You are the Original Asiatic Blackman of The Planet Earth! You gave him birth! You gave him life! You gave him life! You gave him life!

He was "produced", "given shape", "given form", "given life", "given Genesis" from the "genetic" materials that swim across the Holy Primordial Waters of Your Own Divinely Black-

Melanin-Enriched-Testicular-Loins, Black-Man, Black-Man, "Origin"al-Black-Man!!!

Now, who Fathered who??? Who Fathered who??? "Who" is The Real Daddy of "who"? He is "your son", but you running up behind him like he's "your Daddy". Maybe that's why the world is like it is today. They say it all starts from the family. The Father don't even know he's the Father.

Introspection. Should "one grown Man" start whimpering and crying, just because another grown man will not give him a few bread crumbs from his table? "Hell no", is my reply. No sir, this cryin is just not the answer. No sir.

How can we call ourselves MEN?

How can we truly call ourselves "Men" in the face of our Women and children, if we are constantly begging "another man" to take care of us? That is something to deeply think about.

We don't want to hear all of this "The white man won't let us do nothing. He keep holding us back." How does this sound? The whiteman won't "let you" do nothing? "Let you"? "Let you"? "Let-You".

Listen. Well, if you are fool enough to "ask" another man to "let you" live your life, then that man should tell you "No". You deserve what you get. Especially if you are fool enough to ask your proven enemy, the man that has persistently proven to you for over 440 years, that he wishes you, your ancestors, and your children, nothing but "eternal hell" during all the days of your life. Why would you ask him for anything at all? This is not so good, brothers.

By asking somebody else for something, you automatically "give them the power" to say "Yes" or "No". You deserve what you get.

By asking your enemies for something, you automatically "give them the power" to say "Yes" or "No". Can you see this? You give them power to decide the fate of your future. That is really something to think about.

Listen. If I say, **"Excuse me Mr. Whiteman sir, but can I have a job at your company so I can feed my family?"**, and if he then just happens to say "No", does that mean that I and my family therefore will not ever eat again? (Stop-think).

Do you mean to say that I am supposed to come back home to my beautiful wife and say, **"sweetheart, Mr. Whiteman won't give me no job, so I guess we'll just have to sit here and starve to death, because Mr. Whiteman is so mean to us."???** Is this what I am supposed to say? Is this what you are supposed to say and do?

Wait just a minute now. Would **"a Man"** do this? What would **"a Man"** do? Would God starve to death because the devil refuses to give him a job working in hell? If I am **"a Man"**, why can't I go out into the world, and cultivate sustenance for myself, wife, and children, like any other "Man" around this planet Earth would? Why can't I <u>produce a product</u>, <u>perform a service</u>, and <u>create a job</u> for myself? Why does somebody always have to give me something? Huh?

The whiteman was "Man" enough to start his own company...am I not "Man" enough to start my own? Why can't he come knocking on "My Door" looking for a job? Why can't he submit "<u>his</u>" resume' to "<u>Me</u>"? Do I have to live the rest of my life begging him for a little piece of his biscuit, to pass out to my wife and children? Hell, I know how to make biscuits pretty well, my damn self...Thank you.

Look at this, Blackman and Blackwoman. Look at nature. Out of all of the animals in the Jungles and Forests of this Earth, their is no animal who is totally dependent on "another animal" to care for it's own life, sustenance, and success. Do you understand?

Have you ever thought about that? Not even "the animals" of a naturally "lesser intelligence" are as foolish as we have been made to be, nor as foolish as we have decided to stay. The so-called Negro in America.

Do you think for one second that a "Proud Lion" will sit around and starve to death, just because a little "silly monkey" refuses to bring him some bananas down to eat, for He and His Family? No sir, that "Proud Lion" will hunt for it's own food, and if He can't find any food by the end of the day, he might just turn around and eat that stingy little monkey!

What other being on this Earth, do you know of that's sitting around cryin, and waiting on another being to bring it some food to eat for it's life, other than us? What being? What animal? Speak to me?

Yes, I know that a "buzzard" or "vulture" will fly around eating off everyone else's plate, but even that "buzzard" ain't lazily sittin around waiting for somebody to "bring" the left-overs over to him like a welfare check! Even "The Buzzard" will at least get up, and go over, and seek-out the left-overs! But damn, what's up with us? Is we just All Punked-Out or what?

Whose Life is This?

Listen Blackman and Blackwoman. If you truly want peace of mind, love, happiness, success, wealth, and a life of Self-Respect, go get it. Go get it! "Go"! "Get!" "It!"

And if you don't see it out there, "Create It"! "Make it"! Don't you ever, never, ever let "no-thing" or "no-body" prevent you from getting it. Don't let no devil take "Your Life" away!

Don't you let nobody force you into a life of <u>crime</u>, <u>jail</u>, <u>pain</u>, <u>misery</u>, <u>drug-addiction</u>, <u>poverty</u>, self-hatred, no self-respect, and shame...just because they won't give you a piece of what they got! They got you whining, crying, and having a kindergarten temper tantrum on the streets...all punked-out, cause they won't give you some crumbs from they table??? To Hell with "them"!!! Get your own!

It ain't nobody's responsibility to make a Life For You, but You! That's why it's called "Your-Life"! Not "his-Life"! Not "her-Life"! Not "their-Life"! "Your-Life"! "Your-Life"! "Your-Life"!

How is somebody else supposed to build "Your-Life" for You? How silly does that sound? Come on now?

Slavery is over...and you need to act like you know it. Slavery is over in history, but it still exists in your Mind! Slavery is still ingrained in your Brains. Do you hear Me?

Your Massa done been unlocked the gate, but we still standing here on the plantation, acting a fool, mad and upset cause Massa won't give us no more cotton to pick?

"Negroes" better learn how to plant, pick, and pluck they own cotton up in here. You standing on the same soil that you worked to make your Massa filthy rich. The same soil! But, you can't do the same thing for yourself...making yourself righteously rich? Your Slave Massa got you thinking that the soil don't grow food, unless he tell it to. Isn't that something? He got your mind playing tricks on you. Wake-up! Wake-up! Wake-up! Snap out of that Slave-Daze!

Don't let that devil take your life away. He didn't give you life, so how is he going to take it away, unless you let him? How could we let him convince us that our only possible goal or outcome in life is to be a cracked-out, street-hustling, uncivilized-criminal, headed toward Life in Prison or Death in The Grave? It's a trick. It's a mind game.

He made us believe that if he didn't make a decent life

for us, then we just can't have a <u>decent life</u>! And so, we sit here, all punked-out.

The slave and his Massa. The Massa and his slave. You can take the slave off of the plantation, but can you take the plantation-mentality out of the slave? Good Question.

The way you live your life from this day forward will answer that question. It's your choice. You decide.

I challenge us to stand-up and be "Real Men" for Our Women and, and for Our Families. Let us go out into this Earth, to **think**, to **plan**, to **create**, to **cultivate**, and to **produce** a Beautiful, and Abundantly Rich Life for Our Black Families. That is what a "True Man" would do.

And anybody who stands in the way of you being this "True Man", stands in the way of death. No punks allowed!

Big Love to
the Troops!

Mission Statement: What are we doing? We are "Escaping Niggativity" to "Become God".

Problem: Immature Attitude. The crying, the whining, and the temper-tantrums, about what another man won't give us. As Black "Men"; we should be ashamed of ourselves.

Solutions: Clearly state your complaint of dissatisfaction, then use the same energy to persistently change the conditions that leave you dissatisfied. That is not only a mature "re-action", but an affirming "pro-action" towards the conditions you desire for your life.

How do I do that? Constantly-Think. Imaginatively-Invision. Persistently-Plan. Progressively-Create. Relentlessly-Cultivate, and Abundantly-Produce.

(Read the forthcoming chapter entitled "The Changing of the Gods pt. 2 for more details)

Are You a "Black Racist"?

Haven't you heard this question before?   Sometimes Black People ask me these silly questions.

They say: *"Are you a Black-Racist?"*

I **say:** *"No, but it is obvious that 'you' are one, yourself."*

They say: *"...obvious that I am a what?"*

I **say:** *"It is obvious that you are a 'Black Racist'."*

They say: *"No I'm not! I don't hate white people...I love white people!"*

I **say:** *"Yes, yes, yes, I know you love white people, but you hate your own black self.*
You hate your own self and you hate your own people for no other reason than the fact that they were born black, and that's exactly why you hate yourself too. You hate your own blackness, just as any racist-minded person would, except for the fact that you just happen to be the kind of "<u>racist</u>" that is

'black'...a 'black racist'.   You are a 'Black Racist'...a racist against yourself."

They say: "Well, I don't believe that I hate my self. I am proud of who I am."

I say: "Well, who are you? That is the question. Who are you?   Who are you, other than a proud slave to your master?   That's who you are, still just a voluntary slave to your master. Your hair is pressed straighter than his! Your store-bought eyes are bluer than the blue-eyes he was born with!

Yes, you are proud of who you are, but the question is still 'who are you?' other than a cheap imitation of your slavemaster? The closer you get to him the more proud you become. You really don't even know who you are."

They say: "You can't talk to me that way, I know who I am!"

I say: "Well, who are you? What's your name?"

They say: "My name is Sally May Johnson."

I say: "Poor sister, that's not your name. That's the name of a whiteman that owned your great-grandfather. "Johnson".

The slavemaster's branded the 'niggras' that they owned, just like they branded the cattle that they owned. So, they called your great-grandfather 'Mr. John's Boy' or 'Mr. John's Son'...and so now your name is "John-son" or "Johnson". It's the same way with "Thompson", "Robertson", "Jamieson", "Williamson", etc., etc.

I hate to say it, but the truth is that you really just don't know who you are...not even your name...no Self-Identity. You just identify with the master that still owns you...and you are striving to identify with him more and more each day. No Self-Identity.

Sister, it looks like the more we talk about truth, the more you come out looking like a Twentieth-Century slave. You really just don't know who you are, do you? That's a shame the way these people have done us...isn't it? Poor sister, don't even know your name. I guess we are just going to have to start calling you Sally May X?"

They say: *Well, I just don't know about all of that!*

I say: *Yes, well, I'm sorry to say, but many of us really don't know about too many things. That's one of the natural side-effects from being a slave. Here...read this book."*
(From Niggas to Gods Pt. 1)

They say: *"Is this book about hating somebody?"*

I say: *"No, this book is trying to get you to <u>stop</u> hating somebody...Stop Hating Yourself! Racism is an ugly thing...especially when you are a racist against yourself.*
Here...I hope you enjoy the reading."

They say: *"Okay...Thanks...I think?"*

One Year Later...

I see Sally walking down the street looking dignified, dressed respectfully Afrocentric, and she says: *"As-Salaam Alaikum, brother Akil!*

I say: *Well I am very glad to say 'Wa-Alaikum Salaam'
to you Sister Sally May X."*

She says: *I really want to thank you for the book that
you gave me last year. It really awakened me into the reality
of my condition. I didn't realize how lost I was...I mean really,
I just didn't.*

*Since then, I have been reading anything and
everything that can give me a deeper knowledge of myself and
my people.*

*Brother, my life has totally changed and changed for
the better. I have cut away all of the abusive and indecent
habits I used to have. I have principles, morals, and standards
in my life now...you know, a respect for myself.*

*I can see how to make a future for myself and my
family. I am no longer a slave and it feels good to be free. It
feels good to be free...free to be me.*

I say: *"All Praise is Due to Allah."*

She says: *"Yes sir, All Praise is Due to Allah...and
that's real brother. That's real.*

*Well, sir, I don't have much more time to talk. I am a
Goddess Blackwoman on a mission today, and I have much
business to handle. There are too many brothers and sisters
lost out here just like I was. I've got work to do. So,
again...'Thank you' and 'As-Salaam Alaikum', my brother. "*

I say: *"Wa-Alaikum Salaam...and Allah bless you,*
sister."

She says: *"No sir...Allah bless us both!"*

I say: *"Yes, ma'am, thank you. Allah bless us both."*

"Crack" & "Christ"!

"Crack" and "Christ"! "Crack" and "Christ"...two of the biggest hallucinogenic-drugs sold in the Black Community! "Crack" and "Christ".

There are only two people getting rich in these ghettos of America...one "Slangin-Crack", and the other "Slangin-Christ"! One selling "Dope", and the other selling "Hope"! "Crack" and "Christ".

You got the "crack-house" on one corner with a house full of lost and desperate souls, and a "church-house" on the other, with the same.

"Crack-house" got people lined up on the walls, rocking back and forth, moaning and groaning, nose running and mouth foaming with their eyes rolling back in their head...and the "church-house" got the same. "Crack" and "Christ".

"Crack-house" got the people with the broken dreams and lonely lives trying to escape the realities of life...looking for "Crack" to take their pains away. I'm gonna smoke my tears away.

"Church-house" got the people with the broken dreams and lonely lives trying to escape the realities of their lives...looking for "Christ" to take their pains away. I'm gonna shout my tears away. "Crack" and "Christ".

"Drugs" and "Jesus" got us hooked and took! If your brains ain't being "fried", they being "stupified" by a false understanding of your spirituality. If you ain't addicted to drugs, you addicted to Jesus, but you are a poor brain-dead addict just the same. We still talking about "Crack" and

"Christ".

You get up on Sunday, run down to the the "Church-house", with the rest of the addicts, to get your "Sunday Rush"! That's right, getting your weekly "Sunday Rush" of that "Emotional High"!!! Singing, Shouting, Stomping and Spitting!!! Getting fired-up with "Jesus"! "Jesus"! "Jesus"! "Jesus"! "Jesus"! "Jesus"! Everybody in that Church-house just Rocking!...and everybody in that crack-house across the street is rocking too...crack-rocking!!!

Artificially produced and hormone induced!! Emotional Ecstasy is the goal! Escaping Reality is the game, all the same. I don't care if you hooked on "Crack" or if you hooked on "Christ", every last one of you ain't nothing but some addicted lost souls, and you need some rehabilitation. Some of you just traded-in one drug for another...and you know you still just as crazy as you wanna be. Oh, yes you are...just have the courage to listen.

You right here, are getting fired-up on your "Crack", while you over here, are getting fired-up on your "Christ". But both of you got your head all up in the clouds, seeing spooks, spirits, ghosts, and gobblins!!! Mind playing tricks on you...glazed look across your eyes...waiting on your "crack-man" to come back or just waiting on the second-coming of your "Christ"!!! But, hell...can't you see it's all the same? You both losing your mind.

You can't live all up in the clouds forever, hallucinating your life away. Gravity or Sanity is going to bring you back-down one way or another...but you still think you can fly, right?...you flying away to glory, right? You gonna fly up in the sky for the great "rapture" with Jesus, right? Right? Right? You know you crazy.

Well, you just go ahead and jump off that building, flapping your arms trying to fly, and see if Jesus gonna catch you in the great "rapture". Okay? If anything, Jesus gonna be down here on Earth "wrapping" you up in some gauze-pads and band-aids when your lil' silly self hit this here concrete ground! Yes, sir...yes ma'am, you gonna need a Saviour, once your behind hits that ground.

You better wake them brains up! You know you just crazy, but look...this is your brains on drugs...and this is your brains on Jesus. You both looking up in the sky thinking you gonna fly.

Under the influence of "Crack" and "Christ". "Drugs" and "Jesus"...what's the difference??? There is none. The Black Community is full of "Crack-houses" and "Christ-houses", and they are both designed to give you a distorted version of reality. And your white slavemaster enemy gave you both! I said, and your white slavemaster enemy gave you both...your crack and your Christ to distort, discourage, and suppress your intelligence.

"Crack" and "Christ"...putting your mind up in another world to escape the realities of your own. Hallucinating about people with wings that fly...people coming back to life after they die...hellfires burning under the ground...and it got us all strung-out looking like some damn clowns. Yes, this is your brain on "Crack", and this is your brain on "Christ".

It's a shame how they do us. It's a shame how they do us. Throw that pipe away people. Throw that pipe away. Pipe-dreams we don't need. Have the courage to live in reality, instead of emotional ecstasy.

Don't let your slavemaster train you to think that stupidity got something to do with praising Your God. Do you really think that the All-Wise and Infinitely Intelligent God has created the Scientific Magnificence of This Universe, by jumping up and down, crying, shoutin, moaning, and screaming "Thank Ya Jesus" over and over again????? Huh??? Are you trying to say that God is stupid? Talking bout making a "joyful noise" to the Lord...like the Lord need you to entertain Him. You better be trying to make a "joyful future" for the life of your children!

How in the hell did we let these people make such a damn fool out of us???? God is a "Creator", and if you know God, you would be "creating" something in this life too...other than a whole bunch of worthless noise every Sunday morning, while the future of your people is going to Hell.

Slaves better wake up today. I said, slaves better wake up today! This man has tricked you out of your entire life for decades upon decades, and you still don't have a clue.

Your God is more real than you know. Just keep on looking for him, he will prove and he will show. Your God is more real than you know. Just keep looking...but know, that He is no fool...and you will not find him in the midst of foolishness.

"Do You Believe in Jesus??"

I'm quiet. I ain't said nothing to nobody. I ain't did nothing to nobody. But still, everywhere and everyplace I go, people are constantly walking up to me, getting on my last nerve, and aggressively asking me:

"Do you believe in Jesus?!" "Do you believe in Jesus?!" **"DO YOU BELIEVE IN JESUS!!!!!!!!!????"**

Damnnnnnnnn...Negro! Do you believe in <u>Your-Self</u>!!!??? Hell, you running up on me like some NUT that done lost your Mind! Back up off me! Look at yourself! You so obsessed and crazy! Your eyes all bucked open! What the hell is wrong with YOU??? Get a hold of yourself!

You keep asking me if I believe in Jesus, but damn...do you believe in having SOME SENSE IN YOUR HEAD???? Back your fanatical-behind up off me and sit down somewhere, before you make me forget that I'm trying to be a righteous young man.

I'm trying to love you and unify with you for the better sake of the whole of our people, but let me tell you something...you gonna have to get a grip on yourself. I love you as a brother and all that, but hell...don't be stepping up on me like that.

Don't you know that you look crazy? Don't you know that you look like some Religious Fanatical Nut? Is that what you want to look like? Oh, I can hear you talking now..."That's right, I'm a fanatic for Jesus!"

Look, don't disgrace Jesus's name like that. Jesus wouldn't even claim you, acting all silly, fanatical, and insane. Jesus wouldn't claim you. That Blackman's whole mission and teaching is supposed to make you of a sane mind, so don't be trying to put your craziness on him!

Can you imagine Jesus fanatically running up on people talking about, "Do you believe in Me?" "Do you believe in Me?" "Do you believe in Me??????" No, that Blackman is of a sane mind, and is not an insecure individual. But, what the hell is your problem?

Can you imagine the apostles of Jesus fanatically running up on people talking about, "Do you believe in Jesus?" "Do you believe in Jesus?" Do you believe in Jesus????!!!!! No, you can't imagine that, so what in the hell is wrong with you? Back-up!

Talking about some..."Do You Believe In Jesus???!!!" Negro, do you believe in YOURSELF!!! I said, do you Believe In

Yourself??? The whole mission of Jesus is to get you to believe in the divinity of Yourself! Oh, you don't know what that means, so just listen...listen.

The whole mission of Jesus is to teach you to believe in the Goodness of Your Heavenly Father...and if he is your Father, you are therefore his son or daughter, therefore his Goodness is also in You, therefore Jesus is teaching you to believe in the Goodness of Yourself, that you may begin to live your life by that Goodness or God-ness that is within your silly self.

These oppressors have done some serious damage to our brains, and we have got some serious work to do in overcoming our Head-Trauma. It's like we can't even think anymore. We can't even think. It's really sad.

Oh, I can hear you talking again saying, *"Well see, the thinking of man is of the flesh...and see, when we rely on the thinking of man, that's when we go wrong, see...we must not rely on our own thinking...see, we must rely on the word of God. See, see, I am just a man...see, I was born a sinner...I was born in sin...I am nothing. Hallelujah!! Praise Jesus name!"*

What the hell is that???? Talking-bout some, "I am nothing". Hell, you "something" allright...you is a <u>fool</u> for letting somebody teach you that YOU ARE NOTHING!!!

If you ain't nothing but a No-Good Sinner sitting around waiting to die so you can fly up in the sky, then what the hell you waiting on??? If you believe that, then why haven't you just slit your wrists already, so that you can go fly on to glory!!!??? Why? Why? Cause you know in your heart that you talking some damn foolishness. You don't believe in that mess.

Talking about, you don't lean on your own understanding, you lean on the word of God??? Please! Don't disrespect The All Wise God like that, trying to make people think that, as big of a fool that you acting, it is because you leaning on the word of God. Don't you blame that madness on

God!

You know good and well that you ain't relying on your own thinking, nor relying on the thinking of God. There is no thought processing going on at all. God is wise, not a fool. God is not a fool, so why are you?

"But the Bible say...But the Bible say..." Shut-up, you don't know what your Bible is talking about. All that you know is how to be a Damned Slave to your whiteman...looking all dreamy-eyed at that picture of that white Jesus, that he gave you. So, you just be quiet. You are not in any healthy mental state to speak. You need help, beloved.

You run around trying to believe in Everything and Everybody, but Your Black Self. Just a Poor Mentally Dead Slave. And it's really a shame too.

You know, I really love you too. But it's hard loving people when they kind of crazy. You know? It's hard. I'm not telling you these things to make you mad and upset. I just want to make you aware of how you are acting, so that you might get yourself together. A true friend will tell you about yourself, that you might have the chance to correct yourself. Okay?

So, 'do I believe in Jesus?'. Now, to answer your question, beloved brother and sister...I believe in all of The Divine Spiritual Teachers, because I believe in The God that sent them all forth unto us. But, I also believe that they all had good sense in their head...and I believe that we should all act like we have got some good sense in our head too...Okay? Okay. So, please don't walk up on me, or anybody else like that again. Thanks a lot. I appreciate you taking the time out to listen.

In The Search
of Manhood pt. 1
(The Fearful Gangsta???)

Would you believe how many of us are living in fear? Nearly, all of us are. Even some of the roughest and toughest characters on these streets are living in absolute fear. The reason we try to be so rough and so tough, is because we are "afraid" of being seen as weak and vulnerable. Giving effort to being rough and tough is an "act" of defense against an imagined threat. Why do people carry guns? Is it because they are rough and tough? Or is it because they are scared to death?

I would only carry a gun out of defensive fear. So, I tough-up, rough-up, and buck-up, as a front to mask my true self. Is that right? Afraid to be myself. Isn't that what I am? Most times all of this overblown gangsta machismo is an overblown state of insecurity. The "Insecure Gangsta"?

I am deathly insecure about who I really am, so let me project this other character..this hard character...this threatening character. Huh? Look at us. In search of Manhood. In search of Manhood...in search of a strength of character.

Hmmm...it doesn't seem to take much strength to be something or someone you are not. It may take a lot of energy, but not strength. It would seem to take much more strength to boldly be yourself...to be who you really are in the core of your heart, without the fear of being judged by your peers, as weak.

Most of your peers are weak themselves. They are afraid to be themselves too. Punks in the deepest sense.

Most of your peers are just waiting on you to stand up and be a Real Man, so that they can follow you. Your boldness to be yourself will give them the courage to be their true selves too.

Who has the courage to be a Real Man? Which one of you? Which one of us? Are we really just frightened little punks huddling together in little cliques, clans and crews? Afraid, with these little frightened frowns on our faces...afraid to be judged by one another? Interesting. Or are we strong circles of Men coming together to nurture and increase our strength of character...our true Manhood? Which should we be?

We say things like, "Us against the World!", because we are scared of the world. Think about that. "Us to effect the World," is a more powerful attitude.

I'm tight and tense in my gangsta front, scared to relax, always on the defense. Even my offense is a defense against what I "imagine" might happen. That is no way to live. Living in fear.

Fear is the Brains of the devil. Faith (confidence) is the Brains of God. Fearful Brains make chaos. Faithful (confident) Brains make peace. Is our life peace or chaos?

You know...I wonder what percentage of the things that we do in our lives, are out of a "reaction of fear"? Now, how many things have we done in life out of a boldly confident "pro-action of faith"?

Some things, that we really do out of fear, we mistake for courage. A soldier may be honored for fighting courageously in battle, when fear was really his motivation for valiantly defending himself. You might be surprised of how many life decisions we actually make out of shear fear. Very surprised.

Blackmen kill each other everyday out of fear. Think about it. We are threatened by each other. When two black men cross each other's path walking down the street, they both immediately tense-up and tough-up because they are threatened by each other. We are hostile toward one another out of fear, just the same reason that the caucasian has killed us for centuries. Fear. We attack what we fear. We attack what we "perceive" as a threat. Afraid. Afraid. The fearful killer.

How many killers kill to invoke fear into their victims because they are afraid of people not being afraid of them? The fearful killer...insecure about being equalized to a fair competition. They fear equality, for equality may render them less than what they have been superficially fronting to be. Yet, there would be no fear, if they had the real courage to just be what they actually are...no more, no less. Proud to be what God created you to be? That takes the courage of a million lions. Courage to love and be what you truly are, boldly! Boldly!!!

And, who are you, sir????????? A Righteous Blackman!!! A God on Earth!!! A God on Earth!!! A True Blackman!!! That takes courage.

Only a Man can choose to be Himself...no apologies...no need for anyone's approval or acceptance. They can take it, or step the hell on. Allah is sufficiently God.

It's Damn Right You Ain't Got No Money!

Yes, I said "damn right you ain't got no money!" What the hell you gonna do with some money? What you want some money for? Everybody screaming about they ain't got no money! I'm broke, I need more, more, more! Yeah son...right. Why should God bless you with some money and prosperity that you don't know what to do with? What you doing with the little money you got? If you be a fool with a little money, you'll be a fool with a lot.

You want to win the Lottery, be a millionaire, be a billionaire, but for what? For what? You win the lottery today and you'll be broke tomorrow. All these damn Cadillacs, Benzes, BMW's, and Lexuses riding through the ghetto...chrome wheels with gold trim, five-thousand dollar stereo system booming in your ear!!! But you can't even spell B-A-N-K A-C-C-O-U-N-T!

You just blow all your little money as soon as it hits your hand! Blow it on childish foolishness. Soon as the whiteman give you some money, you go give it right back to him. He know this and laughs at us all the day long.

My Blackman...My Blackwoman? "A fool and his money shall soon part." That is the point. A "child" and his money shall soon part. God will not release money into our hands, because we are too foolishly childish to know what to do with it. Billions and Billions of dollars float through our hands, and we have nothing to show for it at all. The more money we make, the more money we spend.

If we would just learn how to productively use the little money that we have, Our God will recognize our maturity and responsibility; and therefore give us more Blackman. You working for money, but your money is not working for you. What do you spend your money on? You spend it on perishable items that give no value in return. Flashing your money and your material items. Showing off to your friends. But what are you showing them other than how much of a fool you are? One fool trying to impress another fool.

Look at the fool with a forty-thousand dollar car, living in a matchbox apartment, 4th-floor, projects USA. Look at that fool with a forty-thousand dollar car, but his children have no computer at home preparing them for the 21st century. I guess they are expected to walk into the 21st century wearing those $200 dollar designer shoes that you bought them; that is if they don't grow completely out of them over the next 30 days! What the hell kind of sense does this make????? A fool and his money, shall soon part.

Do you know what you could do with forty-thousand dollars, and what forty-thousand dollars can do for you??? Do you know what you could do with five thousand dollars, and what it could do for you??? Do you know what can be done with five-hundred dollars??? If you don't, you better find out.

Man, what the hell are we doing? What land do you own Blackman? What corporation do you own Blackman? What industry do you control Blackman? What real-estate do you posses Blackman? What factory do you operate Blackman? What school have you instituted??? What Hospital have you constructed??? What have you created with your money other than a bunch of damn stupidity??? Nothing!!!!! If the whiteman stopped stitching underwear today!...you wouldn't have a decent pair of drawers to pull-up around your rusty behind!!! Blackman? Blackman? Is this the legacy of foolishness you wish to leave your children??? If so, they would be justified in shooting you down as a disgrace! Because you are sending their futures to ABSOLUTE HELL!!! You are murdering their chance at life, by murdering your own. Mmmm...that's a lot to think about.

If you have not devised a fool-proof plan for your money, don't expect God to bless you with more. You will never be successful without Dollars and "Sense", of what to do with your dollars. But if you want to waste your money on foolishness, it's damn right you ain't got no money.

Master a little, and God will bless you with Much. The World is Yours Blackman!!! When you wise up, the world is yours.

Slavery was "Back Then"...This is Today.

"Slavery is a thing of the past." "Let by-gones be by-gones." "Why are you digging up ancient history?" "That was then, this is now." "Slavery is a thing of the past." Slavery was back then...this is today."

Where is this fool, who is talking all of this crap? Come here! You! Sit down...so that you can be taught the proper use of your self! Sit-down.

You should be ashamed to open your mouth to say such ignorance. How in this hell are you gonna open your black mouth to say some "Slavery is in the past...that is ancient history", when the very occurrence of Slavery is the exact reason that you are out of your mind?

Yes, you walk amongst your slavemasters children today freely. Yes, they are your so-called friends, and associates, but this is a reality that you can never escape, with your disrespectful self.

Your attitude is a disgrace...your attitude is a direct spit in the face to every Blackman and Blackwoman who pained, bled, and died at the hands of your murderous enemy, so that you may be alive today! And now you lay down with his children as if everything is just fine and dandy??? Hell, no! You are going to learn something today!

After every Blackman whose neck was hung and stretched from a tree, after every Blackman whose testicles were cut and castrated, after every Blackman whose body was stoked and burned to ashes over fiery coals, after every one of the Blackwomen who was violently gang-raped over and over, after every pregnant Blackwoman who was savagely beaten until the unborn child fell from her womb...you have the nerve...the nerve to open your mouth to speak such vile ignorance? You are a disgust to your race. You need to take your own hand, and just smack the hell out of yourself.

Talking about "Slavery is in the past"? No, "Slavery is in the present!" Locked-up in your slave brains, because you are still being a devil-damned slave to your master today! You just a damn shame.

Listen-up. Let me calm myself, before we go on. Let me just calm down. You know...maybe I shouldn't talk to you this way. It may not be your fault, because this society trains us to think and say ignorant things...you know? Maybe you just couldn't help yourself. Maybe you just don't know any better. But today you must learn.

This is your lesson. Pay attention. "That was then... and this is now"...there is really no such concept. All is connected. Don't you know that everything that you personally did "yesterday" is directly determining the outcome of your "today" and your "tomorrow"??? Do you know that, oh "foolish one"??? If you steal and rob "yesterday", you may get locked up "today", you may get sentenced to prison "tomorrow". See the connection?

Listen, don't you know that you and your happy little nice white friends today have inherited what your parents have passed on to you? You, the children of slaves, and they, the slavemaster's children, have inherited all that your foreparents have accumulated <u>yesterday</u>. The question is, what is the difference between <u>what you have inherited</u>, and <u>what they have inherited</u>?

They are the beneficiaries today of whatever the slavemaster accumulated back then. The slavemaster's children today, are the beneficiaries "economically", "attitudinally", "politically", and "socially".

You are the inheritors of everything that your foreparents accumulated as slaves, "economically", "attitudinally", "politically", and "socially"...which turns out to be a big bunch of pain. You inherited the consequential after-effects of centuries of mental, emotional, and physical abuse, while your white counterparts today, are directly benefiting today, from the suffering of your parents, yesterday.

Your little friends that you compete with today have started off this race many laps and leaps ahead of the game in front of you, while you have started off many laps behind the game in handicapped conditions of injury. And they are still deathly afraid to run against your greatness. There is no true equity.

You <u>inherited the past</u>. As a result of slavery, you inherited "<u>stress</u>", "<u>inferiority</u>", "<u>self-hate</u>", "<u>insanity</u>", and an "<u>automatic social condemnation</u>". As a result of slavery, your little white friends inherited a "<u>self-confidence</u>", "<u>money</u>", and "<u>automatic social status</u>". Yes, "today" is effected by "yesterday".

They are <u>benefiting</u> from what happened then, although they may not directly know it. You are <u>suffering</u> from what happened then, although you may not directly know it.

You hear some of your little arrogant white friends say, *"Okay slavery is over; why don't these blacks get themselves together? They don't want to work. They are lazy, and criminal. I work everyday and I succeed in this country why can't they do the same? We are all the same today."*

Shut your little ignorant minuscule mouth up. Young man, you are sitting on a platform that "I" built with the blood and sweat of "my" black hands. Your America, was built by the slave. But this fact, you want to conveniently blot out of your memory...Correct? You have much nerve...while I am here suffering under the weight of the insanity that you provoked, invoked, and impressed upon me with <u>your savage abuse and torture</u> of my people. How dare you open your evil arrogant filthy mouth to speak? Six damn ounces of intelligence, but always got something to say. Shut up. You are a waste of my time.

Blackman, let me talk to you instead. Yes, I know that you are a successful doctor today, yet imagine what you could have been if your family tree was not virtually destroyed? If your life was "<u>uninterrupted</u>", by the destructive effects of slavery, you could have been a doctor at six years old! You don't know true success, and you don't know your true unobstructed potential. Think about that deeply. Reflect.

Imagine if, your genius would have had no obstruction to it's development? You don't know the true successes you deserve and would have had. But even with obstruction we persist, prevail, and succeed to this day...despite the opposition.. There, is a hinting sign of your greatness.

People, do not "dwell" in the past, but never "forget nor disrespect" your past. Your past is the compass by which you correctly navigate your future; as well as your travels today.

You are no different than the people who lived and died on that plantation...nor any different are the people who enslaved and killed you. You all are the same flesh, and the same spirit transposed in time. Same seeds to earth, in different seasons.

Don't ever sit down on your struggle to be free. The

oppression of slavery hasn't really changed, just the technology of that oppression. Ancient to modern. Yesterday to today. Is slavery "back then", or is it "today"? You choose...by your consciousness, and your actions. It is your choice.

An Answer to The So-called Scholars:

"You're so Smart, You Stupid."

I want to talk straight to you, you know who I'm talking to. All of these so-called scholars who have the nerve to turn their nose up at these writings that God is blessing me to produce for us.

Would you believe, it has been a few occasions here and there, where I've run into persons who have made some pretty silly remarks about "From Niggas to Gods Pt. 1"? Can you believe that?

#1.) I've seen some silly people began an attempt to argue with me over some point they "assumed" the book was saying, without even reading the book themselves.

So, as they argue their point, I would just politely open the book up to a chapter that is saying the exact same point that agrees with what they are trying to argue, time and time again. They see the cover and just assume they know what the book is about. Boy, there is nothing more contemptible than arrogant foolishness that has the nerve to be aggressive. A silly people we are.

#2.) I've run into people who look at the cover, glance through the table of contents briefly, and very pompously say "Oh, well I know all of this already." How foolish this is.

Well professor, if you "know" it all...you should "show"

it all. You don't look like you have mastered the full scope of the principles found in this book. Actually, your attitude clearly displays that fact. If you know all of this already, then why are you not helping the rest of us to know what you already know? I need some help trying to master these principles. You should be trying to help me spread what you claim you already know to those who have not been fortunate enough to know!

As if you've mastered the process and journey of transformation "From Niggas to Gods"! I'm very sorry, but you just ain't looking like God to me, with that foul spirit of thinking. We need some heart-work! Talking about what "you know" already. Look, since "you know already", let me give you an assignment. You go and get all the copies of "Niggas to Gods pt. 1 & 2" that you possibly can, and you go spread them to every suffering Blackman, Woman, & Child that does not know what you already know! Huh? How about that? That should keep you pretty busy, until the next millennium when God may find the ability to reveal some wisdom that you do not already know.

Your people out here dying for a lack of knowledge, while you talking about what you "already know". You miss the whole point. The point is not "what you know"...the point is what "you do" with what you know.

#3.) I've even run into other similar persons who have "claimed" that they have read "From Niggas to Gods Pt. 1", yet they say that they were really looking for a more "scholarly" work. More "scholarly"? More "scholarly"? What the hell is that? God help us! Our people need so much healing.

These so-called "more scholarly" book reading negroes must have failed to read the foreword to "From Niggas to Gods Pt. 1"; for it clearly states that this book will purposely not be written in the "Kings English" with 27-letter words, and all that type of madness. We don't have time for that vain impotent stupidity! Our people are in a state of Emergency!!! Wake up!!! Don't you get it?

I'm not against scholars, scholarly work, or scholastic achievements, but I am against damn fools. Okay? I just am. I don't like fools, because they reproduce foolishness in others; and it is foolishness that is murdering our people in droves. Dead. Dying. Gone. Extinction. Blood is on the streets. Can you get that through that over-stuffed Harvard-head? Is there still a heart somewhere in there? Beloved, sometimes you can be so smart, that you make yourself stupid. It's true. We must be careful.

Listen. "From Niggas to Gods" is constructed to be a bridge to the more scholarly works of our greatest thinkers and researchers. "From Niggas to Gods" is that which will create an appetite in the mass-people to take an interest in the scholarly works and the scholars that we are blessed to have in this era. A bridge is needed.

An appetite must be created. This is the primary function of what is called a "wake-up message". Once this first step is initiated, instituted, and exploded...the people will naturally go out into the world to seek knowledge and wisdom on all higher planes of reality for themselves. This is what is called "resurrection". This is all calculated process. The wise understand this. The thoughtful understand this.

See. <u>What good is the scholar, if the ignorant understand not his teaching</u>? Yet, praise be to God, for the one who makes knowledge and wisdom clear to those who need it most.

Would a "Christian" follow Jesus?

Everybody looking for the return of Jesus...the return of Jesus...the return of Jesus. But, would you really follow Jesus when he returned? I'm talking to the average Christian brother or sister. I said, would you really follow Jesus if he returned?

Well, of course you say *"Yes!"*, but people say a lot of things. You might say, *"I'm following Jesus right now! I praise him night and day!"*. Well, there is a lot we could say about all of that, but we will stick to the point of this subject matter.

You say you are already following Jesus, but really you are just celebrating, praising, and rejoicing over the legacy of Jesus...celebrating the story of Jesus written in the book...praising him as your hero in the story you are reading. That's all you are doing really. That is just true. But, I am not asking you would you follow your hero in some storyline written in a book. I'm asking you would you follow your hero if he materialized right before your eyes today?

I'm asking you, that if you were living during the time of Jesus, living in the actual story of the scriptures, which character would you be? Would you be one of the ones shouting "crucify him", or would you be one of the disciples able to recognize a divinely inspired person in your midst? There were only a "few" of these disciples.

All these religious folks talking bout they looking for Jesus to come back...moaning and groaning about when Jesus come back to take them on to Glory. You don't even know what Glory is. Waiting on Jesus.

But, how are you going to know him when you see him? How are you going to know him when he comes? In the book "From Niggas to Gods Pt. 1" pg. 19, 5th paragraph, it states *"You wouldn't know Jesus if he walked up to you and showed you his identification along with two major credit cards!"*

If you are looking for the return of Jesus, tell me what are you looking for? Tell me? What are you looking for? Let's pause...go ahead tell me. Hmmm?

What are you looking for? Don't tell me you still looking for some dead white-boy that's been hangin on a cross for the past two-thousand years, like in a picture hanging on your wall. If you do see that boy coming back, you better rush him straight to the hospital, cause I'm sure he done lost a lotta blood by now. Better get that boy some band-aids and a "blood-transfusion"...shhh, you think he was a "white" Jesus back then, I bet that boy is as pale as hell by now.

Excuse me for being silly, but this is just the silliness of some of your beliefs. Very silly. Our thinking and analysis must mature. What are you looking for, if Jesus returns? Some of you are looking for some spooky-winged-holy-ghost-spirit flying in the clouds. I will not even respond to that, cause you know that don't make any kind of sense. Jesus...the U.F.O.??? Maybe you meant, Jesus...in the U.F.O.?

You are living in the days of the scriptures __right now__. You are living in the the land of the scriptures __right now__. You should be looking for the man of the scriptures __right now__! You "__looking back__", when you should be "looking around".

How would you know Jesus when he returned? Look at the stories of the book that you been screaming, shouting and crying about. Would a Christian today, follow Jesus? Let's see:

Jesus..."a man born from a woman!". Would you follow him?

Jesus..."a man who made the blind see, and the deaf hear!". Would you follow him?

Jesus..."a man who refuted the religious establishment of his day!". Would you follow him?

Jesus..."a man who refuted the government of his day!". Would you follow him?

Jesus..."a man who traveled throughout the land, teaching and feeding the masses!". Would you follow him?

Jesus..."a man who raised the dead unto life!". Would you follow him?

Jesus..."a man in whom the word, the stories, the legacy, the heroes, and the scriptures of the book became flesh!". Would you follow him?

Jesus..."a man of whom the people hated, mocked, scorned, and ridiculed". Would you follow him?

Jesus..."a man of whom they call evil, a devil, a sorcerer, a madman, a magician". Would you follow him?

Jesus..."a man of whom the authorities sought to imprison". Would you follow him?

Jesus..."a man of whom the government sought to kill". I said, would you follow him!!??

I said, "Would you follow him!!?? You will follow the "words written on the paper", but would you follow the "words animated in the flesh"? You will follow the "hero in the stories" of scripture, but will you follow the "hero in your real life"? Huh? Hmm? Answer me????

If! This! Is! The! Day! Of! Judgement! Should you not be looking for "A MAN", not a ghost..."A MAN" like Jesus??????
If we are fulfilling the prophecy of your scripture, then should not you be looking for "A MAN" today who is fulfilling the stories of the scripture? Not "talking Jesus", but "living Jesus" everyday! Living Jesus Everyday? Stop Looking Back, and start LOOKING AROUND!!! BLIND PERSON!

WHO IS THE MAN IN THIS LAND, that is "making the blind see, the deaf hear, and the dumb speak"?????

WHO IS THE MAN IN THIS LAND, that is "rebuking, refuting, reproving, and reforming the religious establishments of this day"?????

WHO IS THE MAN IN THIS LAND, that is "boldly refuting and rebuking the powerful government of this day"?????

WHO IS THE MAN IN THIS LAND, that is "traveling all throughout the land teaching and feeding the masses of the people, knowledge, wisdom and understanding in this day"?????

WHO IS THE MAN IN THIS LAND, that is "raising the dead drug-addict, the dead prostitute, the dead gang-banga, the dead masses of Blackmen and Blackwomen back unto a righteous life of peace and productivity"?????

WHO IS THE MAN IN THIS LAND, that is "the living expression of the legacies, the heroes, the stories, and the scriptures of the Bible in the flesh"?????

WHO IS THE MAN IN THIS LAND, that is "hated, mocked, scorned, and ridiculed"?????

WHO IS THE MAN IN THIS LAND, that is "called evil, a hateful man, a devil, a "Hitler", a deceiver, a charmer, a sorcerer, a magician, a con-artist"?????

WHO IS THE MAN IN THIS LAND, that is "being continually harassed and investigated by the authorities, looking for reasons to imprison him"?????

I said...WHO IS THE MAN IN THIS LAND, that is "<u>living under the constant threat of murder everyday, risking his life and limb, and liberty to teach the truth to the masses of the people</u>"????? WHO IS THAT MAN???

I said "WHO IS THE MAN IN THIS LAND" like that...like Jesus...like the Jesus that you claim to follow...like the Jesus that you claim to love!? Like the Jesus that you claim you looking for, to return and save you from your ignorance, and from the grips of your enemy, the devil????

<u>LOOK AROUND!</u> Would you follow a Man like that? Would a Christian follow Jesus today? Would even a Christian Preacher, follow Jesus today???

Yes, yes, yes, a "<u>True Christian</u>" would follow Jesus, even today. But, the question is "Would <u>you</u> follow The Jesus today?". Hmmm? Oh, you would...huh? Well, why you so afraid of "Farrakhan"??? Hypocrite.

"Unconditional" Love can go to Hell!
(Death Teachings!)

"Jesus loves me yes I know, for the Bible tells me so?" The hell it does. Have you ever heard these folks talking about "God loves everybody.", "God loves you no matter what", "God is Unconditional Love"??? You is a lie. Stop trying to deceive My People!!!

Unconditional Love? Unconditional Love is a Whore! I said, Unconditional Love is an absolute Whore! Any fool who will allow themselves to enter into relations with just anyone under any circumstance, no matter the "condition", with no type of discriminating standards, is a "whore". Plain and simple. If you will receive just anything that comes your way, you are a whore. Plain and simple. But God is not this "mindless whore" that this caucasian devil and his ideology is trying to teach you. God does not enter into relations with just anybody.

These fools wish that God was "Unconditional" Love, so that He won't kill them for all of the widespread low-down EVIL that they have committed and sustained all around this Earth!!! Hell yes, of course you want God to be <u>Unconditional</u> Love. You can fool yourself if you want to.

These damn deceiving devils Black and White, preach this damnable death teaching of God's Unconditional Love for the world, making you think that you can just live your life any kind of way, and God will still accept you!!! You must be a fool, to try to make a fool out of God! What the hell is wrong with you Mr. Preacher? You are 100% wicked! That's what's wrong.

The God of the Bible, and Holy Quran, and Universe, is not speaking out of no Unconditional Love. God puts forth conditions, standards, and laws that you "must" live by, to receive His blessings! What do you think "Judgement Day" is all about? You will be judged according to "your righteousness" or "your wickedness", whether or not you should enter into Peace or Hell. Otherwise, there would be nothing to judge between!

But some of these fools will have you to believe that the "Sinner Man" and the "Righteous Man" will both receive the same lot in the end. Hell no. Is the "Sinner Man" and the "Righteous Man" alike? I said...is the "Sinner Man" and the "Righteous Man" alike? Do they both deserve the same thing? Have they earned the same wages? If God were to pay them the same wages, God would be unjust. For what benefit would it be to a Righteous Man to be righteous, if he received the same wages as the sinner? Talk to me?

That Bible and Holy Quran names entire cities, towns, or civilizations that were absolutely wiped-off the face of the Earth by God!!! God killed them All! Dead and Destroyed.

In every story, He first sends a warner, a prophet telling them to change their wicked ways. He does this first, out of pure mercy. After a period of time, He blesses and delivers all of those who believed, followed, and lived by the laws of the messenger of God, then he condemns the wicked who would not change after clearly hearing the truth. He kills them for their wickedness and evil...Men, Women, and Children. Look at Sodom and Gomorrah. They are dead. But I thought that you said God's Love was Unconditional? Yeah, you just a fool, trying to make a fool out of me and my people.

Talking about, "God Loves <u>Everybody</u>!" Shut-up. Does God love the devil? I said, does God love the devil???? Does God love the devil and those who align themselves with the ways of the devil? Hell no, he doesn't love no devil! Then it is obvious, that you need to shut-up talking about God loves "everybody"! Mr. Jesus has said, that you <u>can</u> <u>not</u> serve two Masters; you must "love one", and "hate the other". Plain. Simple.

God Hates the devil, and all those that love the devil, and all those that choose to live the devil! America wants Unconditional Love, because she knows that if God's love had preconditions, she would go straight to Hell. She has made it so, that the whole world hates her, and now she wants to preach brotherhood and unconditional love. **America, you can have no "brotherhood" if you have murdered all of your brothers.** It just does not work out that way.

People...you had better get the issues clear in your mind and your life. Yes, God will mercifully "<u>make your acquaintance</u>" in any wretched condition. That is true, and that is the only so-called Unconditional Love that He will give you. But after a certain amount of time, if you refuse to change and adhere to his righteousness after you have clearly heard Him, He will hate you as you hate him. You must meet the criterion by the appointed time.

The Anti-Christs!

Who are the Anti-Christs? They are the Anti-Christs. The Anti-Christs are those who are opposed to your growing up into the mind of The Christ, or into the divine thinking of The God, The Highest Self..."anti", opposed to your "christ-hood" or your "god-hood". The Anti-Christs.

The Anti-Christs are those with the mark of the beast in their head; or the mind of the enemy in their head, or the thinking of the oppressor in their thoughts, speech, and actions. Those that actively oppose your freedom, your growing, your forward motion...oppose your true success are the Anti-Christs. They may be your so-called friends, your family, or your associates. They have death in their minds and in their speech, to oppose your self-development. They don't really love you at all.

They attempt to forfeit your ascension unto mastery, desiring to keep you nailed-down to the cross of affliction and indolence; which is where "they" intend to cowardly stay. You will know them. You will know them, who try to impress their bad habits on you, who discourage you when you are trying to do something positive with your life. Saying "aw nigga you ain't gonna do nothing, and you ain't never gonna be nothing. You ain't bout shit."

I want you to look these people in the eye and tell them

to: *"Shut the Hell up, with that Niggativity! Just because you ain't tryin to be about nothing, don't try to regulate me to your pitiful self! Back the hell up off me! Damn devil.*

If you ain't got nothing positive or encouraging to say about me trying to better my life, then to hell with you.

You trying to murder my brains, and murder the potential destiny of my life. You are a murderer...trying to kill me just because you are dead yourself. You are an Anti-Christ with the mentality of The Beast in you...that same enemy devil beast that seeks to oppress us as a people everyday. You are just another satellite reflection of him. Your brains is worthy of death, trying to pre-meditate my murder. You can't impede me. Back-up."

They oppose what is good, they oppose what is God. They oppose the ascension of your mind, the ascension of your life to "cryst"alize into harmony with The God flow. The Anti-Christs. Skillful and artful, many of them are in their mind-games, their mental warfare.

The Anti-Christs are all around you, waiting to oppose your progress...never wanting "you" to leave the grave of ignorance, that "they" want to remain in. They refuse their own resurrection, and want to convince you to refuse yours. The Anti-Christs are real in everyday life, everyday death. Beware. Vehemently defend your destiny, your future, your life. Defend yourself against those who attempt your murder...the murder of your mind...the murder of your success.

Dead-Prophets can't save You!

Excuse me, but why are you calling on a Dead-Prophet to save you? Why are you calling a dead man's name, while you exist in the world of the living? Have you ever thought about that? All of these religions screaming out the name of dead men to save you. This seems to be a bit backwards, don't you think?

In all of these books of scripture and their stories, the people in those stories had "living prophets" to call upon. You who read the books for their guidance, why do you call on "dead prophets" to save you, when the people you are reading about call upon "the living"?

Dead Prophets did not save the people of that time, and dead prophets will not save you, the people of today. It was a living individual, in whom the principles and guidance of the God was alive and well that saved the people. So, who should you be looking for today? You should be looking for an individual in whom the living principles and guidance of the Supreme God, is alive and animated today...on this realm...in this life...on this plane...in this world. Common sense.

You should be looking for an individual amidst your life today, who reflects the same spirit and mind of the prophets of old.

More deeply, you should understand that no prophet can actually save you; it is and only was the guiding principles that come In The Person of The Prophets, to give you the will and resources to save yourself. These Personalities live, die, come, and go...but the principles and wisdom that they represent are forever living, and always were.

Prophets and Messengers of God are Representatives; meaning that they come to birth at different times in history to "re-present" God's principles to us. Throughout history, they are "re-presented" over and over again until their "presentation" is no longer needed, amidst the people. Think about this.

To "re-present" is to be in the "present", "repetitively". To "repetitively" "present", or to "re- present", as a "representative". Dead Prophets can "presently" present nothing, yet the living prophet can presently "re-present" what the dead prophet presented during his time in history. Read all of that over again, and think.

Listen. Dead Prophets can not save you, so please stop screaming and calling their names. Look for the living individual, in whom the mind and wisdom of these dead prophets are now alive...animated. When you call on the living person, the living person can "act-ually" answer you. The dead can't give you what they don't have themselves...and that is "Life". Let the dead bury their dead, and walk on with the living.

Dead-Prophets. Dead-prophets are honored, respected, and held up high, as their names are constantly repeated on the mouths of the masses. Yet, the Living Prophets throughout history and today, are mocked, stoned, ridiculed, accused, and killed, by the same ones who would honor their greatness after they are dead. Why is that? Why is that? Why is that???

It is because "Hypocrites" hold fast to the names of dead-prophets, for they know that a dead-prophet can no longer demand your righteousness in your face! Dead prophets can't challenge you to live the word you claim to believe in. You can only honor a Righteous Man after he is dead, because he can no longer front you to your face about your own hypocrisy! Only then, all of sudden you want to love him? He is your Hero, dead. He is your Enemy, alive. He is your Hero, dead. He is your Enemy, alive. You praise his name, dead! You curse his name, alive! Bunch of damn devils.

Dead prophets can't save you, but now I'm starting to wonder if many of you even want to be saved from a life of wicked filth. The idle, empty praise of a dead prophet may be preferred by you, that you don't really have to change the sinful ways of your life. You can call his name to appease your conscience, but still continue to live in filth.

You call a dead man, because you know he will not answer you for-real. But you know that a living "righteous man" will answer you if you call "him"...and he will demand that you change your filthy ways. So, you don't call him. Hypocrite. I'm sure that you are sickening before the eyes of your Living God.

You get more respect, if you just boldly be your devil, filthy, sinning, corrupted, sick-self...instead of being a lying deceitful hypocrite. Don't call on God's name, and then live as a devil. Be man and woman enough to call on the devil that you are trying to be. Just say that the devil is your god, instead of being fake. That would be more honest. God will kill you for your mockery, stage by stage.

Only, the dead call on the dead, but The Living call upon The Living. Consider the times.

Why stop being the "Whiteman's Nigga" just to be a "Nigga for White Arabs"???

(Accept Your Own, and Be Yourself!)

My people, my people, my beloved people, how did we become so mentally confused? Why is it that we don't want to think anymore? Why? Can our minds be saved? Can our historical greatness be resurrected from this grave?

Let me ask you one good question. Why would I want to stop being a "mental-slave-nigga" for the whiteman, just so that I may turn around and become a "mental-slave-nigga" for white Arabs? Why would I do such a thing? Why? <u>Do you know that some of my people would try to persuade me to do just that</u>???

Why would I leave one plantation, just to be a "nigga" on another plantation with a different name, and with a different master? Why would somebody invite me to do this? This would be an un-intelligent decision for me to make. In fact, this would be totally insane. Right? Don't you think so?

Well we as Blackfolks have been made so mentally

insane, that this is what one would expect from us, slavery does this you know. We have an imbalanced thinking pattern, because we are thinking from a molested mind. It is sad. The Blackman has been reduced to the mental level of a "slave-nigga" for so long, that he just does not even feel comfortable if he is not being somebody's "slave-nigga". This is such a grievous thing.

We just got to be somebody's "nigga"! Got to be somebody's slave! Won't even think independently! Won't even think beyond the limited intellectual realm of thinking that was taught to us by this racist and sexist whiteman; and now some of us won't even independently think beyond the limited intellectual realm of thinking that was taught to us by this racist and sexist white Arab! True! True! True! True!!!!!

This is the Sure Truth, so just compose yourself, sit still and listen. Come on now Blackman and Blackwoman. Let us be honest with our own selves today. Everything is going to eventually be okay, but we first must take that painful look into the mirror.

Listen Blackman. Listen Blackwoman. Listen to your truth. Everybody is embracing "Islam" these days. But what "Islam" are you embracing, and for what reasons? Are you really embracing Islam or are you just embracing your need for identity??? Some say that they are trying to escape the devil oppressor's religion, but do you know the devil and his so-called religion when you see it??? Better think.

At first we were just mental-slave-niggas with "Bibles" in our hand, and now we are just mental-slave-niggas with "Qurans" in our hand? But notice that either way it goes, we are still the same dumb, lazy, non-thinking, non-productive, non-independent, boot-licking, slave-house-niggas! This has become a problem. Better think. Better just think. It is horrifying to see Blackmen and Blackwomen in this naive condition.

If your religion does not free you from Mental-Slavery, then you have thwarted the cause of Your God, and sustained the cause of your devil. Words to live by. Read that over and over again.

Yet, why do we constantly want to be somebody's slave? Why are we constantly looking for someone else to be our slave master? Why do we not want to think for ourselves anymore? Why are we like children who refuse to maturely grow-up? Why do we not trust our own Black people's Black Intelligence? Why? Why do we not trust our own personal Black intelligence? Why? Why is this?

This is because of the fact that deep-down inside of our sub-conscious minds, we still deeply hate our own black selves and anything that looks like our own black selves. Ever so present, that self-hatred is still alive, well, and wicked. Hatred of Self.

So now you want to ride on the bootstraps of that white Arab, to be a so-called "Muslim", instead of riding the bootstraps of this American whiteman, to be a so-called "Christian"!!! Damned shame, shame, shame, shame.

Why can't we stand-up in our Own Boots to be Our Own Self? Are we not grown Men? Are we not grown Women? Why must we always be dependent upon somebody else? Yes, just the same old slave negroes with a different book in hand, and we really don't understand either one of those books. Don't be offended...be uplifted. This is true.

It pains me to see us so lost. Oh my people, my people, my beloved people, please hear this. Please comprehend this. Please understand these words.   Do not confuse "Islam" with "Arab culture". Do not confuse "Islam" with "Arab culture". Do not confuse "Islam" with "Arab culture"!!!

Can you tell the distinction between "Islam" and "Arab

culture"? Many of our people can not distinguish between the two. Yes, I strive to be "Muslim" (one who submits to God/Righteousness) too, but I am not striving to be an Arab! Please!!!!

But listen...I am an Original Blackman. Who am I? I am an "Original" Blackman. I am not an Arab. I am not that. So, don't try to make me into something I am not. Why would you even try to persuade me to do such? Who do you think I am, a fool or something? I don't want to imitate this man, nor his culture. I am a Man. I am my own Man with my own culture...I am "The Original Man" who fathered all other Men and their cultures...and so are you when you come into the proper knowledge of yourself. You are a bigger Man than you know.

So, don't bring me no mess. Don't bring me no mess, talking about you are trying to bring me some "Islam" from some dressed-up white devil! How in the hell you gonna let some devil try to teach you about your own nature? A Blackman can never be "converted", he can only be "reminded".

"Islam" (submission to the will of God) is the innate, in-born, inbred, inside, internal natural-nature of The Original Blackman and Blackwoman! It may be just a religion to some, but it is the nature of God and God's people. The Original People of the Earth.

Don't let these people attempt to make a fool out of you. Don't let them do that. The word "Islam" simply means obedience/submission to the will of God/Righteousness...not obedience/submission to Arabs and Arab culture! This does not mean that you have to start wearing a beard on your face, fool! This does not mean that you have to start being a male chauvinist, fool! This does not mean that you have to start wearing towels around you head, fool! This does not mean that you have to start talking with an Arab accent, fool!!!

Negro, you know damn well that your Black-behind grew

up down south in Mississippi, so where you all of a sudden get this Arab accent from?!?! What the hell does all of that have to do with serving your God? What the hell wrong with you? Trying to talk like an Arab? Huh? Whitefolks have made us crazy as hell! That's what's wrong. But, almighty God Allah is going to make us as wise as heaven...if you let him. It's okay. It's okay.

Don't you bring me Arab Culture; I said bring me "Islam". Don't you bring me Arab Culture; I said bring me "Islam" (a life of peace). Bring me "spirituality", don't bring me foolishness"; because we are too intelligent today.

"Islam" (a life of peace) deals with the inner mind, soul, or spirit of a person, not the outer shell of a person. "Islam" (the way of peace) deals with the inner heart of hearts. Blackman and Woman, don't let the peoples on the Earth continue to make a mindless-groupie of you, taking advantage of your mental condition...exploiting our ignorance. Don't let them do us like that.

Yes, Yes, Yes, I could wear a beard, talk with an Arab accent, memorize the entire Quran, and pray five million times a day, but does that make me a "Muslim"? While, at the same time, I could be the most wicked and demonic person deep within my heart. Do you understand what is being said? "Islam" (or obedience to God/Righteousness) manifests from the inner spiritual, not the outer garment nor the outer ritual. This must be completely understood in full.

We need to work on our "interior" first, so that we may know what to do with our "exterior". You can be Islamic/Righteous while maintaining and expressing your own particular culture, Black people. You can be a "Muslim"/ "Divine Reflection of God" by just being your true self Blackman and Blackwoman. This must be understood in root. You were born as this, by nature.

We obviously have been trying to imitate whitefolks for so long, that it is difficult for us to break the habit. But still, the habit must be broken. Do not confuse "<u>Islam</u>" with, "<u>Arab culture, custom, or tradition</u>". Let us accept Our Own and be Our Own selves.

Sir, there is just no way in the world I am going to be sitting here trying to be a white Arab. Why would I do that? I have my own identity. This here is Original Man. The Black Mind <u>is going</u> to heal, today. Be yourself.

Much Love.

Jesus & Christianity are two totally Different Things.

(The Final Testament of Truth)

I have been trying to tell you. But it seems as if people are afraid to put 2 & 2 together. You know? Afraid to see the truth that they know in their heart.

But, nobody is really a fool. There are just differing degrees of fear. Why else would you still be holding on to your slavemaster's religion, all the way up unto the turn of this century? Isn't that amazing? I just can't accept the fact that we would be ignorant enough to seek spiritual guidance from the same man who treated us as a real live breathing devil in the flesh for centuries? That would defy the logic of any sane thinking person. Wouldn't it? It is a sick man and woman that will take their religion from a man, handing you a bible with your own blood all over it. Don't you think? He had a whip in one hand, and a bible in the other. He intended to whip you...mind, body, and soul. And here we are today, wounded in every way.

He said it was against the law for us to actually learn

how to read that bible, but we would just have to trust him to tell us what it said. "Preaching the freedom of God, on a slave-plantation"? Doesn't something seem a little wrong with that to you? Hmmm? Do you really think that he gave you the right interpretation of God's word? Of course you don't. But, you are still holding on to what he gave you. Aren't you? But, why?

Well, I have been trying to subtlety hint to you, but the time is about to run out. I will just have to tell you straight out, because you just don't seem to get the point. Your blood will not be on my conscience; I will have tried to tell you.

It is 1996 and you are still sitting in the church. You are still sitting in that little square that your slavemaster erected for you...still sitting there. You are sitting in the modern version of that little church shack that he built for you over in the corner of his plantation...built to train you how to be more of a passive and willing slave to his exploitation. And there you still sit.

You know this, and you betray the truth and dignity of your own soul. That is pretty deep. Who can trust in a man who will lie unto his own soul?...not even he...not even he.

Sweetheart, you are hurting yourself badly. This is not good. This is really sick. Look at us. We send our children to be educated by the absolute <u>same man</u> who made it a crime to teach us how to read...and we wonder why our children come home stupid? We take our religious teachings from the absolute <u>same man</u> who behaved as a savage in human form...and you wonder why we come home from church with no true power to effect real life? This is not to intelligent of us.

Why would you go to a "satanic man", for directions to obtain "God Power"? And, why would you send your children to be mentally "uplifted" by an "oppressor"? Well? What kind of sense does that make? That is an oxymoron.

Betraying your own soul, you have become a Walking

Oxymoron, and a Living Contradiction. You call yourself getting the truth, from a historically proven liar? Contradiction-Oxymoron.

I hate to have to break this to you...but, you call yourself in Christianity worshiping Jesus, and Jesus himself was not even what you call a Christian? There was no such thing as "Christianity"...I'm sorry, there just wasn't.

What "you" know of as "Christianity" was created by a Roman Emperor named Constantine, 200 years after the death of Jesus. You historians out there help me out...isn't that right? Ask your whiteman, he will tell you. He just never thought you would have sense enough to ask him. Check your encyclopedias.

Jesus did not teach what you know of as "Christianity". This is the european's version of a religion that he stamped the righteous name of "Jesus" on. The young man clearly handed you a Bible that said "King James Version". That ought to tell you something? He wrote "his version" of some holy scriptures. They took original scriptures of "truth", and made them inter-woven with "falsehoods". The truth is there to attract you, and the falsehood is there to entrap you. You are attracted by God's true word, but are then enslaved by the philosophy that this devil builds around that word. This is why you can "talk" God, but our powerless to "live" God. Your slavemaster designed it that way. You have been masterminded.

Beloved, baby, precious, sweetest-heart...you got to let it go, and you got to give it up. Let go of this slavemaster, and give up his deceptive religious teachings, that has your mind locked in a knot of powerlessness. Give it up. Give it up, or die away. Your time has all but run out.

You don't have to give up "Jesus"; you just have to give up the mischief-making inequity that your slavemaster built up around "Jesus". According to Your God, your slavemaster and everything connected to him will just have to die...including you, if you still choose to cling to him. And if you choose to cling to a man that has sought to serve you and your people nothing but death...then die slave, die. You have become no different than he. You are already dead and already buried.

But I repeat, you don't have to give up "Jesus". Accept Jesus, and drop what they gave you around his name. You need Jesus, and you need to find Jesus. And you might actually find him if you stop "calling on his name" so much, and start to "call on his character". Don't be afraid. You had a God long before your slavemaster gave you one, and you will have one long after he is gone. It's okay. You need not be afraid.

Jesus and your Christianity are two totally different things. And in order to follow Jesus, you must follow his religion. But, Jesus was/is a man of power. You are a man of powerlessness. Obviously you and Jesus are coming up with two different results, meaning that you are following two different religions, methods, and scripts. Why? Because somebody lied to you, about Jesus. Who? Well, you know who. The same people who have always been determined to keep you powerless.

Well, what was the religion of Jesus? Jesus's religion was called "submission to the will of the Father." His religion was not some sub-title based off of some man's name or title; "Judah"-ism, "Christ"-ianity, "Buddha"-ism. Names and titles come and go. His religion was based on a solid, constant, Universal Principle...that was here long before him and shall remain here long after. That Universal Principle again is "submission to the will of The Father, The Supreme, The One God, The Sovereign of The Universe".

Now, in the original language of the land that Jesus lived, what would he have called this principle and way of life? Would he have said "Christianity"? If not, then what? Read on, you will find out.

I have to say the truth, and let you decide what you want

to do with it. That is what the Judgement Day is all about. May your heart expand unto His understanding. God bless. Peace.

ARE YOU TOO PROUD TO CHANGE?

(The Evil of False Pride)

Do you really want to go from "Niggas" to "Gods"? Are you sure? Do you know that this will involve "change"? Did you know that? Did you know that "change" is the basis of "growth". Did you know that in order to constantly "grow", you must constantly "change"? This is a book of vertical changes.

"Growth" is the "process of change" toward a higher state of being. Okay? Growth involves Change. Growth is Change...and "to change in your life, you must change in your mind". But if you are too "rebelliously proud" to change, it will make you too "ignorantly stupid" to grow. This is a problem. This is a problem with us Blackfolks. This "false pride". This "insecurity" attempting to mask itself as "pride".

Our Blackpeople are naturally "full of pride" but don't really have anything to be "proud" about. We just "proud to be proud"...just silly. We will walk around with our head up, and chest sticking out for no reason at all. We ain't got "no money". We ain't got "no status". We ain't got "no class". And we definitely ain't got "no sense". All we got is some "pride".

I guess our genetic coding naturally tells us that we are "supposed" to be Kings and Queens. But we are Kings with no

Kingdom and Queens with no Queendom. So, in turn, we will just be proud of anything.

We <u>proud</u> of our "new shoes"! <u>Proud</u> of our "new car"! <u>Proud</u> of our "new hair-doo"! <u>Proud</u> cause we "dropped-out of school"! <u>Proud</u> cause we "robbed a liquor store"! <u>Proud</u> cause "we got shot before"! <u>Proud</u> cause "we been to prison"! We <u>proud</u> of "being stupid"! <u>Proud</u> of "our ignorance"! Just silly.

We are actually proud to be a grafted "mentally-dead nigga". This is really a problem.

Some of our people are actually proud of their wicked ways and therefore do not want to "change" or "grow" into a better state of being, even though they are catching hell because of it. Pure devils.

Then, there are some rebellious devils who do sincerely want to change for the better, but they are so wickedly proud, that they can't take the advice of another person who is further along in development than they are. Yes, we have some severe emotional problems to deal with.

We can not "grow" unless we "submit to change", and we can not "change" unless we submit to the higher forces that can righteously guide our change to a higher state of being. Yet, this "false pride" will keep you from all of this!

Sometimes, <u>we are so proud that we would rather drown in the river, than walk over the bridge that was built by someone who walked before us</u>. This is a shame. This is the truth. This madness must be put aside.

Listen up closely Mr. and Mrs. Egotistical Pride. In order "to learn", we first have to admit that we are "un-learned". Okay? In order to "grow more" we first have to admit that we have "not grown enough". Okay?

In order to "become wise", we first have to admit that we are "un-wise". See? In order "to now succeed", we first have to admit that we "have failed in the times before".

In order "to be right", we first have to admit that we "have been wrong". In order "to become civilized Gods and Goddesses" again, we first have to admit that we "have been uncivilized beasts in human form (Niggas)".

Before we "become truly proud", we first must "have something to be proud about". In order "to teach", we "first must learn". Okay? Do we see the pattern?

But some of us are so proud that we think that we have all of the answers all ready! "We know it all!" "We've heard it all and we've done it all!" "We have arrived!" "We have evolved!" "We have ascended!" "I think, therefore I am!!!!"

You dumb therefore you stupid! Please give yourself a break! If you have become all that "complete", you might as well "roll over and die", since your work on earth is <u>finished</u>! You are <u>finished</u> working my nerves, with all this vain madness.

Some people are so full of this sickening false pride, that they will ask <u>you</u> a question, but are too proud to listen to the answer, because they don't want it to seem like you are telling them what to do. Do you know that I have dealt with people just like that? What kind of sense does that make? 'I want to ask you a question, but I don't want you to answer it?' What? What the hell is that?

Listen. I know you proud. And you got a lot to be proud about, but you will never know what you really have to be proud about, if you are too proud to listen and learn of your own ancestral greatness. You have more to be proud of than you know. Listen. I know that you are great. But listen! Listen, Blackman and Blackwoman.

A "great" person does not become "great" because he or she has all of the right <u>answers</u>. A "great" person becomes "great" because he or she has all of the right <u>questions</u>. Think over that.

Hear that Blackman. Hear that Blackwoman. <u>You can not grow to become "true" unless you are **submissive** to "Higher Truth"</u>. <u>You can not grow to become "righteous" unless you are **submissive** to "Higher righteousness"</u>. <u>You can not grow to become "wise" unless you are **submissive** to "Higher wisdom"</u>. <u>You can not grow to become a "God or Goddess" unless you are **submissive** to a "Higher God"</u>. Humbleness precedes growth and change.

Don't be too "insecurely proud" to change. Be too "maturely intelligent" not to change. It's time we grow-on past our pride. We can do it. We have to do it.

Growth is Change...and "growth" is the "activity of life itself". Anything less, is death. Always remember that.

Peace.

Who is Your Leader?

(Polytheism vs. Monotheism Pt. 2)

A man once asked me that same question. He said "Who is your leader?". He expected me to give him the name of a person who leads me, but I did not tell him that. I told him that "TRUTH" is my leader.

Well, of course he wouldn't accept this answer, for he was really looking for a point to attack me on. So, he repeated the same question again looking for me to state the name of a particular person. Yes, and so I told him once again that "TRUTH" is my leader, but that still was not the answer he wanted. He wanted me to say the name of a man.

The reason that this person did not want to accept the answer that I gave him, was because of the way that we have been mentally trained to only look at the surface level of a thing. He thought that just because "he" was looking at the surface of a thing, that I was too. He is silly-thinking, so automatically he assumes I have to be silly in my thinking too.

Being so entrenched with self-hatred, and hatred of anyone who looked like himself, he was sickened to imagine the thought of one Blackman following the leadership of another Blackman. You know?

If I was cutting, shooting, or killing another Blackman,

he wouldn't have a damn thing to say to me...you know? That would be "niggas being niggas" as usual...you know? And, that's okay...you know? But, if I were to recognize the value, and worth of another Blackman of whom I could respect, love, and seek for guidance and leadership...a negro is ready to attack that!

The damn slave will wave his little American Flag, and patriotically respect, honor, and cheerfully follow a white president to hell, but he gets sickened to see a Blackman honor another Blackman. The damnable slave will get all misty-eyed looking at the Pope of Rome, ready to kiss the ground he walks on, but he gets sickened to see a Blackman respectfully honor another Blackman.

No, Mr. Negro, I am not caught up in a cult of personality. I am not a mindless cheerleader, no. You just have never seen Blackmen reverence another Blackman. That is strange to you.

You just have never seen Blackmen respect another Blackman. That is despicable to you.

You just have never seen Blackmen honor another Blackman. That is unimaginable to you.

You just have never seen Blackmen obey and adhere to the guidance of another Blackman. That is a repulsive thought to you!

But you are a trained slave negro, and that is how negroes are trained to think. Never listen to anything as Black as yourself. You have never been taught to reverence the worth of another Blackman, that is why you don't reverence yourself.

No, Mr. Negro, I am not a mindless, hand-clapping, foot-stomping, dreamy-eyed cheerleader being naively led along. No sir. I know that this is what you are familiar with in your church, but such is not the case here. There are brains present and functioning here.

As is clearly outlined in the chapter "Who is Your God" (Polytheism vs. Monotheism Pt. 1), in the book entitled "From Niggas to Gods Pt.1", we are not to just follow '<u>the man</u>', but rather we are to follow '<u>the liberating truths of the plan</u>' found in '<u>the man</u>'.

Jesus said, 'You shall know the truth, and the truth shall make you free.'...he didn't say 'You shall know ME, and your acquaintance With Me shall make you free.'. No sir, he did not say such things. It is the liberating principles of TRUTH, contained within the person of the Jesus, which will make us free. I'm clear on that...now, are you?

Your whiteman did not stop growing in technological mastery just because Albert Einstein died. All that they wanted to do was to preserve Einstein's scientific theories. They were not so concerned about preserving Einstein himself, or rather his outer physical shell when he died. They just wanted to continue drinking from the beneficial wealth of his internal contents, on throughout the decades of time. This, they did.

So, what do you have to say now, Mr. Negro. You are the one thinking on the shallow, not me. I repeat...I follow what dwells in the midst of the Man, not necessarily the physical Man himself. Although I do honor, respect, and reverence the man, in whom God sees as worthy enough to pour himself into, and draw himself up out of, I am clear...now, are you? Sir?

Mr. Negro listen, you just might be able to accept God in the person of one man, when you learn to accept God in the person of yourself. Self-hatred can be a mountain of insanity to overcome, but with a belief in yourself, the size of a mustard-seed, you can authoritatively command that mountain to be removed. The sickness of insanity does not have to be forever. Accept your own, and you can be yourself.

Yes, I know who my leader is. My leader is "Truth"...and

the word took on flesh and dwelled amongst the people. Yes, I'm clear...now are you?

Inter-racial Relationships vs. The Sacred Marriage.

(Part One)

I remember. I remember all that we suffered together. I remember being mobbed, attacked and captured in my homeland, together with this Blackwoman. And when I looked at her, she cried for me.

I remember. I remember being locked-down in the dark nasty holes of slave-ships, laying in puddles of filth and body waste, between living and dead bodies for almost a hundred days, together with this Blackwoman. And when I looked at her...she cried for me.

I remember. I remember being as helpless as a child, chained from neck to ankle, barely alive, walking off that slave ship into this strange land 9000 miles away from home, in the possession of a inhumane beast of a man, a devil. Helplessly, I walked off that ship together with this Blackwoman. And when I looked over at her, she cried for me.

I remember. I remember my body being stripped totally naked, as I was placed up on an auction block, surrounded by, bidded on, and sold by all these yelling savage ghost faces, my mind went into a blur totally humiliated. Together, I was there with this Blackwoman. I looked up. And when I looked into her eyes, she cried for me.

I remember. I remember being slaved, and worked hard in the hottest sun under the constant threat of brutality, day in and day out, day in and day out, day in and day out, damned day in and damned day out!!!!!!!!!!...together with this Blackwoman! And when I looked up, she even cried for me...she cried for "me"!

I remember. I remember being frustrated and angry and broke out of the plantation fleeing, and running, knowing nothing else to do, and the beasts tracked me, caught me and brought me back, in front of everybody. Tied me to a tree naked, burned me with fire-stoked iron prods, slashed me with bloody leather whips until my open flesh just wrapped around the whip itself, as they slid it through my wounds pulling back for another slash. Bloodied and numb, I fell to the ground, broken and defeated again...she carried me back to cover and nurse my wounds. Together we were, again...I didn't have the strength to look at her. She cried, and cried, and cried for me.

Yes, I remember. I never was the same after that. I remember...I remember my woman being attacked and thrown down to the ground, out in the field by one of these white beasts! As this bitch attempted to rape her, I grabbed him by the back of his red-neck and broke his slimy spine with my bare hands! I tried to rip his damn skull off!!!

Half decapitated he lay at my feet, but I did not run. At gun point they walked me to the oak tree, where many had been before me. They swung a rope around the branch and put a noose around my neck. Emotionless, I stood on the platform waiting to hang. And I looked up, and there she was again, looking at me, with one single tear falling from her eye. I remember, our eyes locked it seemed forever...we just looked and gazed.

The slavemaster walked up behind her to snatch her back out the way so that they could hang me, but she wouldn't move. And before he could grab her again she shoved a knife through his throat. Another one ran up behind her, and she cut him down. The whole time she never stopped looking at me. And before my eyes, they shot her to death. And when I looked at her, she died for me. Silently, I never stopped looking at her...I watched...I hung...I closed my eyes.

Inter-racial Relationships vs. The Sacred Marriage.

(Part Two)

Love is an affair of the heart, which sees no outer form. Love sees no color. Love is an affair of the heart, the inner heart. A deep inner love is the basis and fuel of a healthy relationship. True.

But, how can a person have a "relate"-tionship with someone of whom you naturally can not fully "relate" to? It can not healthily be done. True.

Throughout the entire human family, there are an abundance of characteristics and qualities that we all share. And these are shared qualities and characteristics, which can serve as a basis of relationship. True. We have the ability to have a relationship with anyone. But, to whom do you owe your most sacred relationship? To whom do you owe the most inner intimacy of your love, among your various human relationships?

To whom?

Yes, you may find yourself with the ability to "relate" to persons of a different background, on common areas of similarity, but Blackman and Blackwoman...no.

As far as your most inner intimate relationship, you can not "relate" to these other persons without missing something of yourself. You can not fully "relate" to these other persons, with the "whole" of your entire being, because these other persons can not equally "relate" to you on the most crucial levels of your nature. No, they can NOT. You can not "relate" to them with your "entire" being. No.

And, some of you who are in these other relationships know this, while others of you, are so closed off to your own nature, that you are not even aware of the part of you that is not being "related" to, because you are in denial of those central, essential, and crucial parts of your own being! Let's talk to you.

See, if you hate that divine part of you, the part that makes you <u>characteristically</u> "Black", you don't mind living with someone who does not "relate" to that part of you either, because you have divorced yourself from that part of you, your own self! You don't "relate" to what you <u>naturally</u> are. In essence you subliminally say, "Since I hate that Black part of myself, then it is okay for you to hate it too, darling."

Well, you are in hate with the core of your own being, and therefore require not, that your mate be in love with the core of your being. So, your relationship is not truly "interracial", it is just another whiteboy with a whitegirl! Cause you all white, void of color, void of culture, void of flavor, void of spirit! You are void of yourself! You are just void. This is you.

Any being that is not functioning in accord with the nature of it's particular creation, is void. You are not valid. And you can never be validated, by anyone other than your

SELF! And "yourself" depicts, the direct reflection of YOURSELF. Your other half. The other half of a Blackwoman is a Blackman. The other half of a Blackman is a Blackwoman. One without the other is an incomplete soul. You validate one another. You are lost without each other...and these days you are lost "with" each other, because you are lost from your individual selves and lost from your God.

You seek no SELF validation...from neither of the true component/reflections that make up the SELF. Think over what is being said.

Nobody can make you a BLACKMAN but a BLACKWOMAN. Self-validation.

Nobody can make you a BLACKWOMAN but a BLACKMAN. Self-validation.

Your God has made it this way. The further you go away from that, the weaker you get...until you just disintegrate (or integrate) into nothingness...an undefined lump of nothing.

You just can not be a Blackman without a Blackwoman, nor can you be a Blackwoman, without a Blackman. You are both like a sperm looking for an egg in this life...an egg that will birth you into a higher level of maturity and creation. Inside the egg is everything the sperm needs to build itself up in the darkness. In a Blackman, a Blackwoman finds the resources that she needs to build herself up into a True Blackwoman. In a Blackwoman, a Blackman finds the resources that he needs to build himself up into a True Blackman. God specifically placed it there.

Yet, if you penetrate an egg that is not of your own nature, you will find resources, yes...but you will not find all of the resources necessary to make "you" into a complete being of what "you" are. You require more! Without your own reflection, you will only be half-made, a quarter-created, incomplete...never to reach your fulfillment and completion.

God did not make that egg for you, that is why it does not contain what you need for the completion of your TOTAL BEING. The reciprocation can never be equated.

When you are not being your true self, it is easy for you to be with "someone else", because you are being "someone else" yourself. At your deepest levels you will not be known, you will not be touched, you will not be developed.

If you want to find the resources to be made whole, God has placed them in your other half. They are really already in you, but your other half is the only true mirror that can accurately reflect a true image of you back to you, that you may find yourself, in yourself. Think about that. Stop, and think.

Yes, yes, yes, yes...I said YES, I know that this Blackman is CRAZY as hell! And I know that this Blackwoman is definitely CRAZY as hell too! I know you want to run to somebody else's arms cause you can't take the pressure at home. I know...I know. It is enough pressure to make anybody want to run somewhere.

But, the very problem that you are running from, contains the very paradise that you are yearning for. You both want to throw each other away, but you are just throwing away yourself.

I know that we are crazy. I am serious. I know this. We are being sent this book today, because we are crazy. We are actually out of our minds. We are actually not in a state of mental healthiness. This is true. We are literally crazy. I know and openly admit this.

BUT WHO IN THE HELL WOULDN'T BE CRAZY BY NOW, IF THEY HAD UNDERGONE CENTURIES OF THE MENTAL ASSAULT

THAT WE HAVE EXPERIENCED?????? WHO WOULDN'T BE SICK IN THE HEAD???

IT IS A MIRACLE FROM GOD THAT WE ALL ARE NOT DEAD BY NOW, CONSIDERING ALL OF THE HELL WE HAVE EXPERIENCED TOGETHER! TOGETHER! TOGETHER! TOGETHER! EXPERIENCED TOGETHER!

Yes! We are Crazy, but we are crazy together! We experienced HELL together! We were savagely assaulted together! We have suffered, cried, and died together! And the only way that we will ever HEAL IS TOGETHER!!! In the arms of EACH OTHER!!! This is private. This is inner. This is intimate. This is sacred. This is for us...us...us...us. This is home. This is home, like no other.

All those that are foreign to this primeval union, you must respectfully step back. The ground where you stand is sacred. Your trespass is forbidden. You ain't got no juice for a Blackwoman, cause you ain't no Blackman, so just back your ass up. And you ain't got no juice for a Blackman, cause you ain't no Blackwoman, so get off me. Respectfully recede from the premises. Your place is not here.

You know that we are wounded and mentally impaired. You see us running around here out of our minds, trying to be like you, because we have been taught to hate what we are. You see us trying to talk like you, cosmetically altering our appearance to look like you. You know that we are sick.

You know that our minds are not healthy, therefore we have no basis to make healthy decisions and sound judgements. And you also know that this is the only reason we might be with you at this time. You know this. Why, would you take advantage of us, in this state of imbalance? Is this for your own selfishness?

If you claim to truly love that Blackwoman, then leave her alone so that she can go get some sense in her head. You can't give it to her. Since you claim you love that Blackman so much, then get off him. You have nothing for "him". All four of you just weak, and need a knowledge of yourself and an appreciation of your own kind. You all need to find yourself. Yes, you do.

Get on to your own kind, in touch with yourself. We can all be friends. We want friendship in all walks of life. But, as far as this most inner sacred intimate relationship, this is not your place. This is not your place. You just are not welcome in here. Take your place.

No. No. Wait. Wait. Don't think that we are finished. I must explain this thing in detail. See, this Blackman don't want no Blackwoman cause he too weak to deal with her. So, he thought he would take the easy way out..."you". "You" are easy for him. He don't have to be a MAN for "you". All he got to do is just be. A Blackwoman is not satisfied with that.

A Blackwoman will demand that a Blackman be a Blackman, and a lot of Blackmen are afraid of the challenge. So, they run to "you". Oh yes they do. What you have on your hands, is an under-developed God. He is not even meant to be just some old regular man, and you were not given the able resources to make him into what he is actually born to be. You just don't have it. God did not give you that, because you don't belong to him and he don't belong to you. You can't do nothing for him but further domesticate him...weaken him.

And you...Mr. Whiteman with my Blackwoman. I don't even know if I should talk to you. It is difficult for me to hold my composure with you, sir. It is difficult to hold back the murderous rage that boils inside of me when the memory of you raping this same Blackwoman comes into my head. Do you understand me? I am well trained in diplomacy, for your sake.

My Blackwoman is so crazy today, that she has forgotten how "you" repeatedly forced her....she has forgotten the nasty, sweaty, beastial, lustfilled, violent rape that "you" have committed against her mothers and grandmothers. She has forgotten this. Listen, "you" are the direct fruit of your fathers. "You" are the same man as then; this is just fruit of the same seed on a different day. Have you changed, or just the social circumstances around you?

You think about that while I talk with this woman. Excuse me. Blackwoman, listen your ears to this. Your soul. Listen your soul to this.

"All" of those Blackwomen...everyone of your grandmothers who suffered the daily violent assault of rape, to their bodies, their spirit, their minds, their sacredness...they endured all of that for "you", that you may live today...but, that you may live today, to voluntarily lay down for this same man?

You can believe that, everyone of your ancestors look at you today in the desire to kill you...to kill you, because you are killing them. They suffered and died for this? An utter disgrace.

A knife to my soul. My pain, is not remembered. My suffering, not honored. My lovely child. This man has nothing for you, but what he has always had. Give me your hand...touch my pain....resonate, feel the slow depth of my moans. I will always be here. Remember me. I am in you forever.

––––––––––––––––––––––––

Home is primal in your stillest nature. The Sacred Marriage gave you birth, and will grant you re-birth stronger. It is an unspoken bond, never broken. Even ignored, it is always calling you. It is natural. Everything that belongs to you is in your home.

We are the home of one another. None, has experienced what we have experienced together. We are intimated, not because of our color, but because of our shared travels, our days. What we have specifically experienced gives us a compatibility unrivaled. Even amongst other Africans of our own family, but of different background experience, can not fully relate to nor fully understand the specificity of these private wounds. Your wounds have carved you a unique being unto yourself.

Stripped of everything. Stripped of your name, stripped of your culture, stripped of your spirituality, stripped of your self-respect, stripped of your entire self-identity...you two are all that each other has. You are all that each other needs. You are the only home that each other has known refuge. This man and this woman...throughout it all.

You contained me, in every drop of every tear, that falls. I am your reward, and you are mine. Together. Never broken. This Sacred Marriage...the only home I know.

In Peace.

<u>Becoming God Pt. I</u>:
"Obtaining, Knowledge, Wisdom,
& Understanding of Self."

Freedom Has Been Your Enemy.

(Gods with no Training are doomed to be devil.)

Freedom...the right to be God over your life. To be God over your life, can be the greatest blessing...or the greatest cursing. Which has it been for you?

For a lot of us it has been the biggest cursing. If one is given freedom, before they have grown into the mental maturity to know what to do with their free will, they will most likely self-destruct.

What is a man who has the freedom of choice? What is a man who has a million choices, but does not yet have the wisdom enough to choose what is best for his own well being? This is a man in bondage. He is doomed to make choices that he is not prepared to make. He is doomed to make constant mistakes; creating mischief in his life.

Most of us are being plagued by the self-created circumstances that we have foolishly put ourselves into. We have had free will, but we have had no wisdom to "profitably" exercise that free will.

To be "God" over your life, is to be the "Guide" over your life. But what if you have no "guidance"? You are doomed.

As children and as naively thinking youth, we desperately desire independence. We, "pre-maturely" desire an independence that we can not yet handle, but foolishly think we can. We don't take the time to master the skills and wisdom of life first, we just want to get in the driver's seat of this thing, and go. Thus, we wreck our lives.

The greatest injustice you can do to a child, is to give it freedom before it is prepared for that freedom. The greatest injustice you can do to a child, is to give it freedom before it is prepared for that freedom.

What would happen if you left a child, to live by his own free will? What would happen if you left a little child, left a little toddler in a room by himself, where there is a loaded-gun sitting on the table? The child would eventually kill himself! One might call "you" a "murderer" after that incident.

(So, now you understand why your enemy gives guns to you. He knows you are a child. He knows that we have no guidance, no mental maturity, no common sense. So, he leaves a few guns, some liquor, some drugs in the Black neighborhood, knowing that it will only be a matter of time before we blow our own brains out.)

Freedom to a child, is like poison candy. You hear the bible saying, if you spare the rod, you spoil the child. The "rod" does not only describe a means of "punishment". The "rod" describes "the law of discipline". A "rod" is something that is "straight", "strict", and "firm".

Discipline and Law is like a firm mold, that contains wet clay. If you remove the mold before the clay has fully dried and hardened into the "desired form", your creation will fall apart leaving it "deformed"...undesirable.

Here we live in a world of "deformed" human beings, producing "deformed" lives. How did we get this way? We had no discipline, no law, no guidance...or we chose to refuse it when it came.

We wanted so-called "freedom" from any guidance, and that freedom led to a our own Self-Arrest.

The greatest curse you could have ever had was to be "Made The Master", before you "Learned Mastery"...to be "Made God", before you "Learned Guidance". Powerful beings you are, yet Gods with no training, no discipline, no wisdom. Just power off course. Rage off course! No "coursed-rage" (or courage)! Just fearful, emotional, reactive, insecure rage off any productive course! Mischief makers in your life and your world. Your enemy is a god off course. That is what Lucifer the fallen angel was and is. He is an angry childish god off-course, making mischief in the house, refusing the guidance of his Father.

Only the restrictive law can guarantee our success. If you want Freedom...if you want True Freedom, which is the freedom to choose, along with the Guiding Intelligence to know what to choose; know that Freedom is born out of Restriction. If you first sit still long enough to learn the laws of where "not to go", you will be wise enough to choose for yourself, where "to go".

Gods with no training are doomed to be devil, while Gods with straight and strict guidance are destined to be Master of Success. Which will you choose for yourself? Wise men love to be reproved, while fools despise to be corrected.

We Have No "Self"-Esteem

(Polytheism vs. Monotheism)

We have esteem in everything and everybody except our Self and our Kind. No "self", "self", "self"-esteem, but rather we have "other"-esteem in things outside of Self. This is the root problem to any and every unhealthy human being. This means you and I and us all. We all suffer from different degrees of the same illness. We suffer from a disbelief in God, or in other words low, or no Self-Esteem.

To disbelieve in Self, is to disbelieve in God and His Purpose for creating Self. That is a heavy statement to decipher level by level, but it is true on all planes.

Whatever you place your esteem into is what you believe in...it is your God. To place your esteem, is to place your confidence, faith, assuredness, worth and hope into a person place or thing. A lot us place our esteem into the wrong point of reference. We place our esteem into persons, places, and things other than The True God who created and recreates us everyday...thus we fail. It is the wrong point of reference.

A person, place, or thing can assist you at building esteem, but they actually can not give it to you. For, they are outside of self, outside of the true point of reference.

When you have no point of reference, you have no definitiveness, no reality, no being, no root, no base, no sense of self in any way, form, or location. In this state we just float aimless and rootless cause we don't know where we are, where we have been or where we are going.

Even if we say we know where we want to go, it is useless. This is because with no point of reference as to where you are, you don't know how to get to where you want to go. You might claim to want to go somewhere, and you are already standing right there! Many of us are searching for the very place that we stand, and trying to find the very thing we already are. Lost. Can you imagine trying to read a map, and not know where you are, having no point of reference. Such is the case of our lives with no knowledge or appreciation of "Self".

I want to go to Chicago, but I don't know how far I have to go to get there? Why? Because I don't know what city I am currently in (no point of reference). I could have 300 miles to go, or 3 blocks before I hit the city limits. For all I know, with no point of reference, I could be standing on the South Side right now. You may already be there.

Here says the Blackman; I demand my Freedom, Justice, and Equality! Okay, well who are you demanding it from? From where are you seeking this esteem? From self? From other? What is the point of reference?

Freedom, Justice, and Equality??? Stand still and Exercise Your Freedom, Be Just to Self and your Kind, and you will Have Equality to all. Instead of continuing to search and search for Freedom, Justice, and Equality, why don't we just try looking in our pockets? There may be some God given rights in there. Accept what is naturally our own by birth, and be what is naturally already ourselves. You just might already be free.

Yes, you just might already be free. You just might already be equal. You just might already be happy. You just might already have power You just might have already attained inner peace. Have you checked your pockets for what you are looking for?

Too often we "needily" attach ourselves to people that don't deserve our acquaintance, not realizing that we have everything we "need" already. Just stand still and Be.

We may not even have to go "From Niggas to Gods", we might already be divine. Maybe we just need to just stand still and Be. Hmmm...I think we have something there. Stand still, and just be, instead of searching all around for the recipe.

Where is Mecca?

(Spiritual vs. Ritual pt. 3)

Where is Mecca? What is Mecca? Why is Mecca important? Where is the true East? What is the pilgrimage? Why do Muslims make the pilgrimage to the holy city of Mecca? What does this signify ("sign"-ify)? These are very good questions. They are even better questions for those who are ready to transcend "ritual", and on into the "spiritual".

Listen, it is time that we reason with one another on this subject, because we are trying to grow in our intelligence today. To be quite blunt and to the point...we could spend all of the money that we "don't have" to travel to the "so-called" (used to be) holy lands, if we wanted to. Yes. We could run through the hot desert sun making circuits around a big Black Box made of stone, if we wanted to. Yes, we could do all of that, if we wanted to. But allow me to ask the critical question.

After we have done all of that, what have we really done??? What have we really accomplished??? Well??? What???   What???   What??? Nothing really. We haven't accomplished anything but a big elaborate ritual for the sake of symbolic tradition. Even after all of that, <u>we still have yet to make the "real pilgrimage"</u>. It is time for us to arise into a higher realm of consciousness. Our thinking must grow, if we are to grow. "Thinkers" is what we want to become, not just blind "doers".

But, where is Mecca? Where is Mecca? Look at the condition of our people. Be real. You know that we can't go to no brother living hard life on the streets and say to him, that in order to be a Muslim, he has to have a lifetime goal of making a pilgrimage to the geographical city of Mecca, so that he can run around a big Black Box in the hot desert sun!!! No! No! No! That brother would look at you and I as if we were crazy as hell, and he should!!! Oh, yes he should.

Again, be real. Ain't nobody got no money to be traveling all· the way over to the "so-called" Middle East (formerly north-east Africa before the manufacturing of the Suez canal), to go sit down on a rug to pray and chat with some folks you don't even know! Please! Not today! You better take that same money and them same prayers and lay that same rug down in the middle of "downtown-ghetto U.S.A.", where that same money and those same prayers are needed the most! Talk to me?

The last thing that "we" should be worrying about is trying to run around a box in the hot desert sun! It's hot enough right here in the concrete desert hells of North Amerikkka!

The next time we take all of our life-savings to make a trip back "over-there", is going to be the day when we go home for good, not just to visit! And we will not be returning to run around in the sand either, but rather to righteously build, erect, and establish a civilization...a Nation...the Kingdom of God on earth even as it is in (a state of) heaven! Yes.

Look, we need not even waste time on this subject matter. Human Consciousness is evolving on this planet today. This is "spiritual vs. ritual". Don't get foolishly caught-up in the mis-understanding of all of these customs, traditions, and rituals. We want the Root of Truth. ALL "RITUALS" ARE JUST SIMPLY SIGNS AND SYMBOLS OF SOMETHING THAT

OCCURS WITHIN THE HEART AND MIND OF A "SPIRITUAL" PERSON. Take it, or let it alone.

Too often we get ourselves crazy and start floatin all off in space with this fantasy foolishness type of mind-set. That mind-set is hurting us, underdeveloping us, and leaving us ill-equipped for a real future. It is time to re-set your mind on reality. You could have stayed with the slave-master's "version" of Christianity, if you were still looking for a Hocus-Pocus Religion. You know?

I mean, the Reverend could have still been dunking your head in that tap water to "so-call" baptize you in the name of a "white" impostor Jesus, and save you for God's glory! Which really he was just dunking your head into the abyss of ignorance to brain-wash you and save you for the mental enslavement of your slavemaster. The coffin is comfortable isn't it? I know. But why change your religion, if you are going to maintain the same mind-state that kept you stagnated in the first one? Enough about that.

A return to sanity please. This is "Spiritual vs. Ritual"...and what is our lesson here? Too often we only embrace the "outer" symbol of a ritual instead of studying the "inner" substance and meaning that the ritualistic symbol is symbolizing! Right. This is why today's "rituals" have no sincere "spiritual" value. And they are having no real reforming effect on the religious society.

There must be conscious awareness of the meaning of the ritual, to extract any true spiritual value. This is why we get no juice, no nourishment, no true fulfillment. All that we get is the emotional elation of the idea of having completed the particular mechanics of the religious ritual. Ego gratification of your conscience. But where is God in this equation? This is "you", elating "yourself". But where is God in this? But you don't want to hear this do you?

The power of the "Spiritual" must be <u>EXTRACTED</u> from the "Ritual", or else you have nothing. How can a piece of fruit nourish it's possessor, if it's possessor refuses to peel back it's skin? Maybe the possessor was never looking for true nourishment of the soul in the first place, but only the assumed prestige of identity that comes from simply being holder of the fruit. Thus, he is satisfied with mere "possession", feeding his vanity, as his soul shrinks.

Mecca....is what we need, and Mecca is where we need to go. Mecca. Yet, we will never actually get there, by the path that most would have you travel. No.

Could we ever imagine that maybe, the true West is the exterior/outer/material world? And, maybe the true East is the interior/inner/spiritual world? Turn toward the East? Maybe, within this True East is Mecca? Maybe "Mecca" is a pure and righteous mind state (Holy City/State); and within the holy lands of Mecca, is the "Kaba" or the house of God, or the soul of God, or the throne of God? Maybe? Is it possible that the "Kaba" is the Brain/Mind, and within the Kaba is the Spiritual Center? Or maybe even the Spiritual Center of the "Black Stone" is the pineal gland saturated with Black neuro-melanin, which allows a person to see or perceive the true heavens and true reality of the living God? Is that possible? Possibly, the "pilgrimage" itself is simply the journey of life that a righteous person travels to achieve the spiritually elevated illuminated mental mind state of "Mecca", and bear witness that Allah is God...stoning the pillars of Shaitan (sinful establishment) and making spiraling circuits around the Principle (and Principal) of Allah God? Imagine that? Could that be? Could that actually be it's significance ("sign"-ificance)?

I heard it said that Brother Messenger Elijah Muhammad used to teach that no devils could go to the holy city of Mecca. What could he have meant by that? He could not have been talking about going to that geographical location called "Mecca" in the so-called Middle East...could he?

Just maybe he was talking about the fact that most devilish type caucasian people have a non-spiritual mind-state that prevents them from ascending into the Mecca state of mind? Maybe that meant that neurologically they have over-calcified or dormant pineal glands that are non-functional because of the caucasian person's general lack of ability to produce complex melanin molecules; therefore creating a biological obstacle in the ability to receive and perceive certain vibratory realities of energies, in addition to, and as a result of their historically perpetual evil state of mind and behavior that has been socialized into their culture being inbred over generations of history from the beginning, that they may not be equipped or qualify to experience the same spiritual revelations as The Original People, without that necessary quality of chemical hormones needed, deriving from the key chemical of carbon required to receive the illuminating spiritual sunlight that reproduces and transforms itself into the strong magnetic gravitational pull of electrical/magnetical spiritual energy divinely animating the material bodies of those who are in submission to the will of Universal Law (or Allah) by nature, because of their bio-chemical abundance of the above said, in concert with a righteous mind-state? Maybe he meant something like that? You think? Maybe...I don't know.

Or, maybe he just simply meant that "anybody" of any color, with an un-righteous heart and a wicked thinking mind, could never grow-up to recognize the divinity within their own selves and others? Maybe that is what he meant? Maybe he meant all of that together at the same time, when he taught that no devil could ever go to Mecca? Maybe? Maybe.

Now, what is this spiritual in the ritual??? Tell me

Blackman and Blackwoman, "Where is Mecca?" And what is "The Pilgrimage"? The pilgrimage is the pathway to your soul. Mecca is your mind, the Kaba your soul, the pilgrimage...your pathway there...your journey of life. This is spiritual within ritual. Make and complete your pilgrimage.

Mecca...is what we all need. Mecca is where we all need to go. "Where is Mecca?" "<u>There</u> is Mecca." Your pilgrimage began, the day you journeyed out your Mother's womb...in search of you...the harmony with God.

What is My "Real" African Culture?

Even this resurrection is a process that will take time, stages, and phases. It will take some time for us to mentally restore ourselves in full.

As we, the slumbering Blackman and Woman re-awaken from our sleep, we desperately scramble around searching for our Self-Identity. In that search for identity, we tend to grasp at anything that we can find; anything that can fill the abandoned void.

Awakening to the fact that we have been raped of our African Culture, it is natural that we scramble to reclaim what was once ours...our Self-Identity. Yet, as with all other things.......when we rise and take hold, we must rise and take hold to the right things, for the right reasons. We must what? We must rise and take hold to the "right" things, for the "right" reasons. Okay.

Yes, even in this struggle to reclaim our African Culture, we sometimes lose sight of the overall picture and goal, getting lost and misdirected in that desperate search for Self-Identity.

Remember this. Often, our mistakes may not have "solely" been because of "what" we have grasped onto, but more so "why" we have grasped onto it. Directionless naivete' will cast us to and fro, like a journey with no compass...well traveled but still homeless. Thus, caution should carry on through all of our stages of consciousness, regardless.

The relative point is that, even as we navigate to reclaim our African Culture, my beloved Brothers and Sisters, we have to be "discerning" and "discriminating". We have to be what?..."discerning" and "discriminating", meaning thoughtful, critical, and analytical of what you embrace and consume...lest we be lost all over again.

Very thoughtful we must be. Very mindful of the destination, focus, purpose, point and goal we must be...as we reclaim our Culture. Discerning and Discriminating as we navigate.

Bluntly...you don't just consume anything, just because somebody says it is "African". You don't just embrace anything, just because somebody labels it as "African". See, you just don't know how crafty this devil is.

As you reawaken into the awareness that you are an "African People", this enemy will try to teach you about what "he" recorded of your African history leading you off of the true path of your resurrection. He knew that the day of your reawakening was coming, and planned many mental detours to distract (dis-tract) and slow-down your resurrection process. Not only does he give you distorted images of Africa to dissuade you. His tactics have advanced. You would be surprised at what is placed in your path to pacify your mind's attention, to keep you "unproductively" occupied with the insignificant. Think. If you don't know the time, and what must be done in that particular time, man is lost. Think.

Man can be "lost", thinking that he is now "found", simply because he is not in sync with the times, and the needs of that time. Therefore, he is unsuccessful. Yesterday's "right", is "wrong" today...as is tomorrow's "right" is "wrong" today. You can not be too far behind, nor too far ahead. Successful man "must know the time". Oh, you don't hear this do you? Okay. Let's just go on.

So, how do we escape the pacifying distractive deceptions of our enemies? How do we stay focused-on and in-sync with the urgently significant...in sync with the times? By remembering "THE PURPOSE" for which you are reclaiming your past culture. What is that purpose? To make you a better effective human being at creating your present life and future. Don't forget that.

Admittedly, it is true that, when you look at "Africa" today, you are not looking at a Great People. No, I'm sorry. You are not looking at a Great Civilization. No. You are looking at the barren remains of what once was a Greatly Civilized people, driven all the way down to the bottom of this world.

And even as we read our African Histories, in all of it's GREATNESS, don't - forget - that - you - are - reading - the - history - of - the - fall - and - destruction - of - Black - Civilization. Yes, we have to think about that. Think. Think. Think.

It was a shock to me, when I heard it said that The Honorable Elijah Muhammad has taught that, even the great pyramids of Kemet (Egypt), in all of their technological genius, was what we built during our fall from "Higher" civilization! Can you believe that? We were indeed "great", but not near the total measure of our true "greatness"? That is something. That is something. That is something to think about a long time.

So, what do I do? "Which", "how" and "what" of my African Culture do I reclaim? The Blackman has history and culture that expands the length of time itself, so where do I indulge? Where do I establish a base and paradigm? These are good questions.

See, there is more to this story. In the midst of sifting through our different histories, our many cultures, our natural ways, our varied customs, our varied languages, and our many tribal heritages, we have to "think". How did we get into all these little groups and tribes? We did not always exist in such a fractionalized disarray! Your Nation of People used to be One People of a High Civilization before the timed hand of fate came down to smite that unity, into broken pieces of peoples fleeting into the jungled interiors of the continent of now called "Africa". Oh yes, I know you remember. I know you remember.

It is a shame but, even as we seek to reclaim our "African Culture", we have to ask ourselves "what really is my African Culture?"; as even the continent of "Africa" was named by and after a european explorer and conqueror. Even everytime we call ourselves "African", we are calling ourselves after a derivative of some whiteman's name. What were the original names of that continent? From what period of a vast history shall you seek to reclaim your history?

So listen, why is all of this being said here today? The bottom-line message is this. Do not suspend your analytical thinking! Don't allow us to get side-tracked with the insignificant. Never forget "THE PURPOSE"!

As we reclaim our African culture "in whole", let us not get satisfied with beating some drums, chewing on tree-roots and sticks, stringing shells, beads, and saber-tooth tiger teeth around our necks, pouring water on the ground, tribal dancing, sweating and singing at feasts and festivals, eating yams and some damn curry rice! Do you hear what I'm saying? Man, we are dying!

I mean, do you really think we have been suffering here in the hells of North America, because we forgot how to beat the African drum??? Because we forgot how to pour libations??? Because we didn't have enough feasts and festivals and fertility dances??? Is that why your people here are suffering? Is that what they are missing?

I mean come on now? Don't get carried away! All of that is wonderful and great, Black people. But don't get stagnated and satisfied with that! I mean, 'do you think that that is all that there was to us?' Sometimes we get so lost in a search for Self-Identity, that we just don't know who the hell we are?

You meet people today who think that they are so "Cultured", so "African", so "Natural"...that they think that going back to "Africa" means we gonna go back living in some damn grass huts with dirt floors. Talking about we have to reclaim the ways and customs of our ancestors! Fool, you don't know Your Ancestors! You don't know nothing about your ancestors, you are looking at the "destroyed" remnants of your ancestors...deceived by your enemy.

Do you really think that I would be taking my time to talk to you about reclaiming Your Greatness, if I thought that the "root" of Your Greatness is living in a grass hut, cooking in a pot outside, cutting warrior marks on your face, going to the river carrying water back and forth on your head!!!??? Is this what you think it means to reclaim Your Culture? Your Greatness???

Man, please...if so, then we are wasting our time. Don't you understand? You created irrigation and indoor water-works thousands of years ago in advanced civilizations. Don't you understand? So, don't bring me this 'water carrying on the head' business. All that we did during that time of water carrying, was survival tactics to endure and live after being destroyed from the light of high civilization...that we originally created. And, we were Most Wise, Most Noble and Most Beautiful even then...yes, even then, even then. Extremely so! Even in our lesser state, we were and are a Great People, today. But we don't understand the "vast expanse" of that greatness

No. This we don't understand.

When I call you the Mothers and Fathers of Civilization, and when The Honorable Elijah Muhammad called us the Gods and Goddesses of the Universe, what kind of civilization do you think that this Mighty God and Mighty Goddess built????...a civilization of grass-huts and beaded necklaces??? You better get a clue! Don't let your enemy fool you.

I love my Afrikan Drums, I love my Afrikan Dance, I love my Afrikan Culture, but I can not get "satisfied" with just beating some damn drums...thinking that I have returned unto MY WAY!!! You think that that is the way of your ancestors, but who are the ancestors to your ancestor's ancestors??? Huh? Do you know?

See, I know my ancestors! MY ANCESTOR(S) IS THE SUPREME GOD OF THE UNIVERSE! THE SUPREME BEING! THE ORIGINATOR OF THE HEAVENS AND THE EARTH!

RIGHT THERE, IS YOUR CULTURAL ROOT, SUN OF MAN! THERE IS YOUR HISTORICAL LEGACY! THERE IS YOUR ROLE MODEL, BLACKMAN & BLACKWOMAN! THE SUPREME BEING!

"That" is why "I", as an Original Blackman, am called the Father of Civilization. My history is a loooooooooong history. My ancestors come from the Circle of God Himself...men and women of a High mentality and consciousness governing their Universe. There is my culture!

My culture is not just in little trinkets, customs, and clothings! How can this contain Me? My Culture is an Eternal State of Mind! I am a Far-Reaching Dark Consciousness that Births Creations of Light from Pure Will! I am The Thought which Upholds The Heavens, and The Hand that Forms This Earth! I am The Vibration of the Atom that carries the Sound of My Afrikan Drum! I am The Energy you hear in it's lingering "Hummmmm"! You don't know my culture, you don't know my sum. You just don't know my sum. And who am "I"? I am

"YOU"...I am <u>The Black Man</u>!...I am <u>The Black Woman</u>! I am. I am...you...the Universe in person. Wait. What is my real Afrikan Culture?

What if I told you that you created water, and sand, from a few components to make molecules with your hands. Do you really know what it means to be an Original Blackman? Do you know who you really are? Do you think that your enemy has worked night and day to oppress you, because he's intimidated by some beads and some drums? Is that what he has been trying to stop you from doing? <u>What is it that he really fears about you and your potential</u>? It is beyond words. It is beyond words.

Male and female alike, remember. This Universe itself is the unfoldment of our Black Culture. The Supreme God, His Universe, His Way, His Sciences, His Immutable Laws, is Our Black Culture.

Not only do we "honor" our ancestors, but we live "honorably" because we are somebody's future ancestor. We not only <u>study</u> history, we are here to <u>make</u> some history. Where is our legacy?

Never forget "<u>THE PURPOSE</u>". Never forget that...we only **return to our ancient past for the "purposes" of carving out our modern future...carving out our modern future.** Grasp hold to that which will productively and progressively contribute to your present life and future. That is your compass, so navigate. Words to live by.

What is your real Afrikan Culture? Your roots are deeper than we know. Stay digging...digging deeply.

The Universe is Yours,
as is Afrika, a shiny jewel
in your shimmering crown.

Imagine
a Nation
of Your Own.

The population of a unified Germany is near 78 million. The population of Nigeria is near 105 million. The population of Japan is near 121 million. Imagine that.

The population of Great Britain approximates 46 million. The population of Ghana is near 12 million. The population of France is close to 54 million. The population of Libya is stands near to 3 million. The population of Israel is merely 4 million. New Zealand has near 3 million; Greece 9 million; Egypt 50 million. The Nation of Canada has near 25 million. The Nation of Australia has near 15 million. The Independent Nation of Kenya, 21 million. Imagine that.

The collective population of the Blackman and Blackwoman in America estimates between "<u>40-60 million</u>". Can you Imagine a Nation of Your Own?

It has been said that the collective economy of the Blackman and Blackwomen in America estimates 190 Billion Dollars per year making you the 8th richest nation on the Earth. And, there are a lot of nations on this earth. But you are the only homeless one.

Imagine-Nation.   Imagine-Nation.   Imagine-Nation. Imagine land on this Earth of your own. Imagine the entire area.

Imagine the square mileage. Imagine it having an outlet to the sea. Imagine the sea coast of Your Land. Picture it.

Imagine your own righteous set up of government. Imagine your own elected Honorable President or Noble Prime Minister.

Imagine the diplomats of your own Nation traveling abroad to represent you, as masters of statesmanship.

Imagine a body of sincere representatives in your own National Congress, making appeals for your own concerns. Picture it.

Imagine regional government officials. Imagine qualified local government officials, elected of your own family, friends, peers, and associates...improving and maintaining the structure of your own community. Just picture it.

Imagine an organized and unified body of people, making up your own Mass Society, spanning from one border of Your Nation to the other. Picture it.

Imagine your children awakening in the morning to go to schools of their own. Imagine your children being masterfully instructed in their own curriculum of True History, Relevant Mathematics, Universal Sciences, African Arts & Culture!

Imagine these healthy, balanced, mature, articulate, intelligent, geniuses at 6 years old, 10 years old, 18 years old...prepared and ready to compete and succeed in the international market. Imagine your children. Picture it.

Imagine yourself succeeding in a career that is contributing to and uplifting the commerce of your own nation. Picture it.

Imagine feeling proud every morning, to go work for a company, corporation, or business owned by your own kind...or even owned by yourself. Picture it.

Imagine the sky-line of your own city. Imagine the tall and elegant, masterfully crafted buildings that were creatively designed by our own architects. Picture it.

Imagine all of the friendly, clean, and respectable businesses that make up your own downtown marketplace...woven in and out of that sky-line. Picture it.

Imagine the alluring bakeries, the little outdoor cafes and juice bars, the top quality restaurants, the righteously stylish clothing shops, the fresh vegetable markets, healthy food stores, the cultural theaters, the majestic hotels, the internationally respected banks, the clean swept sidewalks, the artistically manicured greenery, the visiting tourist groups walking around in amazement at the wonderment, the grandeur, the energy, and the excitement, of such a thriving, progressive, peaceful, proud, clean, polite, respectful righteous society of people. Picture it. Just picture it. Can you see it? Imagine this Black Nation of Your Own.

Imagine beautifully laid-out parks and neighborhoods designed by your own city planner. Imagine your well built homes. Imagine the neighborhoods and neighborhoods of newly designed houses in spacious communities. Imagine the spacious yards for your children to play. Imagine the mannerable and friendly neighbors, who respect you, your family and your property. Picture it.

Imagine the hospitals full of your own highly trained nurses and physicians, masters of the mind and body...serving you with delicacy and care. Imagine that.

Imagine the Libraries with volumes and volumes of knowledge and wisdom spanning back unto the beginning of time discovered.

Imagine Your Own media systems designed to uplift, inform, educate, enrich and inspire minds of humanity, instead of oppress, depress, degrade and mindlessly distract the minds of humanity.

Imagine Your Own Agricultural Engineers scientifically

overseeing the acres upon acres upon acres of organic farmland crops that abundantly feed and nurture the entire Nation, as well as other Nations around the World. Your Own wheat, beans, and corn. Your Own orchards of apples and oranges.

Imagine the various manufacturing companies, factories and laboratories, producing high quality products to be sold all around the Earth, bringing the highest in "civilized" technological advancements to the world.

Imagine Your Own automobile manufacturers producing progressively engineered vehicles that function from clean, natural, and unpolutive sources of fuel and energy. Imagine that.

Imagine Your Own Defense Military of Air Forces, Naval Powers, and Armies of Specialized Troops in Military Artistry...to secure and protect us.

Imagine Your Own Airports and Space Travel Programs. Yes, it is true. Who do you think was the first to establish, chart, and to travel the stars?

Imagine a society of people whose personalities were that of a mutual love and respect for one another. Persons of a high civilization, high intellect, high spirituality, high moral development shall become commonplace, yet forever reaching higher toward advancement.

Imagine a people whose consciousness was the circumference of the Universe itself, whose home was the expanse of the Universe itself, who lived in accord with the laws of the Universe itself, who had become masters and maintainers of the Universe itself, and whose National Flag is the symbol of the Universe itself...the Sun, Moon, and Stars.

Imagine Nation. Imagine Nation. Imagine Your Nation. It is clear. You will see it, once you "believe" it, and once you "believe" it, you will achieve it. "Belief" is powerful.

For those of you who can see it, it is your divine

objective and duty to achieve it. Yes, it is. Your Quran says that, '(God) Allah puts on no soul, a duty beyond it's scope'. Create your part. Create it well. Imagine Nation.

Master Fard Muhammad?

(God is a Mind)

Master Fard Muhammad? Who is this person? Well, as you already know, The Honorable Elijah Muhammad said that this is the person who taught him, for three and a half years. This is the person that taught him the Supreme Wisdom, and gave him the mission to awaken the sleeping masses of Black People within the wilderness of North America. The Honorable Elijah Muhammad said that he himself was taught by God, in the person of Master Fard Muhammad.

Uh-Oh, now what did our brother Elijah Muhammad mean when he said that he was taught by God? Many of our parents thought that Elijah was crazy. They thought maybe Elijah might have been fasting a little too long and started hallucinating or something. We knew that Elijah was wise but he just might be taking this "Mooz-lim" stuff a little too far. Right? Isn't this what we thought at one time?

How could God be a Man? And if God was a Man why would he come amongst us Negroes? "Elijah, I admit that you be telling the truth about that whiteman, but I think you might be a little confused about this other man being God." Isn't this what we said? Isn't this how we were thinking?

Well, considering the fact that our own mental

healthiness is ("<u>extremely</u>") questionable, we really don't have too much of a basis to question the mental-health of this wise man, The Honorable Elijah Muhammad. We disputed his teachings about meeting with God. We disputed with him, as if we knew God personally or something. We did not know anything at all about God. How can a fool question, the wise?

Just a few minutes ago, this devil had us worshiping a pale-faced impostor of Jesus, that we thought was God! The devil had us worshiping his wicked self, but we did not know any better! We don't even know our real names, and at the same time have the nerve to argue with a wiseman about the realities of God! Is that right? You a Black Mud man, and you walking around here calling yourself "John Jones", in this modern day in age? Who the hell is "John Jones"? What kind of sense are you supposed to have? Huh? See, this is our condition, beloved one. Do you see what I'm trying to communicate to us?

So, from what basis of knowledge do "we" have to argue with anybody, when "we" don't even know our own self-identity? Please give me a break, and yourself too. I know that it sounds crazy at first, but we need to stop all of this critical arguing and start some critical thinking and analysis! Come think with me Blackman and Blackwoman. Open up and listen. Open up...listen...think.

Now, let's talk. Who is God? Think. What is God? Think. Where is God? Think. These are some serious questions. Right? Right. Well let's think about this together. Maybe we will find some new insight.

Do we know anything at all about God? Let us see. Now, who and what is God? <u>Some</u> of us say that God is the "All-Mighty". <u>Some</u> say that God is "Supreme Wisdom". <u>Some</u> say that God is "The Highest Intelligence". <u>Some</u> say that God is "The Best Knower". <u>Some</u> say that God is "The Highest State of Mind". <u>Some</u> say that God is "The Spirit of True Love". <u>Some</u>

say that God is "Pure Righteousness". Some say that God is "The Harmonious Rhythmic Natural Laws of The Infinite Universal Sphere of Life".

Some even say that God is "the combined collective consciousness of our ancestral intelligence that is locked within the central genetic core, seed, and root of our true inner essence, that can only be interpreted and expressed through the perception of our mentally resurrected spiritual third eye, which will only be activated by the inner peaceful unification of all mediums of our sensory perception centers, so that 'thine eye' will be single and our body shall be filled with the illumination of light, which will animate our material manifestation on this physical plane to a spiritually guided life of inner and outer peace". Yes, this is what some say.

Okay, so now who is right? Who has the correct description as to "who" and "what" God is? Which one of those descriptions provide us with a true perception of God? Who is right? Good question, huh? Right?

Well let us see about this thing. It's kind of difficult to pick one of these descriptions of God over the other, because all of these descriptions are true and correct at the same time! Yes that's right! God Allah, is "all" of that and then some more! Huh? Why can't God be all of this simultaneously? Well, He can and He is. The "All" in "All".

Yes! Allah God is, "Supreme Wisdom", "Pure Righteousness", "All-Mighty", "The Highest Intelligence", "The Best Knower", "The Highest State of Mind", "The Spirit of True Love", "The Harmonious Rhythmic Natural Laws of The Infinite Universal Sphere of Life", and "The Combined Collective Consciousness of our Genetic Ancestral Intelligence", all combined into ONE!!! Do you perceive that?

Yes, Allah God is all of that combined into "One", but Allah God is all of that combined into "One" what? "One" what?

"One" spirit in the sky somewhere? "One" spook in space somewhere? "One" 2000 year old dead white-boy hanging on cross, turning the other cheek and loving his enemies, somewhere? "One" Holy Ghost floatin around under sheets getting young virgins pregnant, somewhere? Or is it that "One" Holy Ghost that makes Black folks jump and shout at the local Baptist Church on any given Sunday morning? Well? Well? Well? No!

We are not as ignorant as we used to be, when the slavemaster tricked us into believing all of that. We are trying to be an intelligent thinking people again. So, we have done away with the ghost-stories. We want intelligence.

So listen. Yes, God is "Supreme Wisdom", "Supreme Intelligence", "Supreme Righteousness", and "The Spiritual Love Supreme" all combined in ONE, but wait.

We know that we have never seen wisdom, intelligence, righteousness, and a loving, nurturing formless spirit floating in the sky. Wake-up! You know good and well, that in order to produce any type of wisdom, intelligence, righteousness, or loving spirit, you first have to have some BRAINS to produce it.

Ghosts don't have heads and shoulders, so where are their brains kept? In order to produce Supreme Wisdom, Supreme Intelligence, Supreme Righteousness, and Love Supreme, you must first have a Supreme Heart and a Supreme Mind to produce or manifest these Supreme attributes!

You can not have a Supreme Mind unless you manifest it from some Supreme Brains! And you will not ever find any functioning, alive, living, thinking, Supreme Brains, unless they come in the head or skull of a Supreme Being!!!!! Oh, wait a minute now.

Please think about what is being said, beloved Blackman and beloved Blackwoman. Please patiently see into the inner meanings of these words to fully perceive this.

When The Honorable Elijah Muhammad said to us that he had met with God, he was not talking about all of that mystical type of stuff. No, sir. No, ma'am. Due to our mental condition here in this country, we have acquired such a childish viewpoint of things which leads us to a web of misunderstanding. As we gain a more mature type of thinking, we will be better able to understand Mr. Elijah Muhammad's teachings to us.

Think with me. Our dear brother, Elijah Muhammad, told us that God came to us, in the person of Master Fard Muhammad. This man, Master Fard Muhammad placed the seed of life (truth), into the mind (womb) of The Honorable Elijah Muhammad. This was a very, very immaculate conception.

Master Fard Muhammad raised up a simple Blackman from among us, and then he breathed the breath of divine wisdom into his nostrils, making him a living soul...a living mind. (This is spiritual talk, now. This simply means he taught the man, not blowing breath. Keep it real.)

Then The Honorable Elijah Muhammad was commissioned (co-missioned with God) to mentally awaken the sleeping masses of Black people, who are mentally trapped within the wilderness (wild uncivilized lifestyle) of North America. What is so difficult to understand about that?

Allah God came to us "in the person" of Master Fard Muhammad. This is what Elijah has said, now what does all of this mean? This simply means that The Intelligence, The Wisdom, The Love, The Peace, The Mercy, The Spirit and The Mind of Allah (God) came unto us, up inside of the material flesh of a Master Teacher named W. Fard Muhammad. You believe that the devil has the power to possess individuals, but don't believe that the Supreme God has the power to place Himself on the inside of an individual as well????

The Mind of The God came unto the lost sheep, the

Blackman and Blackwoman mentally lost in America...God came to teach us something through the vessel of this Man. Visualize. Isn't this always how it happens?

Thought...how else would God choose to communicate to us, but through a Man? God has good sense enough to know that He could not speak to us from the clouds in the sky, because God is intelligently thinking. And Wise God knows that in order to communicate with us directly face to face, he must have "vocal-cords" from which to produce an audible, plus an intelligible sound in the form of the Spoken Word, for us to best comprehend his message! Huh? Can't be speaking in "tongues", unless you mean the type of "tongues" that is defined as the "dialects" or "languages" of the people? he spoke in many "tongues".

Plus The God knew that, if he tried to speak to us from the clouds in the sky, He would have scared the hell out of us!!! We would have all died of a heart-attack, if we heard some voice rumbling up in the sky! Yes, you know it's true. Thank God for common-good-rational-sense.

Straight talk. God is a "mind". A "mind" manifests through a "brain". A "brain" lives in a "head". A "head" sits upon a "body". Yes God is a "spirit", but "spirit" vibrates and emanates from the core/center of a "being". "Spirit" lives in a "house". It is time that we mature enough to stop looking at the "container" and start looking at what is "contained" inside of the "container". Think.

God is a mind. Mind is a Man/Woman. You are not flesh, blood, and bone. You are the essence of what animates the flesh, blood, and bone. Your body is just a platform, stage, or finite vehicle of expression. Right? Right. So, are you the "Temple of the Living God" or are you "the synagogue of satan"? What is manifesting from your vehicle of expression? Who is coming "in the person of you"? Stop, and let thought commence. God is a Mind. God is a Mind.

In patient time, we will soon understand who we are once again. And we forever give thanks and holy (pure) praises to Allah, for coming in the person of Master Fard Muhammad to re-ignite our minds into mental illumination, after this devil has wickedly snuffed-out the light of truth.

We thank Allah for the seeds of wisdom. And we thank our beloved brother, The Honorable Elijah Muhammad, for skillfully, obediently, and carefully planting those seeds among our people. We are those seeds! Watch us grow! Harvest time is coming soon, by the light and love of Allah who came in the person of Master Fard Muhammad. Wisdom is known of it's children. Watch. Time. Unfold. Peace be unto you.

God "is" a Scientist!!!

Many of us believe that so-called "science" and so-called "religion" are in direct conflict with one another because of the supposed vast ideological differences between the two. Right? But nothing could be further from the actual facts. Upon deeper thought, we will recognize that it is truly our own miscomprehension of both of those fields of study which has actually caused the conflict in our understanding.

Question: What is at the root of this construction called Universe?

Answer: It is "Mathematical Science" that is at the root of this construction called Universe.

Question: So, with that being true, what would that make The Creator of this Universe?

Answer: With that being true, The Creator who constructs this Universe must be a "Mathematical Scientist" Himself! Plain. Simple. True.

You live in the midst of Science. I said, you live in the midst of Science. You live in the midst of God's genius. Whose genius? God's genius. God, The Scientist.

Everything of "Bi-ology", "Ec-ology", "Ge-ology", "Astr-ology", "Cosm-ology", "Psych-ology", "Anthrop-ology", "Soci-ology", "Zo-ology", "Meteor-ology", "Ide-ology", and every other type of "ology" is rooted in the study of "The-ology" (Theology). This is because "The-ology" is "The"-science above and beneath all other sciences! It is the seed before the root, as well as the seed inside the fruit. It is before and after all things. Alpha and Omega. It is "The"-science that encompasses all other sciences collectively. Theology. "The" Science. God Science.

Your God's Science is the Master Root to all other sciences. He has Created it "all" with the stroke of His pen. Your God has absolutely "authored" all that is in this existence. You exist in the midst of his mind, his genius, his science. He is The Author. This Universe is His volume...his eternal edition. His Book! The One Book! The Universe! "Uni"-"Verse"! The "One"-"Verse", in which all other verses are birthed and contained!!!

Therefore, just because your vision might only allow you to read one page of His written book, doesn't mean that the rest of the pages have no validity. True Spirituality is Scientifical, as True Science is Spiritual. There is no conflict. Our limited vision/wisdom might only allow us to see so much at certain stages in our development, but nonetheless God is a Scientist.

More than ever today, we must sincerely and comprehensively understand the reality of Our God. And that understanding is born from the unified study of "science" and "spirituality". The unified study of the "rational" and the "intuitive", will provide a balanced stimulation to the Left-Sided Rational Hemisphere of the brain, as well as the Right-Sided Intuitional Hemisphere of the brain. This brings a balanced mental vision in which we can better perceive the total balanced reality of God. This is truth.

Yes, <u>back to reality</u> is the path of our travels...the reality of God. Understand that The Supreme Being is not only "<u>a</u>" scientist, but rather is "<u>The</u>" Scientist. The Supreme God is not guiding the evolution of the Worlds using no hocus-pocus type of magic-spoof! Wake-up slave! The God is masterfully evolving all of the Worlds using a much superior form of mathematical science. A science of which he is Master and

Creator of. Yes!

Your little enemy devil knows that God is a scientist. That is why this devil has tricked us into wasting our time worshiping an imaginary spook in the sky, while he is wisely spending his time studying the scientific realities of this Universe toward technological genius; and far exceeding the rest of the World. The devil wants to keep God's science a mystery to the majority population of the world, so that he can deceive, control, and exploit the population.

Therefore, this means that after we come back-down into reality from outer-space worshiping an imaginary "Mystery God", we have to <u>pay money to,</u> <u>take orders from,</u> and <u>seek assistance from</u> this devil who has mastered the realities of this material/physical world in which we all have to live. Isn't that something? While we were chanting, singing, dancing, and burning incense trying to contact God, the devil took over the earth trying to be God. It is <u>he</u> that the world population bows to.

He has subdued the air, sea, and the land. He took over agriculture, commerce, and educational institution. So after we are finished chanting, singing, dancing, and praying, we have to go to this devil to get food, money, and an education. Yet he is that same one that sent us up into space wasting our time looking for a white-spook-mystical-space-God in the first place. Something is wrong here, don't you think?

Your devil is trying to master the sciences of divine so that "he" can become Lord of the Worlds. And he thinks that the evolution of time will be guided by his wicked hand. His wicked plans are laid in this way, because he understands that in order to supplant The Supreme God he has to become a Supreme scientist. Your devil understands that God is a scientist and that he created the Universe based on scientific law. He understands this.

But where is the Blackman and Blackwoman??? We are all down at the church, mosque, or synagogue being taught about a Mystical Mystery God, while the enemy is in the laboratory learning about a Real God. He is studying the construction of the chemical compounds and molecular structures that make up the creation of this Universe, so that he can better learn the knowledge of "The Creator" who created it...The Real God, and the Realities of That God!

All the while, we Blackfolks are in the church basement, after Sunday afternoon worship service, arguing over whether or not Jesus rose on the third-day!!! Hell, if "WE" ain't rising, then what does it matter!? That is a shame, brother and sister.

Or either we are sitting around the mosque trying to calculate exactly how many wives the Prophet Muhammad of Arabia had, while the whiteman is calculating the distance between Earth and Mars, so that he will know where best to orbit his telescopic satellite to photograph the planet's surface! This man has taken over the world, while we have sat non-productively debating the insignificant. That is a shame, brother and sister.

Your enemy is the one who put you on this wrong course, to distract you! He is trying to make it to God before you do! What makes you think that "he" would give you the proper interpretation of your spirituality? He tells "you" to find God one way, and then "he" goes off to dis-cover God another way. Why does he have all the power, and you have all the problems? Why does he have to answer to no one, and you have to answer to him? You had better listen.

Your enemy. Your opposer. Your deceiver. He is "realistically" meditating on the true living realities of The God, as we only meditate "ritualistically" on an imaginary formless spirit. It is clear, that we are deceived. We are deceived from our front-side, from our back-side, from our right-side, from our left-side, and all the way to the in-side of our own minds. We have been led astray. We have been led astray into the insanity of a mental imbalance. Obviously.

So now what? How do we get back on the right mental course? How do we get on course to a holistic knowledge of God? How do we get truly connected to the peace and power of The God?

Answer; if we are truly in pursuit of the total Will of God, we have to truly be in pursuit of the Mind of God...not just the Heart of God, but the Mind of God. The Intelligence, not just the Emotional. The Science of the Spiritual, and The Spiritual of The Science.

We have His Word in our hands, but we also exist in the midst of His Word. To know Him, is to know it all. He is The Author of it All...and therein awaits His Power, His Peace, His Balance. All Realities belong to Him. It is not beyond our comprehension.

The Changing of The Gods!

(Are You Preparing to Rule The World?)

Wise up god! Can't you see what I'm, saying? Can't you see what this is all about? Don't you know what time this is? It's time for the changing of the Gods! One god going out, and One God coming in! One god coming down and One God raising up! One god at war with righteousness, One God at war with wickedness! The Original God is getting Up Out of The Grave to return to his rightful place. This means you!

Here comes The Original Suns, The Lights of The World! The Creams of The Planet! The Gods & Goddesses of The Universe! It's time! It's time! So, raise up, God! Wise up, God! The Sons & Daughters will rise in the West, as the Mothers & Fathers once rose in the East...coming forth by day.

But hold up...hold up. You gots to wise up, to raise up...wise up, to raise up. True. Wisdom must precede...must precede. So, let us crack them brains apart, and start this.

Our question at hand today? Is this Mighty Sun <u>ready</u> to rise? Is this Mighty Sun <u>preparing</u> to Rise? I'm talking to you. Is the Original Blackman & Blackwoman <u>preparing</u> to take <u>his & her post</u>, <u>his & her throne</u>, <u>his & her rightful place</u> on top of civilization? What up God? You gonna resurrect or what?

The longer the Sun sets buried in the shadowy grave of this Earth, the longer the pale moon rules the sky...prolonging this night time, these dark ages of ignorance death, and savagery. Is God dead forever, or shall He return as He said in his prophetical word? Tell us? You gonna resurrect or what? Will there be a second coming, Blackman? Humanity is in desperate need.

I said, <u>are you preparing to Rule the World</u>? Do you know what it takes to be The Lord of the Worlds? Do you know what "the Worlds" are? Speak! Speak! Speak to me! Do you know what it means to be Yourself again??? Let us prepare the lessons for them Gods gettin up out of that grave. Do you know what it means to be "The Lord of The Worlds"? And do you know what "Worlds" you are to be Lord of? We must know this. This is all so real.

Listen. What is a "world"? What is a "world", that you may rise to rule it? A "world" is a sphere of existence. A "world" is a functioning sphere of activity governed by it's own laws. A "world" is an organized system of activities working toward a common goal and objective. Now, just listen. Follow this.

In This Larger World, you have many "smaller worlds" contained inside of "The One Universal World". The Universe is a World. This Planet is a World. This country called America is a World. All of these are spheres of existence inside of other spheres of existence. Worlds within worlds. You are a World, yourself. Now, listen, listen, listen. If you are to raise up to rule "<u>The</u> World", there are certain "little worlds" inside of "<u>The</u> World" that you have to master in order to <u>Master The One</u>.

In this World, on this planet, or in this sphere of existence, you have different little systems to govern all the activities of this One World...the little worlds that make The Whole World go around.

Look around...inside of This World called Society. We have the "World of Business and Commerce". You have the "World of Government or Political Science". You have the

"World of Education or Scholastic Science". You have the "World of Manufacturing or Industrial Science". You have the "World of Food Production or Agricultural Science". You have the "World of Health Services or Medical Science". You have the "World of Law or Judicial Science". Do you see what we are saying?

All of these are "worlds and systems" that make an organized society function and run. And this point has to be made clear, in order for us to see the realism in this.

The thought of The Blackman and Blackwoman returning to the top of civilization, is not an idle, vain, nor empty ideal. It is an inevitable fact, attached to an implemented plan. The question is are you preparing for the inevitable? Are you preparing for your participation in the inevitable?

The point is that we must master these smaller worlds, to Master The Universe, again. This is what it really means to be "Lord of The Worlds"...to be master of all spheres and systems of activity that makes the One World go around. You better think about these things. This is real. Once you master each smaller world, it shows you the real possibility of mastering the next elevation, on to the next, on to the next.

Blackman. Blackwoman. I said are you preparing to rule the World? Our Nation must produce a Master, a well equipped, well trained, Master Scientist to oversee each one of these little functioning worlds. Do you understand what I'm saying? This is serious life. We will build our Own Society for our Own Nation. We will do this. It is either do this or die...and we will not die.

We must prepare and produce a **God** or **Goddess**, for each realm! We must produce and purposefully educate a **Master Scientist**, to righteously rule the "**World of Commerce and Business**". We must produce scientists to righteously rule or oversee the "**World of Government**",

"The World of Education", "The World of Manufacturing and Industry", "The World of Agriculture", "The World of Medicine", "The World of Law and Justice", "The World of Communications", "The World of Spirituality and Theological Science", "The World of Architecture and Construction Engineering Sciences", "The World of Warfare and Military Sciences", "The World of Mechanical and Modern Electronic Technological Sciences", "The World of Waste Management or Waste Recycling Sciences", etc., etc., etc!

These are all worlds and sciences that must be mastered by "you", "you", "you", or "you".

You, The Nation of Righteous Gods and Goddesses, who were dead and asleep to the knowledge of your self-identity and purpose, but are now being raised up to recivilize the World again, after the savages have spread their savagery and unrighteousness to the ends of the Earth..."You" must produce a God or Goddess to righteously rule each one of these worlds, under the guidance and law of The One Supreme God firmly established on The Throne. The One Supreme God, from whom's wisdom we all nurse ourselves to divine strength. He is the Head of this class, and is "The" Master that prepares us to master His many realms of activity. This is His Universe-ity. Only a Master can make you a master. (He is the One who will make Pharaoh let His people go! Your bible has come to life.) So, prepare for your life on the other side of this thing.

Each one of you that are born, are born with a specific gift and talent. This is for a reason. Each one of you are born with a specific attribute of The God, that is to prepare you to function in your specific area of expertise. You are of natural talent, in your specific arena of mastery. This is where you serve society and make your contribution to the world.

Yes, you and I are little masters standing in a circle around The Master Supreme, who feeds us the wisdom to master our own field of endeavor. You have to hold your specific post or rule over your specific world, that helps to balance and maintain the entire system, circle, and entire World. I know you understand what I'm talking about . This is nothing new to you, I'm just trying to spark the memory of a sleeping God.

Now, just why is all of this being said to you here today? Look, the point is that we can't be slipping and tripping, acting the fool, like we ain't got some business to handle! That is the point! God you got much major business to handle! There is not time to loaf or leisure.

Do you know how long you been laying up in that grave? Your eyes all crusty, brains all rusty! But it's okay, that's to be expected. That is to be expected. We didn't know any better than to be acting a the fool before now! All that we knew was that we was just the whiteman's "nigga". It's so shameful.

Nobody told us that we ourselves, were that crucified God awaiting resurrection. Nobody told us that we were the true Body of Jesus. Nobody told us that. We didn't know! So, of course we just acted a fool! Here we are sittin up in Hell with our devil, and we just figured...if you can't beat him, then just join him! We tried everything else? What else were we going to do? You know? Sittin here in hell, I figured I might as well raise a little hell myself, right? Maybe that's what I was supposed to do? It didn't quite feel right, but they said I was born in sin, so I figured "Hey, what the hell???" Yeah, that is exactly what is was, "exactly hell".

But now that you know that the only sin that you were born into, was the sin of your oppressor's moral-less society, and shaped in the inequity of his rebellious mind-state and character, what you gonna do? Are you going to continue to raise hell with this devil, or are you gonna raise up out of hell with your True and Living God?

Now that you know...the truth of this message will never let you go! The truth will "make you" or "break you", depending upon your reaction to it. This is "The Changing of The Gods" Today! Are you prepared to take your post, with your Supreme God? Blackman you gots to come real. Blackwoman you gots to come real. The time is set. What you gonna do? Live or die? This is last minute.

Now that you "know", you have to "act" like you know. When you don't know "who you are", you automatically do not know "what your function is". But, I am telling you who you are! I am telling you all your names! You are the Sons and Daughters of the Supreme Ruler of The Universe, The God! No debate. That is your Father, and you are the fruit of Your Father.

All of you are just different manifested parts of Your Father. Yes, you are! And you are named after Your Father, like any other child would be. I know the slavemaster took Your Father's name from you and gave you his own, but I'm going to remind you of Your Original Name!

Now, when I call your name, don't raise your hand, "Raise Your Mind" and do what your Father created you to do! I will tell you your name and I will tell you your Father's name!

You. You right there...your name is "Aziz", which means you are the "Powerful" of God! You are created to master the Military Sciences. You are the protector of the Nation, the protector of peace and order. Now, you get prepared to take your honorable post and await further orders.

You over there...your name is "Rasul", which means "Messenger" of Your God. You are created to master the Science of Communications and Information Exchange. Prepare to take your honorable post, and await further orders.

Your name right here...your name is "Shaheed", which

means the "**Witness**" of Your God. You are created to master the **Science of Spirituality**. Prepare and train to take your honorable post, and await further orders.

Sister, come here....your original name is "**Alimah**", which means the "**Knowing**" of your God. You are created to master the **World and Science of Education**. Prepare to take your honorable post, and await further orders.

And you sitting there...your original name is "**Hakim**", which means the "**Wise Judge**" of Your Father. You are created to Master the **World of Law and Justice**, of course. Prepare to take your honorable post, and await further instructions.

Brother, your name is "**Razaaq**", which means the "**Provider and Sustainer**" of Your God. You are created to be the **Lord and Scientist of Agriculture**. Prepare to take your honorable post, and await further orders.

Oh, and you Blackman...no sir, I did not forget you. Your name is "**Malik**", which means "**King**" for Your God. You are created to master the **Art of Rulership**, the **World of Political Science and Righteous Government**. Prepare to to take your honorable post, and await further orders.

See, when you "know yourself", you "know your name". And when you "know your name", you "know your duty and function" to your life...your "duty and function" to your people...your duty and function to Your God. And when you "know <u>who</u> your name is from", you "know <u>who</u> gave you your duty and function". And you know to whom your praises are due forever.

"All" of these righteous names belong to "Your Father". "All" righteous names belong to "Him", so instead of trying to call him by all 99 of His attributes, he said to call him Allah (All-ah). Because he is "The All". He is "the All in All" existing simultaneously at the same time. We are projected particle parts of "The All". "<u>Individual Sunbeams</u>" of light, projected from "<u>The One Mighty Sun</u>, <u>The One Mighty Light</u>". You better know yourself.

Check the time. This is the **Changing of The Gods.** The caucasian is being relieved of his duty around the planet, bit by bit. His time has run out. Now, are you preparing for your return to duty? Don't sleep. Your enemy knows what time it is, and that is why he is doing everything within his power to keep you "unprepared" and "unworthy", so that he can get an extension of time to his rulership of The Planet Earth. You better listen to me.

Your Supreme God can not restore you to your rightful place if you can not handle the job! You must cultivate an Intelligent Brain and a Righteous heart to manage the world. You must be a worthy candidate. Now, who's gonna take the weight?

They
95% Less than
God!!!

(Ode to Hip-Hop...Blackman Victory Chant!)

Attention Devil:

Your 32-degrees is still frozen. Iceman impostors can never replace the chosen.

Pure Sun of God, I exist as fine mist. If mentally blind, my reality you will miss.

Three-Sixty degrees requires the God throne. You can not approach, so just leave The God alone.

Pack your bags, hang it up, abort your mission...against God Allah, you validate no competition.

Six thousand years, I lay my head down to rest...but on the seventh day, you will plead "no-contest!"

For the slumber of God will be up, be resurrected. A Saviour is born, God Allah be manifested. Now, check it.

They 95%, Less than God!
They 95%, Less than God!
I said, they 95% less than God!
And you will never defeat...The Sons of Allah!
(Repeat)

"Niggas"
Ain't God Yet!
(Spirit + Matter = Life)

You are The Original Blackman and Woman. Cream of The Planet Earth. God and Goddess of The Universe.

Yes this is true. This is true. This is true, but so what?! Yes, biologically, chemically, physically, or materially you are supreme amongst beings, but so what? So what? Soooooo-what!!! Who cares???

Listen. I want to talk to those of you who already know that you are the Original Man and Original Woman, but yet got the nerve to walk around ignorantly boasting and bragging about it!

I want to talk to those of you who already know that you are bio-chemically supreme, and think that this single fact alone has qualified you to righteously declare yourself as a divine Black God or Black Goddess!

I want to talk to those of you who are constantly bragging and boasting with your silly mouth. "Look at me, I'm Black!" "I'm Black!" "I'm Black!" "I'm The Black Man!" "I'm the Original Man!" "I'm the First Man!" "I'm the Cream of the Planet Earth!", "I'm God!" "I'm this!" "I'm that!" Negro...please. Please...negro. Negro...please. Please sit down somewhere. "Allah God loves not any self-conceited boaster". We surely die for a lack of understanding.

When you walk around boasting and bragging about "The

Blackman is Supreme!" or "The Blackman is God!", you are just making a severe FOOL out of yourself. Boasting and bragging, setting yourself up for a great fall. Here you are shouting out loud, "The Blackman is God!" "The Blackman is God!" And the whiteman looks at you and just laughs.

He says, "look at my niggras over here talking about they God. These niggras still ain't figured it out." He laughs, because he has the intelligence to recognize that deep-down inside, you really don't actually "believe" in what you are saying. He knows that you are just the same old nigga singing a new song. You ain't no threat to him. You ain't no sweat to him.

You just talking. Lip-service. Boasting-mouth. Idle-words. Hot-air. You just talking. You ain't no threat, and you ain't no sweat. The presence of God should make a devil sweat, but ain't no devils sweating while you walking around loudly boasting... "I'm The Original Man!" "The Blackman is God!" Your devil ain't afraid of that. Why should he be? Afraid of what?

Why should one little devil be afraid of another little devil that's walking around immaturely repeating something that he has heard, but doesn't understand? Children always "mindlessly" imitate and repeat the words they hear, but that don't mean they saying nothing. You don't have to take their words seriously, because they don't take their own words seriously. I said, "You don't have to take their words seriously, because they don't take their own words seriously."

So, what's all of this lip-serving, "mindless" boasting all about? What's that supposed to do? Niggas don't believe they no Gods! And anybody of intelligence can see that! That's why your enemy just sitting back laughing at you everytime you open your mouth to a "mindless" boast of your divinity or supremacy.

Your enemy says, "Yeah...Yeah...Yeah nigga okay, so you

are God...now what?   Yeah, you are the Gods of the Universe...yeah...yeah, so what?"

"Yeah, yeah, you can be Gods of The Universe, The Second coming of Christ, or whatever the hell you want to be, but you niggras just better not forget who "I" am, when it comes time for you to pay my rent money at the end of this month! You hear me boy?"

"Yeah, yeah, you go ahead and be The Lords of the Universe, and I'll just keep on being your Landlord!"

"You niggras take the Universe, and I'll take the money. Okay, niggras?"

He has every right to laugh at us, as we childishly make a fool of ourselves. Any self-conceited boaster is a fool. Niggas ain't God! You can't authentically claim the divinity of your ancestors when you do not realistically exhibit their righteous thoughts and conduct. No, Niggas Ain't God.

Your "physical characteristics" may reflect those of the Black Divine Gods and Goddesses of antiquity, but your "mind and spirit" does not. You may look like God, but you acting like "nigga", and Niggas Ain't God. If you are God, then adhere to the Laws of God Allah (All-law).

Do you think that your ancestors were divinely great, just because their material form was "Black"? Is that what you think? If so, then what's your problem? You "Black"...now where is your greatness? Where is your power? Where is your divinity? Good question. Where is your divinity? Open your mouth and talk to me, Blackman! Stop playing son! Your God is Real! And our people are dying as we play these damn games.

Listen.   Obviously, it was not the fact that your ancestors were "Black" in physical skin pigmentation, that made them divinely great. Striving to create their mental genius and uphold their moral character, is what preempted their greatness. It was their works, deeds, and actions that made them great!

Just because we are their physical offspring, does not automatically declare us to be great. The question is, 'Are we their intellectual, spiritual, and moral offspring?' Now, what's the question again?

It would be foolish for you to pre-maturely boast and brag about being Gods and Goddesses. That is not so wise, beloved. When you begin to manifest the mind, deeds, and actions of divinity, we will all know it, without you telling us. Thank you. You have to earn those righteous titles just like your ancestors earned it for themselves. No, we have not yet ascended.

The Son of Man must know that (Spirit + Matter = Life). Spirit plus Matter equals Life. What good is the material "form of God", void of the internal "mind of God"? No-good at all...because (Spirit + Matter = Life). You will have no True Life, one without the other.

To have no Life, is to be considered Dead. The Blackman is now considered to be Dead...a Dead God? Spirit + Matter = Life. We have the Matter, but void of the Spirit that animates the Matter into the true expression of Life. Half of the equation will not do.

What good is The House of God, if God is not Home? This is like having a beautiful church, mosque, synagogue, or temple worth millions of dollars...but yet inside of the temple, having a congregation of corrupted little devils that aren't worth a damn dime collectively. God does not live there anymore. His spirit/mind has been evicted. Now, where did God go? Materially rich, but Spiritually poor...no, not good enough. Spirit + Matter = Life.

You have yet to breathe in the breath of Life, Son of God...Daughter of Allah! Your brain is like a highly-tuned super-computer, but you have not yet even learned how to turn it on. The instruction booklet is entitled "Knowledge of Self", but we have not even internalized the first page because we are too busy talking about "I'm the Original Man!" "I'm the Original Woman!" We just the "Original Fool"!

Void of Life. Void of Greatness. Void of our Divinity. Why? Because, Spirit + Matter = Life. Understand that in order to get this super-computer to perform up to it's divine potential, it has to be plugged in first.

Spirit (or the activity of the Mind) is Electricity. The Master Engineer has laid the Supreme Circuitry all throughout your Material Being. Your being is not only a Super-computer, but also a super-conductor of electrical spirit. Everybody is producing an electrical current, but the activity of your mind will determine the quality of the frequency and/or the voltage at which your electrical current will flow.

In order to activate the higher living functions of your material super computer, you must generate a higher voltage or higher frequency of electrical spirit. In order to generate a higher electrical spirit, your mind must be rotating on a higher plane of thought. <u>In order for your mind to rotate on a higher plane of thinking, you must consume a higher quality and quantity of higher knowledge, while living a life of higher moral virtue.</u>

Only this can bring us the other half of the equation needed to give us "True Life". Just the material shells made from dust, awaiting the breath of "True Life", we have been. God stands on Two Legs (Knowledge & Virtue).

When properly disciplined and guided, our minds will produce the energy/spirit, or breath of life needed to Supremely Animate our Supreme Material Form, brain, bone, and blood. Only then is the Supreme Being alive...God on Earth. Moral and Mind. Anything less, is death. So Resurrect!!! Yes sir, the Blackman is God, as soon as he believes it true.

Respect The Whiteman!

(The Purpose of A True Revolutionary.)

What do you think all of this is for? Do you think this is just a bunch or "ranting and raving" getting excited over nothing? I mean what is this for? I hope that you don't think that this is supposed to make you mad at the whiteman, and now you are a Revolutionary because you walk around with a little frown on your face. No beloved, that is not the purpose here.

Tell me something. What is walking around with an angry frown on your face going to do about anything? You are correct...absolutely "nothing". The things that you learned in "From Niggas to Gods Pt. 1", and other subsequent reading since that time, are not designed to make you into some little walking time-bomb of hate. You ain't gonna do nothing but blow-up on "yourself"! You just wake-up "fuming", go to bed "fuming", and "fuming" all the time between! Pretty soon you have "fumed" your life away, burning up from the inside out, and this devil ain't even broke a sweat. He out playing volleyball somewhere, and you catching all the flames from "his" hell-raising.

No, that is not the way this thing is supposed to work, neither is it designed for such. The truth is designed to free your mind from it's current ignorance, not to enslave it unto the bitter emotion of anger; at what has been done to your people. Yes, any sane individual with a sincere heart will become EXTREMELY ANGRY AT THE MASS ATROCITIES ASSAULTED

AGAINST AFRIKAN PEOPLES across this World!!!! If you don't get angry, there is something severely wrong with you.

Yet, what is your proper response to your anger, as well as what should be your resulting action to your dissatisfaction? Do you want to take a little-bity semi-automatic assault weapon and start a civil war? Urban Warfare in the streets is exactly what they would like to provoke you to do, therefore having an excuse to turn their Military Forces inward toward a wholesale Mass Murder. That would be very convenient, wouldn't it?

Of course if it comes down to life or death, we have to do what a Man does. But, do you think that Urban Warfare is simply like popping your little pistol at some "niggas" cross town? No sir, it is about jets firing missiles on your home, helicopters dropping chemicals on your head, tanks rolling through your community; cutting off your water, your gas, and your electric, your food supply etc., etc., etc. Are you ready for that? They only sold you enough ammunition to shoot yourself and them niggas across the street. It's so ignorant, I don't even want to talk about it...the way we are killing each other. It's ridiculous.

The question posed is this, "What is your proper response to your anger, as well as what should be the resulting action to your dissatisfaction?". This is neither a passing fad for you to pump your Black Power fist for a few years, and then go back into utter foolishness. What is this all for, and what is a True Revolutionary???

A Re-evolutionary, is a person who strives to constantly "re-evolve" self, and the realities around the self. This is a person who is dedicated to the onward development of self and society. To "re-evolve", is to evolve over and over and over into greater stages of maturity. The first cell of life is a "revolutionary" in the womb of it's mother. God is "The Revolutionary".

This is about "growth". Now, are you "up" for the "struggle"? It starts in your chest, then to your head, and out to The World around you.

Listen.

There is an art to war.

Respect your opponent.

He has accomplished great things.

He did what his god created (or "made") him to do, and then some. You do what your God created you for. He was obedient to his maker. You be obedient to yours.

He has great power. He has great knowledge. He has a Nation, and world of his own. Respect him. He has everything you wish to have one day.

Don't wear your politics on your sleeve, so much. He knows that it is your time. If you were wiser, you would learn from him, all that you could. He learned all that he knows from you? Didn't he? Then he came back and whooped you with it. (Smile). But, he had no problems learning from you...back then. So, are you too proud? He'll teach you. He loves to teach...he can't help himself.

"A wiseman is a teacher to a few, but everyone is a teacher to a wiseman."

Respect your opponent. Be a wise "revolutionary", on all levels. There is an art to war.

You so Busy Hating The Devil, That You Forgot to Love God!

(Polytheism vs. Monotheism)

In our juvenile stages of development, we go "through" phases. Sometimes though, we fail to go "through" stages, and get "stuck-in" phases. Food for thought.

Blackpeople why do you want to denigrate the teachings of The Honorable Elijah Muhammad? Yes, he said that the whiteman was the devil. Yes, he taught this. But sometimes you act as if that was all that he taught, when that fact was only .003% of what he was teaching to you. What about the other 99.997% of what he was teaching? You know?

You want to focus on one part, and forget the rest? You want to focus on the easy part, and ignore the hard part? Yes, he said that the "The whiteman is the devil.", but he said it in juxtaposition to the other statement, "The Blackman is God". But you want to denigrate this man's wealth of wisdom down to

"The whiteman is the devil"? No, that is not right. That is "your" madness of misunderstanding, not his.

Everything has it's proper seasons, for proper reasons. But, you got yourself all caught up in that, by only being half attentive. Don't you know that "hate eats away at it's host"? So, if your focus is all about "hating", and you have nothing that you are "loving", then you all messed up partner. Just end up sour. By doing this for too long, you actually end up worshiping the very devil you say you hate, by giving him all the attention of your mind-energy. Doing this gives him more power. And doing this, is a symbol of your fear of him. You only "hate" what you "fear". Pretty soon, you will end up pathetic, paranoid, and powerless. "Hate eats away at it's host."

Yes, it is natural to hate the opposite of what you love, but "You-Must-Love". You must "love"! Your mental "focus" must be on what you love and not what you hate. The rest is peripheral vision. It is not the point, nor should it be your focus.

You may love the sweet-smell of a flower, and hate the foul-smell of cow manure. But if you are walking through the field only "anticipating" the smell of what you hate, you will find what your mind is focused on, and pass right by the flower. On the other hand, if your mind is focused on the sweet-smell of the flower, you will find the flower and walk right pass the cow manure. Do you understand? It's all in the mind's power of "anticipation". But still, always be careful where you step. Such, are lessons for life.

The point is this. You can not have a theology based on hate for the devil, it can only be based on the love for God, and the God Way. Why is this? Because, you become whatever your mind focuses upon. (Stop-Think)

What does God look like giving all of his time and mind to worry about a little insignificant speck of a devil??? God got

Universes to build!!! He ain't got no time for little petty drama. God is busy building His Light, His Universe, His Kingdom!-and if the devil get to close, He just kick'em and get right back to work!

Devil who? Devil where? I can't see no devil! I'm too busy kindling My Light! Why? Cause once My Light is fully kindled, not one speck of darkness will exist again. That is God's attitude. See, once the Sun has arisen to it's zenith, the world will forget that there ever was a dark time of night. God knows this.

"Optimism" will give you the proper optical-vision, when "pessimism" will be a pestilence of blind hopelessness. You see darkness, cause you walking further into it. You see light, when you are walking toward the light!

We said that, you can not have a theology <u>based</u> on hate for the devil, it can only be <u>based</u> on the love for God, and the God Way.

You don't want to spend all of your time, "re-acting" to the latest whimsicals of your devil. **You want to spend all of your time "pro-acting" on Universal Principles of God!** Right? Right. God is One.

God The Supreme (State Of) Being.

3-Stages of Man

A wise man once said to me, "The Original Blackman fell from a triple-state of revolving".

There are three spheres of being.   One sphere is inferior.   One sphere is transitory.   One sphere is superior. This is just as the moon revolves around the earth, and the earth around the sun.   One sphere is death.   One sphere <u>has</u> life.   One sphere is life.   One sphere repels the light.   One sphere absorbs the light.   One sphere is the light.

Our brains.   Our brain's mind.   Our brain's power.   Our brain's potential.   Have you ever heard that we use less than 10% of our potential brain power?   Isn't that something?   And I really think that 10% is a very generous figure.   This 10% probably only applies to the so-called "genius" of this present day world.   We average people who make up the oppressed masses probably use much less that 10% of our brain's potential power of operating strength.

But I want us to deeply think this over.   The figure given is 10%. Think about all of the technological genius in this world and think about the figure 10%.   Think over that.   If you double this 10% you have only 20% of your brains potential.   If you triple this 10% you only have 30% of your brains potential.   If you quadruple this 10% you only have 40% of your brains potential power and that is less than half of the brain's full potential. Even this mere 40% far, far, far, far exceeds the given realities of this world's genius. Think over that very deeply.

It is no wonder that the whole world is miserable, depressed, and dis-satisfied. We are so mentally <u>under-developed</u>, that it is like we are in a vegetable comatose state of being. More than 90% of our brain's vital signs of life have been snuffed-out. We are the walking-dead.

We do not have life or know life in the way that we were created to have it. We obviously were created to have a very highly qualitative state of life. We are living less than 10% of the quality of life that is naturally due to us. Our low quality of life produces a lower quality of being, while our lower quality of being produces a lower quality of life. It is a constant perpetual cycle towards deeper and deeper states of mental death. Will we choose to reverse this cycle?

It has been so long since we have really known "true life", that we don't even realize that this is "death". So, we end up thinking that this "state of being" is absolutely normal. You only know that something is dead by comparing it to something that is living. And we have had no true "life" to compare ourselves to, that would clearly show us our "death".

You are only as good as what you are compared to, and you are only as bad as what you are compared to. Take this for example. At your job you were totally satisfied with your salary until you found out that the person who worked there before you made much more money for the same job that you do. After learning of that, you immediately demanded a raise in pay!

Well, after you learn about your true history and the true knowledge of your true self and therefore your true potential, you will immediately demand a raise in the quality of your life and the quality of your state of being! Yes, you will!

You will compare how much productivity and power that your ancient ancestors got out of their Brains, and then demand the same from your own Brains.

Well just how far up have we got to go in order to raise ourselves? We will know that once we understand how far down we have fallen.

See, "<u>dissatisfaction</u>" with the status-quo has to come first, in order to create the desire to change! Many of these writings are designed to make you so disgusted with the present self, that you will either change and excel, or die in disgust. Truth is Judgement. It will make you do or die...make you or break you. The choice is ours. And we choose to RAISE THE DEAD! We choose to LIVE AGAIN! Is that right? Well, let us proceed with this resurrection.

As stated before, the Original Blackman and Original Blackwoman have fallen from a triple state of revolving. We have fallen down three complete stages in our human development. And since everything that exists, exists in three major stages (solid, liquid, and gas), this means that we have fallen to the very bottom stage of our potential development. We are at our lowest quality or lowest state of being, and we don't even know it.

Listen. Let us just get straight to the point. When you hear about the Original Black People of ancient times being called Gods and Goddesses, that is <u>not just a bunch of talk</u>! No! No! No! That is very real.

Remember that you and I, during this present time, day, and age, are using a very small portion of our brain's potential. Well at those ancient times, we used a much, much, much, higher degree of our brain's potential to accomplish things and display powers unseen to this present world. There was a <u>totally different realm of possibility and reality</u>. I said this is not just a bunch of talk, so listen!

Your ancestors not only "mastered" the internal divine powers of themselves, but they were masters of the very Forces of Nature itself! Ohhh...you can't handle that. You don't want to know what I'm talking about, do you? You afraid of that, right? Well, you are afraid of yourself.

See, once your inner Universe is mastered, you have thereby mastered the "control panels" to everything that you see in the outer Universe. Do we understand this?

You don't know how that mountain outside of your window got there. You don't know! You say God put it there...but "who" is God? You don't know how that ocean outside of your window got there. You don't know! You say God put it there...but "who" is God? You don't know how that moon over your head got there. You don't know! You say God put it there...but "who" is that God you are talking about? You can't answer that question using less than 10% brain potential. That means that you are only acquainted with less than 10% of yourself. I think we might be too afraid to answer these questions. Enough about this for now.

Well, the point to understand is that this same divine potential of Black excellence is still very much contained deeply within us all. It is just that we are not truly awakened to the knowledge of what lies undiscovered within our own personal selves.

We all have the potential to exist in one of three states of being. We can exist on the level of BEAST, MAN, or GOD. Inside of all of us is the potential to manifest the lowest savage qualities of the common beast, all the way up to the highest divine qualities of a God or Goddess. You have a full dose of wicked potential as well as a full dose of righteous potential. It is up to us as to which potential we will feed and manifest.

Beast, Man, and God. Instinct, Intellect, and Inherent Wisdom. Move by Appetite, Move by Reason, Move by the grace of High Intuitive Knowing. Solid, Liquid, Gas. Ice, Water, and Steam...lighter than a feather. Beast, Man, and God.

In between the state of "BEAST" and the state of "GOD" is "MAN"...mortal "MAN". This state of mortal "MAN" is a transitory state of being that is experienced between your upward climb or either your downward fall between "BEAST" and "GOD". "MAN" is a state of motion and time traveling between these two points. This is why they say that "in life there is no such thing as standing still, because you are either moving further ahead or falling further behind".

Think about this. I know that this whole thing might sound a bit different to some, but it is really quite simple to understand. This is no vain type of teaching, except to the vain who take it vainly. Relax.

Remember when the preacher in the church used to teach us about a God in the sky and a devil in the ground? Well even though the preacher didn't know what he was talking about, he was still telling the truth in a symbolic way.

"God" does live in the sky, if you understand that "sky" only represents the highest realms of intelligence wisdom and understanding within the mind.

"Devil" (Beast) does live under the heaviest atoms of the earth, if you understand that "under the earth" only represents the lowest realms of savagery, beastial behavior, ignorance and moral-less mental death within the mind.

"Man" does live in the atmosphere between the sky and the earth, with God living above us and Devil below us, but this is only symbolic of states of mind and states of being.

Our lives are but a measure of motion and time in which we struggle between two forces that exist above us and below us and this is all within us. Our motion and time is either spent in submission to the lower gravitational pull of the earth beneath us, or in a struggle to submit to the attractive life giving light that is beaming down from above us. The light on your chlorophyll/melanin makes your stem stand strong and straight, as you "flower" wide open and "flower" straight upward.

While when death comes, gravity pulls...leaving our blossom sagging toward the ground. Resurrection is due, in the cycle. Resurrection is due.

This measure of motion and time called life, is where we struggle to cleanse our hearts and minds of the heavy material mass debris that weighs us down toward the pull of the lower earth where the beasts roam.

That is why our ancient ancestors of Black Egypt (Kemet), gave us the symbol of the scales with a heart on one side and a feather on the other side. They did this to let us know that if we wanted to ever rise to the level of "divine genius" and "Black excellence" that they attained, our hearts would have to be as light as a feather.

And, in order for our hearts to be this light in weight to escape the pull of the earth's gravity, it would have to be thoroughly cleansed of lower earthly waste. Our hearts and minds have to be cleansed of the heavy burden of guilt and sin, in this beastlike moral-less state of being, in order to ascend the divine states. This is true.

Of the three states of being, GOD, MAN, and BEAST. God is the Supreme state of being. Supreme in Peace. Supreme in Power. Again, this Supreme potential exists in you. All of the greatness that you have ever attributed to God, should be attributed to something that exists deep within; that unexplored brain potential of yourself. All of the displayed genius of God's creation is a sign of the masterful creative genius that exists deeply within you, when you are quickened to the developed potential of your own brain's mind.

A Beast signifies an "under-developed" human mind. Man/Woman signifies a developing human mind. God signifies a developed "humane" mind, awakened to it's eternalness. Okay. We have yet to be "human" or "humane". Yet, all three of these spheres of existence can manifest from you and I, depending upon our level of developed mental/spiritual maturity. One sphere repels the light (moon), one sphere absorbs the light (earth) and one sphere is the light (Sun).

Adam (Atom, Atum), the Original Man was split. Your moon/caucasian was blasted/grafted out the fertile Black earth/Original Black Man to give us a knowledge of what lower evil potential lay dormant within our own selves. This in turn would motivate us to willingly submit to the higher life-giving potential within us to escape this lower manifestation of what is also within ourselves. We would much rather revolve around the sun's light than the moon's pale light. Right?

If we lived revolving only around the moon's little light, just about everything on earth would die over time. Right? Well since we have been only revolving around the recent little moonlight mentality of your young caucasian, Man has died to the potential of himself. It is only when we begin to revolve around the illuminating divine Black genius of our ancient ancestors, will humanity receive that sunlight that will give us life. That light is coming again. It is on the other side of this thing.

We have yet to travel the depths of the other 90%-95% of our inner space. But with the mapped out guidance of our ancient ancestors, we can find our way back up home to God the Supreme state of Being. There, is Guidance.

The scripture says honor thy Mother and thy Father that thy days may be long. Well really, "who" is my Mother and Father, that know something about making my days longer? Good question.

We have only honored the extremely young technological knowledge of the european, while dishonoring the ancient wisdom of the original Blackman and Blackwoman who is the Mother and Father to all in existence. This is why we die.

Under the dominance of the western european world, everybody is now savagely living a carefree cut-throat lust-filled life on a quest for an over abundance of material possessions and material wealth that we can't even take with us once we die away from this material form. These young men have set up a worldwide uncivilization of money, sex, and murder that results in mischief, bloodshed, and chaos. Shamefully, it's everywhere now.

This is what happens when you only utilize less than 10% of your brain's potential and force everyone else to follow your footsteps, to be governed by no moral law of divine discipline...repelling the light. You will fall from God to Beast. You then become a devil, the spiteful rebel. And since misery loves company, you then seek to pull the whole world down to hell with you, which is the utilization of less than 10% of your brain's mind. His aim is to make sure that no one else's intelligence develops to outshine his own, during his time of reign. He is the god of his world, the underlord. Darkness has now covered the earth, with only a pale moonlight to guide us through the night. God help us.

And behold! As the Blackman and Woman lay mentally asleep, the time quickly approaches. The awakening is now come, as we prepare to meet the Eastern Sunrise again...rinsing our mouths, nostrils, ears of all debris from this world, in preparation for a New Day...washing our faces, our heads, our hands, and our feet from the old world, getting ready to meet and greet the New World in a new way; The Opening...entering the doorway of Light at a speed of one-thousand thirty-seven and a third miles per hour! Are we ready for This Morning

Prayer? Let us hurry! We want to exist within God, The Supreme State of Being.

Pause-Reflect.

You are such a Wonderful People.

What is God, without knowledge of Himself, but mere mortal Man? What is mortal Man, without knowledge of himself, but mere animal, a beast? Yet when Knowledge of Self does comes to him, he becomes the Light of The World, the life giving Sun of Man. You are much more than you think. Your potential awaits you.

WHY IS GOD, GOD?

God is God, because He is in perfect obedience to His own divine laws. He exists in harmony with His Creation, and with Himself. This stimulates Peace. This amplifies Power.

God is accepting His Own and being Himself. Should not we do the same? Be God. Be God.

God Is Still "Self-Created".

Lessons of life. The God is a "Self-Created One" existing "Self-Securely" in and of Himself. The God is "Self-Sufficient" in need and in want.

He has "Self-Created" Himself out of a state of Nothingness onto an Organized, Prioritized, and Purposeful state of Somethingness. The God is Self-Created.

So, how do you expect for yourself to be created? Nobody can do it for you because they can only assist you as a guiding resource themselves. A resource only helps you to help yourself. God helps those who help themselves. You will also be self-created.

After The God Self-Created, Organized, and Prioritized Himself, He created, organized and prioritized all of His creation around Him, the World...His World. In other words after God created Himself into Divine, He made His outer atmosphere to reflect his own inner beauty. Lessons.

As we go "From Niggas To Gods", our journey is an uplifting act of "Self-Creation" as an individual person, and as a whole Nation. Collective assistance is only to be used toward the development of Self-independence, which will prepare you worthy enough to be a point of Inter-dependence for your people. Yet, we first must grow to stand up straight on our own one foundation; becoming a strong enough link to be added to the chain. This brings equal balance to the whole community, by requiring that everybody carry their own weight of personal responsibility to the Nation (society). Monotheism. God is still Self-Created. God is still Self-Created.

You are The Prophet.

You are "The Prophet". Who is The Prophet? You are "The Prophet". You are prophetically telling the future. You are prophetically telling the future right now, prophesying about the future of your life right now as we speak. Everytime I look at you and listen to you, you are prophesying to me exactly what is going to happen in your near and far future. You are The Prophet.

Everything that you think, do, and say habitually, is determining exactly what, when, where, and how you will be doing in your future. Your future is predictable, and you are predicting it. The thoughts that you are having right now, are connected to and because of the thoughts you had yesterday; and are leading you to a particular thought pattern tomorrow. This is all connected. Connected by time and calculation (mathematics).

The Messenger has taught the Blackman & Woman in America, that our ancestors (God-Scientists) wrote their history in advance (prophecy). They would do this for every 25,000 year cycle. The God/Scientists, writers of scripture, tap into the thinking of the people and can therefore determine their history in advance. Well, on our baby level this is not much different.

This is calculation or mathematics sped-up. Your brain is faster than you are right now. It is more powerful as a creation than you are as it's creator, because you have been put to sleep to the fact that you are it's creator. So, when you release your control of it, going to sleep at night, it is on automation. It will bring you visions and communications that you and I have not yet learned how to call-up at our own will. On automation, it will sometimes give you a vision of the future of some sort. But most times it just happens, and we are mystified as to how it happens.

Well, when you take a common calculator and you ask it how much is 986 multiplied by 236, and all of a sudden the screen says 232,696. This is no mysterious, mystical feat. A hundred years ago, it may have seemed mystical, but today it is just the normal mechanics of an adding machine.

Well, are not the brains that made-up the adding machine, and it's mechanics, more powerful in intelligence than the machine itself? Sure it is, no doubt. No creation is more powerful than it's own Creator. So, all of this to say that your brain has this same calculating power and much more. When you receive vision of the future, a brain has taken all of the information it has stored (knowledge), and multiplied it times all of the information it now sees (perception), and systematically calculates what kind of circumstances this will bring about (prophesy).

Our brains receive in, much more information and stimulus than we are consciously aware of. We get hunches, feelings, and intuition, but don't know where it is coming from. Sometimes we say the ancestors are talking, or God is talking, (and that may be true at times)...yet most times it is your own self talking, because your anatomical system is more intelligent than you know. You and I just have not been taught how to tune-up to our own nature yet. This creation that we are is so powerful that it has been <u>driving us</u>, instead of us being intelligently powerful enough to mount up on it, and <u>drive it</u>

where we will to go.

You can look at a person and tell if they are sick, have cancer or something like that. Your brain is seeing all of the symptoms that the modern doctor can not see without using all of his machines. The physical man has to "make" an eye to see, but the original/spiritual man is an eye that sees. The brain/mind already knows things that we have yet to consciously access. It's all there already. Like a library of stored information. Taking more in everyday. Brain is a tape recorder, we just haven't learned how to fully play it back. But sometimes it does it on it's own, or somebody else will play it back for you. That is enough about all of that. Dreams. Visions.

A scientist-mind will tell you that one circumstance plus another particular circumstance, will bring about another circumstance, that will lead to another circumstance, that will ultimately create this particular circumstance. This "cause" times this "cause" = This Effect. We call it prophesy, but it is really mathematics (The discernment, processing, and calculation of perceived information to reach a final summation).

Well, you the prophet. You the mathematician, adding up the results of your life destiny. Whatever you are doing in your life right now multiplied by what you do in your life tomorrow, will equal what you get in your future. You determine the results. you are in control, whether you know it or not. You are in control, whether you are mature enough to handle that control or not. You are in control.

This is why your adversary/enemy never worried about giving you freedom, because he knew that you didn't know what to do with your freedom. He knew that he had stripped you of the knowledge of how to guide or drive your life. So, he stuck you in the driver's seat knowing that you would eventually just wreck yourself. He laughs, as he watches you wreck yourself and your community, attempting to justify his saying that negroes can't do anything for themselves.

But with the knowledge of these things you can do all things. When we are fully conscious of the fact that everything we do today is prophesying our future, we began to behave a little different. We begin to think more, and train ourselves more. We say "hanging on the corner drinking beer, multiplied by wasting time with my friends that ain't going nowhere, multiplied by no goal or purpose in my life, multiplied by five years, equals a drunk-aimless-five-year-older-fool. Is this the type of future I want for myself? Wait, let me find some different type of calculations."

"Building my mind up with knowledge about business, multiplied by building my mind up with my particular skill, trade, or interest equals money, a career, and possibly my own business".

"Cleaning up myself, multiplied by cleaning up my mind, will equal or attract the respectable woman I desire as a wife and partner."

'Disciplining my mind with spiritual and moral law multiplied by disciplining my body with proper law and maintenance will equal open accessibility to the powers of my being, giving me the maximum ability to recreate life around me, growing each and every day."

All of these things multiplied times ten years will equal a productive, respectable, righteous, human being with money, career, good homes, healthy family, and friendship in all walks of life, a sense of equitable community around the world. In other words, heaven on this Earth. All we really want is to be happy.

Math & Science, son of Man. If you know the future that you want for yourself, you better see if the current thoughts, habits, and actions will add up to what you want for yourself. Add it up. You are writing your future in advance, as we speak. You, "The Prophet"!

<u>Becoming God II</u>:
"Understanding The Ways & Method of God."

Little Elijah and his Strange Religion?

(The Messenger came, but did we get the Message?)

Why do we even need to understand this man here? Why do we even need to discuss an Elijah Muhammad? Why?

It is because it was "he", Elijah Muhammad, who re-introduced the concept and possibility of "Becoming God" to our people again, back in the 1930's. But blackfolks didn't know what the man was doing. We didn't know. Yet, the intelligent rulers of this world knew exactly what he was doing, and hated him for that.

I mean, come on now. Do you really think that Elijah Muhammad was just trying to bring you another religion? Is that all it is? Is that all it was? Is it all that simple? Was Little Elijah just trying to bring us another strange religion? I don't think so. Why would he attempt to bring Blackpeople some more "religion", when it was "religion" that helped to get us so ignorant in the first place? That wouldn't make sense.

Elijah Muhammad was not teaching "religion" as we know it to be. Can anybody see beyond the surface of things? **This man was giving Blackmen and Women a structured method of achieving a successful life. He was** teaching us a practical methodology of living, that would lead us unto a peaceful contentment of mind. It is true. He said that he taught "Islam". Right? This word sounded strange to us at first. But, this word "Islam" defined at it's root, only means "peace". "Peace". And "peace" is the destined and promised achievement. That is all that we want.

Elijah has said to us that our "Heaven" was to be achieved <u>in this life</u>. He said that "Heaven" was, "<u>money</u>", "<u>good homes</u>", and "<u>friendship</u>" in all walks of life; during this life! Doesn't that sound good and practical??? Yes, I think so too.

This was the basic goal that he aimed to achieve for his people. And this is what you and the masses desire today. This is all that you want. "Sufficient money", "good homes", and "friendly relations" is what you really want.

Why does this content your soul? It is because, having all of these things, leaves you "undistracted" on your road to spiritual inner peace, development, and happiness. "All I really want is to be happy". Don't you? Well, that is what he is teaching...the road to peace...the road to happiness...the road to success and fulfillment in life. Simple. Very simple.

No, he was not some fanatical religious nut, trying to take us out in the sky to find some mystical make-believe place. This man was trying to improve our tangible everyday for-real lives. <u>Real life!</u> You know?

Sometimes we can get so "mystical" and so "spiritual", that we lose sight of the "obvious" realities. Is that right? Yeah, I know you deep...I know you meditate all day...I know you can read minds like a psychic...and I know you can see off into the future. Hell, you probably can levitate above ground! But damn, can you hold down a steady job??? Huh? That's the question! That's the question! That's all your wife and children want to know. That's all Elijah Muhammad wanted to know from you Blackman. The real. The real.

He wanted to know, "Blackman, can you take care of your family? Can you love, honor, and protect your wife? Can you guide, teach, properly raise, and provide for your children? Can you be a real Man to your family?" This is the root of what he was teaching you and I.

For those of you who have studied his teachings, his community sampling, and his example, you know that he was not just teaching some vain religious preaching, for you to follow one day out of the week. No, not this brother. This man taught you <u>how to wake up</u> in the morning, <u>how to eat</u>, <u>how to live</u>, <u>how to think</u>, and <u>how to act</u> all during the day, and <u>how to lay your head down in peace everynight</u>. He taught not mere "religion", he taught "life"...life!..life!..life! Your "life" is seven days a week, twenty-four hours a day. Pay attention. This is not a typical one day in the temple, hypocritical religious exercise. We need Life Skills. We need training. This is what he presented to you. Practical guidance.

After our enemies have worked night and day to un-civilize us, we need to be taught! Do you agree?

You need to be taught <u>how to eat to live</u>. Guidance. You need to be taught <u>how to maintain the best of hygiene</u>. Guidance. You need to be taught <u>how to respect the sacredness of your physical being</u>. Guidance. Oh, yes you do. We all do!

You need to be taught <u>how to speak</u>. You need to be taught <u>how to conduct yourself</u>. You need to be taught <u>how to present yourself</u>. You need to be taught <u>how to carry yourself</u>.

You need to be taught <u>how to think of yourself</u>. You need to be taught <u>how to properly deal and relate to your own people</u>. You need to be taught <u>how to properly deal and relate to white people</u>. Yes, all of that.

You need to be taught <u>how to create employment for yourself</u>. You need to be taught of <u>how to pool your resources</u>. You need to be taught <u>how to be self-reliant</u>.

You need to be taught <u>how to properly maintain and guide a family household</u>. You need to be taught <u>how to be respectful of yourself and other</u>s. You need to be taught <u>how to discipline your life</u>; in all ways.

You need to be taught <u>a knowledge of yourself</u>, and <u>knowledge of God</u>, and the devil. You need to be <u>taught</u>! You need to be <u>taught</u>! You need to be <u>taught</u>!

Yes! Yes! Yes! We need to be taught all of these things after being lost from the light of civilization...lost from the civilized ways of life that we originally devised. This is what Elijah Muhammad was doing, preparing us to be placed back upon the top of civilization itself. The lost sheep now found. This man was not simply trying to religiously argue with you over some Bible. He was just trying to loosen you, from the mental grips of your master. No. Elijah was not just trying to bring you another religion for the sake of religion itself. His work was much greater...much greater. Can anyone see beyond the surface of things?

You should understand that, if Elijah Muhammad was just another religious nut preaching stupidity, this government would not have worked night and day to destroy his efforts. *The government don't care about negroes becoming "religious", they gave you your religion. But, what they do care about, and are frightened of, is having an intellectual and an economical rival that is out of their control. Particularly, their ex-slaves of which they enjoy exploiting today.*

If Elijah was just teaching you some regular little silly fantasy-world religion, your enemy would have no problem with that. But Elijah, was not just teaching Blackmen and Women to just "praise" God. He is teaching Blackmen and Women to "Be" God!!! Be God! Rule, Master, and take righteous control of your Life, your Planet, and your Universe! Get up and Be God! That is "praise". Be a "Righteous God" and go out to challenge the wicked ways of the "Wicked god" of this world...the whiteman. There is your religion. That is Elijah.

See, Elijah Muhammad was never teaching you to get on your knees and just pray to Jesus to make your life better!!!!!! No!!!!!! If you want your life to be better, get up, go out, and make it better for you and your children! The planet belongs to the Original Asiatic Blackman, the Maker, the Owner, and the Cream of the Planet Earth...God of The Universe!!!!! Now, act like it!!! Move out!

Yes sir, and yes ma'am, now that's Elijah's teaching. And that is precisely why your enemy did not want him teaching you. You can not mentally enslave or manipulate an individual who thinks like that. No. Now, just imagine a whole nation of people 40 million strong, unified in that kind of stream of consciousness, one day. Imagine. Imagine that. That is a powerful thought.

Now, you can see why Elijah's teaching scared the hell out of the whiteman. He could clearly imagine the 40 million strong in his head. He is knows that, if these teachings sincerely took root amongst our people, it would automatically uproot "him". He knows that "these" teachings are that which could really produce "his rival", and better. He knows the potential, and so he feels threatened. He feels that your success means his doom. This is how he feels.

He knows this potential, because he remembers what it was that raised "him" up from the bottom of civilization to the top. He has the benefit of a comparative view. Mistakably though, he judges you by the paradigm of himself; thinking that you will do the same with power, as he has done. Yet, he should know, the spirit of God is a million ways opposite the spirit of Satan.

But you Blackman and Woman...you should know...simply by the reaction of your slavemaster, you should know "what" and "which" has the power to liberate you from his grip. His nervous trembling should let you know that someone is present on the plantation, who can actually set you free. You should embrace, what he vehemently rebukes. The reaction of your oppressor is your sign.

Can anyone see beyond the surface of things? Are we understanding Little Elijah any better, at all? Are we getting his message? Let us continue to see.

Now, if we can clearly see that, it was not merely "religion" that Elijah Muhammad was teaching, then what was it that he was teaching? He said that he was teaching us "Islam". Okay. Well, "Islam" is a religion...isn't it? Isn't it? Well? No, it is not. "Islam" is not a religion. What? Listen.

Studying the root of a thing, shows you that "Islam" is not a "religion". "What? How can you say that?" No, "Islam" is not a "religion". "Islam" is <u>much, much, much, more than that</u>. "<u>Islam</u>" is "<u>a way of life</u>." A way of life. A righteous way and method of life, that leads to success!

Yes, you will know the true believers, for they are the successful ones. And it is this success, that Elijah Muhammad is seeking for the Blackman and Woman in America. Are we understanding Elijah any better now? This is all he wanted for us. And for this, he strived with his life.

Many people disagreed with his prescription/methodology of teaching what they thought to be "Islam", but none could disagree with the results. Many dispute without knowledge and understanding, but none can dispute the results of his community sampling.

Many people misunderstood the point and the purpose of his teaching altogether. This still goes on today. And, in this misunderstanding, the Blackman and Woman may be missing the very salvation (guidance) that we have been praying for all of our lives.

You better be mindful of what you pray for, cause you may not recognize it when it comes. Little Elijah and his Strange Religion needs to be looked at all over again.

One day you will understand what we all have felt in our hearts all along. It will be verified.

Peace to the Pure at Heart.

The Heart of an Elijah Muhammad.

(Do they condemn him???)

Some of them say that they are "too intelligent" to be taught by an Elijah Muhammad. Some of them say, that "those are baby teachings". Some of them say they "know that already". Some of them say that they are "beyond what he has taught". Some of them say that "that was good for then, but this is now". Some of them say that they are "too deep for that now".

They say that they have too much knowledge to be guided by an Elijah Muhammad. They say they <u>know</u> "volumes of history", now. They say they <u>know</u> "volumes of scriptures", now. They say they <u>know</u> the "depths of the ancient sciences", now. They say they <u>know</u> the "ins and outs of world politics", now. They say they <u>know</u> the "inner workings of global economics", now. They say they <u>know</u>. They say they <u>know</u> it all, now. They say they <u>have</u> it all, now! They say they "<u>have</u>" it now!!! Huh?

<u>But</u>! <u>What</u>! <u>Does</u>! <u>God</u>! Say???????????????? God! Says! Have you not "LOVE", you have "NOTHING"!!! And have you not "LOVED"...you have done "NOTHING"!!!

Well now. For those of you Big Headed Scientists that <u>know</u> it all, and blindly see Elijah Muhammad's teachings as child's play...afford me the opportunity to speak with you today.

Elijah Muhammad? Huh. Elijah Muhammad??? "In his Heart, is the Hiding of His Power." You think about that. Think long, and think hard.

You, who sit on the mountains of knowledge in your little secretive circles, stroking one another with your knowledge...from what high and mighty position do "you" judge an Elijah Muhammad? Huh?

You, who say that your knowledge is more abundant and far beyond Little Elijah...from what lofty place do "you" condemn this man? Huh?

Who are "you"? You are so high up on your mountain of knowledge, that I can not see "you"!

Where are you? You are so closed up and secretive in "your" little social club, that our paths have never crossed.

What is your name? You have never taken the time nor consideration to acquaint me with "you"...so, I can not honor "your" name, because I don't know it.

But, "he"...."he" of whom you say that is "less" in knowledge than you, I honor "his" name. I "honor" his name, because I "know" his name. "He" introduced himself to me, the average, everyday Blackman trying to survive.

You say that "he", Elijah Muhammad, is not as knowledgeable, or as wise as "you". But, I beg your pardon. I said, I beg your pardon, sir!

According to the little bit of understanding that "I" have, I would say that "this" man, Elijah Muhammad, is a VERY wise man. Yes! I say this because it is "he" who took the mind, the time and the heart to share "his" knowledge with "me". "He" did this, not "you". I don't know "you". Who are "you"?

"He" took the little knowledge that you call insignificant, and "he" broke it down into a language agreeable to "my" ears...a language that even "I" could understand...that

"I" could comprehend! "He"...did this..."for ME". Who am "I"? I am the average, everyday Blackman trying to survive.

Yes sir, that is right! "I" say that this man "Elijah Muhammad" is a VERY wise man. "I" would even go so far to say that "he" is a bit wiser than "you", sir.

"I" would say that "he" is wiser than "you" who sit on your high and lofty mountains, selfishly hoarding your knowledge all unto yourself. Yes, Elijah is wiser.

Elijah is wise enough to know that a day is coming. Elijah knew that the book of scripture described a day, when all the "high places" would be "made low"...when "the first" would be "made last", and "the last made first"...when "the mountains" would be "brought down", and "the valleys raised high". Elijah knew this, but did you know? But did you care?

But you, who sit atop your mountains of knowledge all unto yourselves...what will you do when your mountain is brought down to the feet of the masses who starved before you? Starved for knowledge? You would be fortunate, if they do not eat you alive!

What will you have to say to me, of whom was not worthy enough for you to break your bread of knowledge with???? Nothing!! If you consider yourself to be truly knowledgeable, you will have nothing to say to us. We don't know you. You are a stranger to us.

Wisdom should tell you to close your mouth, today! Respectfully close and refrain your mouth from ever uttering a word of condemnation, dishonor, or disrespect of a man who stretched and extended himself to feed knowledge to us! To us!..the average, everyday Blackman trying to survive.

A man of whom had the LOVE ENOUGH to come down off the mountain, to a people who lay low in the valley...breaking down complex wisdom into simple truths that could nurture our understanding. We, a mentally dead people who died for a lack of the knowledge, you had! What do "you" have to say against an Elijah Muhammad? You have nothing to say against that good man. Why would you condemn a man like that?

How arrogantly ignorant can you behave? Do you really think that, you and your mountain of memorized information is supposed to make you <u>more intelligent</u> than an Elijah Muhammad??? Is that supposed to make you to be <u>smarter</u> than an Elijah Muhammad??? Is that supposed to make me <u>honor</u> and <u>respect you more</u> than Elijah Muhammad??? I don't think so. No, I don't think so. No sir.

Let <u>this</u> <u>child</u> teach "you" a little bit of wisdom that might have tumbled down off of your mountain one day. Out of the mouth of babes, okay? Listen.

In all due respect sir, we the children...the average, everyday Blackman & Blackwoman trying to survive...we respect, honor, and recognize an Elijah Muhammad, because he respected, honored, and recognized us. The true origin and measure of intelligence is found not in your brains, but in the heart of your brains. The Motivation is what defines.

See, my Grandfather was acquainted with who Elijah Muhammad was, because Elijah <u>poured his wisdom out</u> to the masses of the Blackman...for his generation.

My Father was acquainted with who Malcolm X was, because Elijah had prepared him to <u>pour his wisdom out</u> to the masses of the Blackman...for his generation.

Today we are acquainted with who Farrakhan is, because Elijah prepared him to <u>pour his wisdom out</u> to the masses of the Blackman at this time...for this generation.

Knowing that we all were dying for a lack of knowledge, they all strove, and strive today, even against deathly opposition, to spread their mental riches amongst us, that we may be able to help ourselves and our condition. That is LOVE to a people like we! And for this we are thankful...for this we are thankful. We thank The Supreme God.

See, we understand that "God" is a verb. We understand that, "God is not what you know...God is what you do". Repeat that, please. "God is not what you know...God is what you do". God is what you do with what you know.

Yes, we understand that God is not simply what you know in your head, but God is what you do, and why you do it. And what did Little Elijah do?

"He" came down to "us", while "you" wanted only those who could come up to "you". Well, maybe had you thrown us a rope that we could grip, we might have gone with "you"...but up came a little lamb with The Master's Grip, and now we stand on a Mountaintop with "Him", who stood for "us".

In "his heart" was the hiding of "his power", and in "his heart" was "His love". The heart of a saviour. Motivation defines.

Peace.

He called you "Muslims" By Nature?

(Jesus, The Black Muslim)

"<u>All Black people are Muslims by nature</u>." This is what The Honorable Elijah Muhammad has taught. Well what did he mean? How can that be? What is a "Muslim"?

Now before you reject that label of which you really have no knowledge of...before you say, "I ain't no Mooz-lim!", find out what a "Muslim" is first. You may be rejecting something that is very good for you.

Do you know what a "Muslim" is? Do you know what the definition of the word "Muslim" means? Well, if you don't even know what the word "Muslim" means, how are you going to say that "I ain't no Mooz-lim"? To be perfectly honest, we really do not know who we are at all. You can't trace your family tree back pass the state of Mississippi. Think about it. Just open your mind and think about it beloved Blackman and beloved Blackwoman.

Listen. Before we reject the title of the word "<u>Muslim</u>"

being put on us, let's understand what Mr. Elijah Muhammad was saying to us? Let us see.

The word, label, or term "Muslim", is actually a spiritual description. The root definition of the word "Muslim" means "<u>one who is in submission to the will of God</u>." This means, "<u>one who is in submission to the will of Righteousness</u>." This means, "<u>one who is in submission to the will of Truth</u>". This means, "<u>one who is in submission to the will of Supreme Wisdom</u>." This means, "<u>one who is in submission to the will of the Universal Laws of Nature</u>". All of this put together means, "<u>one who is in submission to the will of God</u>" or one who is "<u>Muslim</u>".

All of this describes the innate divine nature that every Black child is genetically born with.

It does not matter whether or not you say "God", "Christ", "Yahweh" "Allah", "Jah", "Jehovah", "Buddha", "Krishna", "Ptah", or "Amen-Ra". If you are in submission to the will of Righteousness/God, you are called "Muslim" in the Arabic language, which is one of the forgotten languages of our ancestors. Don't forget who the original Arab was before the arrival of the destruction of Black Civilization. You are the Original Man of those lands. The word "Saudi" means Black itself. Black Arabia. That belongs to you Allah.

The word "Muslim" describes the righteous nature of the Blackman and Blackwoman. This is looking at the inner "substance" of a word, instead of looking at the outer "symbol" of a word. Do you fully understand? Let us move on.

Let's decipher this. Quickly..."You" are already Muslim, but just don't know it. We were already born into the righteous Nation of Islam but just didn't know it because we didn't know our own self. You have actually been a "Muslim" for trillions and trillions of years every since the Creator first created and perfected his own divine essence into a Supreme Being, in whom you existed only as a neutral state of potential awaiting the proper time to materialize. A Blackman or Blackwoman can not convert to be a "Muslim". All that we can do is come into a knowledge of self and submissively unite with the central essence of our own being.

The God created us to exist in harmony with the righteous Universal Laws of Creation, that we may not find peace in any other way besides the right way. This is our natural mind state under our natural circumstances and natural atmosphere. This is when we can accept our own and be ourselves. Who are ourselves? We are the "Righteous", or "Muslims" by nature.

So how can we, the Blackman and Blackwoman, become our natural selves again, in this un-natural circumstance? This is not our natural atmosphere. If we have the ability to conceive the question, we have the ability to perceive the answer. Righteous will shall be done. True. True. True.

So all that The Honorable Elijah Muhammad meant, when he said that all Black People are "Muslims" by nature, was that we are a naturally "Righteous" people instinctively, under our normal/natural circumstances. We are born with an instinctive (or genetic) inclination that leans towards peace and righteousness. Simple. Now, we can better understand Elijah.

Why stop being the "Whiteman's Nigga" just to be a "Nigga for White Arabs"??? pt. 2

(A Messenger of Our Own!)

Listen, listen, listen. I just want to talk to you. You may not want to believe it, but The All-Wise God Allah, has specifically blessed "u s" with pure mercy. You may not want to believe it, but this pure mercy was shown to us by sending us a personal teacher of "Islam" (which simply means a life of peace) who looks just like us, who thinks just like us, who shared the same experiences as us, who loves us, and who is of us. Of course, this great teacher and guide that I am speaking about is our Brother Elijah Muhammad, who is worthy of much honor. Time brings all understanding and reveals all truth. Many of our scholarly or learned brothers and sisters have shunned his teachings, because he proclaimed his teachings to be "Islam". So naturally, after learning of the white Arab's assault in the destruction of the Blackman and his civilization, they would want nothing to do with white Arabs or "their" religion. That is intelligent. That is proper. But who said that Islam was "their" religion? And who said that Elijah Muhammad was teaching that which would propagate and glorify white Arabs and their culture???? Elijah Muhammad is nothing remotely close to a fool. We need to look at him closer before hastily dismissing him and his blatant success, in resurrecting Black people from the dead.

I said that Allah God (The God of The Blackman) has prepared "us" a teacher...just as he has prepared teachers for peoples of the past. Pay your attention to this, with all defenses down, if you can please. I will say this as briefly and succinctly as possible. You can receive it, or let it alone, by your own choice. Your rejection, or adherence to the truth will not give or take one atom's weight from the truth. Truth stands heavy on it's own merit. There is no threat...it's okay. So, just listen.

Look at the terrible conditions of your Black People. Do we not need a helper, a saviour, a messenger, or a prophet just as bad as any uncivilized or oppressed group of people has ever needed one in the past? Does our condition not warrant the same attention? Would God-Allah ever consider sending a message and a messenger to The Blackman, as well? Would God love us enough to send "us" one? Let us see.

Little Elijah, huh...Little Elijah teaches "Islam" (a life of peace) specifically "for" the Blackman and Blackwoman, "to" the Blackman and Blackwoman, "from" the divine wisdom of the ancient Blackman and Blackwoman. Yes, this is true. So, knowing this fact to be true, would naturally tell you that his teachings will be distinctively different from the method that God Allah used to ad-minister Islam (a life of peace) to civilize the white Arab from the days of their barbarism. Of course, it is going to be different. Our barbaric situation is different than their barbaric condition was, centuries and centuries ago. True.

You need to know this. What is called "orthodox Islam" is based on wisdom revealed 1400 years ago. It is based on the beautiful revelation of the wonder-filled Holy Quran to the holy Prophet Muhammad ibn Abdullah (P.B.U.H.), of Arabia. We thank Allah for the revelation of the Holy Quran and the righteous example of Prophet Muhammad of 1400 years ago. True.

But the lost/found original Blackman and Blackwoman need to deeply understand that if this wisdom was "<u>revealed</u>" to Prophet Muhammad of Arabia, 1400 years ago, then that tells you that the wisdom of Islam must have already been here before it was "<u>revealed</u>" to this messenger Prophet Muhammad of Arabia. People "say" that they understand this, but they don't "act" like it. Who is the angel Jabril, and where did he and his people come from? Can you handle this?

"Islam" did not just start 1400 years ago with the revelation of the Holy Quran; for the Holy Quran itself speaks of Abraham as being "Muslim" thousands of years before there was a such thing as (what you know of as) a Holy Quran. The vain, don't like to talk about that, but you will not mislead my people today. We are too intelligent today. All praises due to Allah.

Listen now. "Islam" itself (a life of peace), did not start with Prophet Muhammad of 1400 years ago, it just started amongst white Arabs (or the fratricidal warring tribes in Arabia). This is just like the continent called North America did not just start with Christopher Columbus, he was just the first whiteman to find out about it. Think about that, beloved Blackman and Blackwoman. God is not new, nor is His Earth new; nor is His Truth new.

So, if "Islam" was in existence "originally" before white Arabs were taught of it, then "Islam" (a life of peace) must have already existed amongst the ancient "Original People" of the Earth. That means "you" Blackman and Blackwoman. Elijah Muhammad has taught that "Islam" (submission to the will of God/Righteousness) is our very nature. You can not convert a Blackman to "Islam", you can only bring him into a knowledge of himself...or bring him into an understanding and acceptance of his own nature (which is in submission to the laws of the Creator and This Universe). We are dealing with the nature of The Blackman & Blackwoman.

This is why Allah has blessed us specifically with a teacher who's wisdom is not singularly based on 1400 years ago, but rather we have been blessed with a teacher who's wisdom originated from millions and billions and even trillions of years ago! He "literally" teaches histories from more than seventy-trillion years ago. The wisdom given to him originated with "our origination". We are an old ancient Black people, so we require old ancient Black wisdom to properly re-stimulate our Black minds and Black hearts back into Black divinity. Allah is an old God...older, wiser, and larger than the little compartment that you want to put Him into. Allah is not a recent little "religious" invention. Allah is "The Inventor", before you had a religion. All praise is due to Allah.

The wise amongst us know this. Our honorable brother Elijah Muhammad, teaches you and I a revealed wisdom from way back before the revelation and/or compilation of the Bible or Holy Quran. This is because "we" ourselves are from way back before the Bible and Holy Quran. We are the Original Mothers and Fathers of those Prophets and Messengers written about in these books of scripture. The learned amongst our people know this. It takes a highly placed sunlight to move the Blackman's planet.

You can not limit Allah, with your limited understanding. Allah knows what He is doing. He best knows how to heal, and what methods. Although we do need the wise scripture of Bible and Quran, we need more...our own pre-script-ion. I said, our "own" pre-script-ion. We need a root understanding of those scriptures. <u>We need a pure and practical understanding from the original Black mind that produced the book.</u> Would you agree? Speak up, I can't hear you! I said, would you agree? Well allright then.

So, listen. We need not to be "mental-slaves" for anybody anymore. Right? We now have Our Own teacher and guide, to guide us back into the Divine Mind that we once had before the destruction of Black Civilization. God knows what He is doing, although many may not understand. He, Allah is the Best Knower. So, let God Be God. He knows best his methods, and his reasons.

As for Little Elijah...he came to his own, and his own received him not. This happens over and over again all throughout the Quran. The people never want to receive a messenger, who is raised from the midst of themselves. But God knows what He is doing. He is freeing your mind from captivity.

The Religious World of today has been corrupted into an instrument of Mental Slavery. Spirituality is not meant to enslave the mind. This must be abolished. Little Elijah does not selfishly teach in a way that will make us dependent upon his mind for wisdom. This is no cult of personality. He is selflessly teaching us how to become intellectually independent again, that we may become self-empowered, self-sustained, and self-contained through the ancient divine wisdom of The God within each and every one of us. He is teaching us how to think and do for ourselves again. But first we must become students. We must come as a child. We must humble ourselves to superior wisdom, so that we may be taught all over again to become "Mental Masters" instead of "Mental Slaves", who will not think beyond the aid of the whiteman. It is time for us to grow up out of this childish dependent type of mind state.

Rejoice...you don't have to be a "nigga" for the whiteman, the white Arab, or a "nigga" at all anymore. We can now command respect from the whiteman or the white Arab, or anyone else. But most of all, we can now earn, implement, and emanate our own Self-Respect!!! All that we have to do is accept our own Black teacher and be our own Black selves. Only then can the world respect us. Only then will we truly respect ourselves as Men and Women.

We as a Black Nation will have a relationship with Europeans, Arabs, and all others in the world community, but that relationship can no longer be as a slave to Master, or child to an Adult. No sir. No ma'am. We must mature. And if the World community can not love us, accept us, and have a relationship with us as an independent thinking Black Nation, then to hell with them all. Yes, to hell with them. To hell with the wicked, and to heaven with the righteous! There is no God but Allah! And thee alone will we seek for guidance, sustenance, and strength.

I mean, how the hell were you going to go unite with some Arabs and have not yet even attempted to unite with your own Black People? I just do not understand that. Don't go traveling-off somewhere, until you have taken care of business right here amongst your own troubled family! Never forget that.

Love God, love self, love family, and then others...(in that order). Accept your own and be yourself first. And only then will the world respect you as a Man and Woman. The truth is just the truth. You can take it, or flee. All praise is due to Allah.

The Religion of Hip-Hop

(In the beginning, was...)

That African Drum has never stopped it's hum, son. Day to day making them heads sway back n' forth, forth n' back. It's talkin...it's talkin. Hypnotic repetitive rhythm vibrates the atom's-sphere. There is science in my beat. There is science in my beat. There is plan in My Hand. The Religion of Hip-Hop, ya don't stop.

My Universe moves on a Hip-Hop loop...boom-bip, ba-boom-bip. Not one slip. Fluid Motion and Perfect Time, the mathematics of my natural mind.

The drum drills in the song of my poetry, my story, straight to that subconscious level. I penetrates. I penetrates...to depths of your soul, and take control of where your manhood was sold. Testosterone, aggression, and beats. No Fear! Testosterone, aggression, and beats. No Fear!

Generations nursed from the milks of fear, that the enemy placed in the minds of our Black Mothers! Poisoned we drank. Poison passed along and along, the manhood was gone. A chemical castration...an impotent frustration.

But Allah is Born, God! ...with beats, bass, and rhythm, my surgery is precision on the hearts of The Original Man. My vibe is liquid...it can't be stopped, cause it pours straight through your system, your system. It's heart-surgery for a

Black Manhood. Testosterone, aggression, and beats. No Fear! Testosterone, aggression, and beats. No Fear!

Remove the fear of one generation, in the face of it's enemy. Beat it out...the fears, with them beats that I hear. Testosterone, aggression, and beats. No Fear! My manhood was sold, but now The God is in control with His open heart-surgery. They don't understand The Man...nor His methodology.

My God is beats, bass, and black with a pulse in his hand bringing the dead to life. First, I form his body in sound emotion, then his mind with the breath of intelligent...this is my experiment...until completion, until completion. Be patient with the skill of my hand, my plan. Man is Music, inside dust, dirt, and sand. It is "I" who make Man, again and again.

Knowledge Ain't Enough!

(Spirit + Matter = Life) pt. 2

Today is a good day. Our beloved beautiful Black people are beginning to awaken from the depths of mental ignorance. We are blessed to have this information explosion, in which we are now attempting to re-claim our legacy of Black Greatness. So now everybody is aggressively working to add to their reservoir of knowledge. This is good.

We hear things like "Knowledge is the Key!" or "Knowledge is Power!" Well, this is true, but this is true only to a certain extent. Upon deeper understanding we will find that "mere knowledge" is not enough. No. No. "Knowledge is not power". I would say that, "Knowledge used powerfully, is Power." That is better. Interesting. Think.

But why is it that this mere "knowledge" is not enough to restore healthiness to our minds? Why? What is knowledge anyway? Well in today's world, the word "knowledge" is commonly defined as meaning, an accumulated body of facts information or data. But why is a body of accumulated information not enough to give life back to our minds? This is still because only SPIRIT + MATTER = LIFE. That is still the equation.

If we understand knowledge to be an accumulated "body" of information or data, we can symbolically parallel that to a physical/material "body" of accumulated matter. And we now know that a physical body of matter material ain't enough. Matter needs some spirit in order to animate it into an expression of living life. Is that right? An inanimate piece of matter is considered deceased...it has ceased and doesn't matter anymore. Right?

So, our paradigm equation is still, SPIRIT + MATTER = LIFE. Well since a body of Knowledge (data/information) is a kin to a body of MATTER...in this analogy, what is a kin to SPIRIT? What is the missing element to the equation; "X + Knowledge" equals = "True mental awakening" (or "true mental life")?

"X" = "Wisdom". "Spirit" = "Wisdom". "Wisdom" + "Knowledge" = "True Mental Awakening". "Spirit" + "Matter" = "Life"!

See, "Wisdom" is that element that brings out the best potential in "Knowledge", and "Knowledge" is that element that brings out the best potential in "Wisdom". They both can only exceed so far independently. "Knowledge is in need of Wisdom" and "Wisdom feeds Knowledge".

Well what is "wisdom". Wisdom is that guiding force that righteously applies Knowledge. Wisdom moves Knowledge. Wisdom is the intelligent active force that animates a body of Knowledge to move and produce things from the benefit of that Knowledge as a tool. Wisdom is active good judgement much like common sense.

"Wisdom" is the "righteous" application of knowledge. This is because the wicked application of knowledge is not a wise thing to do in a Universe that is created in righteousness. And this Universal governing principle of righteousness will ultimately destroy and overpower anything that is wicked or not in harmony with the One Law (Uni-Verse), in which it was created.

Listen, beloved Blackman and Beloved Blackwoman, the simple point is that mere knowledge/data or information is dead unless you have the wisdom/common sense/or good judgement to know how to properly use that knowledge. Wisdom (righteous application) gives animated life to knowledge. Knowledge alone, is just not enough.

Are you understanding this in full? Let's use an example to better understand the point. Then we can go on. Okay? Okay. Have you ever seen a person who is very, very, very, smart in the way of book-sense? You know what I mean? I mean they are filled with memorized knowledge, data, and information with all types of masters, doctorates, certificates and degrees. You know what I mean?

Have you ever seen a person like this who is so smart, but yet will turn around and do so many dumb things? Yeah, I have seen this before too. The person is so full of "book-sense" (accumulated knowledge and data) but cannot utilize it because they ain't got no "common-sense"! All of their "book-sense" becomes "mere irrelevant trivia" because they "use it so trivially". So, their accumulated knowledge is dead. Their body of knowledge is life-less. Knowledge Ain't Enough.

Well on the other hand, there are those of us who are very rich in common sense (wisdom), but poor in "book-sense" (accumulated knowledge/data). This is still a limited situation. This is because our common sense (wisdom) can only travel so far and only so effectively with a limited amount of knowledge/data or information through which to express itself. Knowledge is the tool in which you use to express higher forms of your common-sense or (wisdom).

There are a lot of people on the streets with profound wisdom (common sense) but with no accumulated knowledge (book-sense) through which to display that wisdom, so they remain dead. There are a lot of people at the colleges and universities with profound accumulated knowledge (book-sense) but with no wisdom (common-sense) to activate that knowledge, so they remain dead. Only SPIRIT + MATTER = LIFE. And only Knowledge + Wisdom = Mental Awakening .

Those of us with knowledge need to intercourse our time with those of us with Wisdom, and those of us with Wisdom need to intercourse with those of us with knowledge; that we may all give birth to a True Mental Awakening in which is Mental Life. We all need one another to assist ourselves in bringing out the best in ourselves. We want mental Life and we want it more abundantly.

There must be a horizontal balance between complimenting dualities such as Wisdom to Knowledge, Spirit to Matter, and Heart to Brains. But on the well balanced vertical plane, Wisdom is the God over Knowledge, Spirit is the God over Matter, and Heart is the God over brains. Understand this dual balance. There is a Horizontal and a Vertical balance in everything, when you observe closer. The Center of the Horizontal Balance is God. And the Top of the Vertical Balance is God. The apex of a pyramid is centered horizontally but resting atop the axis vertically. God is top and center. Balanced and Prioritized. Only then can life flow freely uninhibited.

You Produce God! pt. 1

(Divine Genetic Engineering)

Man and Woman are two halves of the Force of Nature itself. When these two come together, they have the capacity to reproduce "God", or reproduce "rebellious devil" through their seed.

Even though, sometimes "the seed runs wild"...the quality of the condition of the Man, determines the quality and condition of his seed, therefore the quality and condition of his offspring. Such is the same with the Woman.

Everytime you put poison into your physical body, you are decreasing the life of not only yourself, but of every child that might be born through you. You could be killing generations in advance.

Everytime you put poison thought into your mind, you are producing poison hormones in your blood and brain; plus you are rewriting the genetic coding of yourself and of any child that you may produce. You could be retarding the mental growth of generations in advance.

But, when you place knowledge into your mind, it will not only benefit you in this life, it will benefit those produced in your family-line long after you. Your knowledge and thoughts are literally stored chemically in your body, like data on computer disks. This chemical-water is what your offspring will use to build themselves up out of the darkness of their mother's womb. What you add to that water, determines the resources they will have to work with during their life's time.

Your enemy knows these facts to be true. This is why during slavery, a bright, brilliant, courageous, and rebellious Blackman was always castrated by the white slavemaster. They would literally take a knife, and cut off the testicles of a Man like this. Why? Because they did not want him to produce more children like himself, of whom they could not control. The slavemaster knows the reality of genetic engineering; or genetic breeding. He bred you. Think about that.

You as a Blackman today, a Blackwoman today; you do not live your life simply for yourself. You live today, for generations and generations far off into the future. One generation passes the baton of advancement on to the next generation, that the entire race may move ahead.

Just as you have been directly affected by your parents, and foreparents; what "you" do today has real implications and effect on the times and lives of your children in the future. In reality, you are really preparing a life for yourself, in the future. Justice is eternal.

You are literally a genetic Scientist and Engineer. Everytime you think a thought, you are altering a reality in your own being. You are constantly either building yourself up, or tearing yourself down. Nevertheless, you are always altering your genetic pattern for better or for worse.

Each child that you produce will be a reflection of your own human development, at the particular time that you conceived that child. This is why you often read of God asking his prophets and messengers of divine mind, to produce physical children in that state of mind. This is so they may pass their seed of greatness at a time in their lives when they have achieved a greater level of human development within themselves. Greatness reproduces greatness, on down the wheel of time.

Verifiably, your Bible and Quran speak of Jesus, son of Maryam, son of Joseph, who was the son of such and such, who was the son of such and such, son of King David of such and such, son of Abraham...etc., etc. This person begot that person, and that person begot that person that begot that other person that begot this one. I always wondered why the book of Matthew opened with the genealogy (family tree) of Jesus, but now I know. Greatness produces greatness. I always wondered why the whiteman castrated Dr. George Washington Carver, but now I know. Greatness produces greatness. I always wondered why some of these divinely guided persons in the Bible and Quran produced children from more than one wife, but now I know. Greatness produces greatness through a genetic seed multiplied.

Well, since genealogy is so important, what legacy are we passing on in our own genealogy? Everything that you place in your Head, Heart, and Body is producing the future. What are you genetically engineering for your people? Are you preparing the way for a Saviour to be born from your seed, your womb, your flesh, your mind?

How else will a Saviour be born, if not "through you"? The only immaculate conception, is when you take an immaculately kept woman, with an immaculately kept man, who will produce an immaculate conception. Clean-up your thoughts and your Body. Make yourself "immaculate". Then every child you produce will be from an "immaculate conception". Every child you produce will be like a Jesus (Isa, Yeshua)...a divine child of God. Divine Genetic Engineering...is how a saviour is born.

You Produce God! pt. 2

(How is a Saviour Born?)

Question: Is devil "Spirit", or is devil "Flesh"?
Answer: Devil is "Spirit in Flesh".

Question: Is God "Spirit", or is God "Flesh"?
Answer: God is "Spirit in Flesh".

You have heard it said that the devil was grafted out of the Original Blackman. You have heard this, and know this now. This devil was produced from the lower character, and the lower materials found in the genetic seed of the Original Blackman...grafted from the worst in your "spirit" and "matter". He came from you. He came from "what is in you". We have learned this, accepted this, and gone on. Okay

But Now! I want the Real Question! I want to know! FROM! WHENCE!? COMES!? GOD???? FROM WHENCE COMES MY SAVIOUR??? FROM WHENCE COMES OUR SAVIOUR???

Let me ask you a question today. If you believe that it is possible to produce devil from your loins, what about God? I am talking to all of you who understand the realities of genetic engineering. I am talking to you Blackman & Blackwoman.

If I have made the lowest in my own character to materialize before my eyes, can not I also materialize the best in my character before my eyes? Can I? I am the Human Collective Mind, and I am asking questions now. I have heard it said that "God is Within"!

If God is "in" my Mind! If God is then placed "on" my Mind? If God resonates on the water (bio-chemicals) of the Brains of my Mind! Can, THIS, SPIRIT, in, chemical, form, travel, ACROSS, my, spinal, column, THROUGH, A, SEED, released, in, to, HIS, WOMB, to, take, MATERIAL, FORM???? Speak to me? And the Spirit became Flesh, and dwelt among the people! Whose Spirit? Whose Flesh? What People? A blessed people.

From "What Pyramid" (or Man/Mind of Divine Order)...from "What Mountain" (or a Man/Mind of Giant Greatness), does God Come from? I said, if you believe that it is possible to produce rebellious devil from your loins, what about God?!?!

As a slave We were! And When We cried in Our Mind, cried in Our Heart, cried in Our Soul for God to come save Us!...Who? Heard? Our? Cry??? Who heard us!!!!?? My Beloved Blackpeople!!! Pay attention to the GOOD NEWS! I have heard it said that "God is Within", now how can we pull him out? We need Him.

God on your Mind. God in your heart. God in your soul, heard your cries. You called HIM. You called HIM into FORM. You called HIM from the WOMB. You called HIM into MATERIAL EXISTENCE. You called Him from a place in YOU that you perceive not. God on your Mind. The Inter-networking of your collective spirit sent messages to a mind/seed/womb/and spirit on the other side of the planet in heaven. And you moved those forces of nature (men and women). Your message was, "prepare us a body"...prepare us "somebody"...prepare us a "Saviour"!

And out of the best of YOUR COLLECTIVE CHARACTER! Out of the best of YOUR COLLECTIVE WISDOM! Out of the best of YOUR COLLECTIVE LOVE! Out of the best of YOUR COLLECTIVE ANCESTRAL GREATNESS!!!...a Saviour was Born! Born unto who? Born unto YOU!

You are more powerful than you know. In your cries, you worked a Plan, and in your mind you made a Man. And He appeared unto you. A conglomerate-consciousness in One Man/Mind, drawn up out of "your water", to seek and to save that which was lost. Beneficence and Mercy coming to a people who had known neither. I have heard it said that "God is Within"!!! Oh, surely this is Good News, to a people who perceive!!!

Master Fard Muhammad? pt. 2

(He caused an Effect...Resurrection is constantly)

Intelligently we resurrect, from the depths and graves of Self-Hatred, and lack of Self-Respect. No knowledge of self is the blow of death, suffered by us at the hands of a devilish man. Who will be a Saviour to this, The Original Man?

Cries of pain made plain in the ears of God, moved mercy out to finally seek us. The Cycles were spinned and initiated. Rejoice. Praiseworthy, He came.

With a far reaching plan of the eye. He dropped pebbles in a pond, rippling out to cause an effect of the future times to come. The God Mind is patiently wise in His, the best of plans.

In the top of your head Original Man, is the Ocean of the Universe. In the balance of your mind, He dropped teachings that would ripple out to the children, the generations soon to be born from the core of your seeds. His Word dropped from on high, make waves in your water. If you don't perceive, your sons and daughters will perceive and do perceive. It is calculated. Re-cognize Master Fard Muhammad. God is a Mind.

If He is not talking to you, He is talking to what is in you. If you choose to remain a valley, a mountain shall stand in your place one Day, The Son of God, The Daughters of Allah. They will say, I heard you speaking words back in time,

Allah...speaking to the ears of my father. In the water I lay, until the time came for I to be born. Sound waves traveled space and time on water. I was there. Now, I am here. I am Your Son, Your Daughter. This is what our children will say to the Man who came like a ghost, faintly perceived, mostly Unseen. They will call Him, Father. Yes, your holy ghost defined.

You might not know what goes on inside of you as you read this word. Impression is made, and form is shaped that He has planned. From a pebble dropped in water, a Tidal Wave is born on the other side. The Best of Planners, planning from a mind that the mortal eye refuses to see. Resurrection will be. The Scientists have met, and they have agreed, resurrection will be.

The Master concurred and said "Be..and it is"...currently working on these hearts and these souls and these minds...all from the touch of a hand of a Man of a Mind, The Mind. Masterminded we think, act, and make motions from a cause we did not see. You and me, we, in sync to a series of times...His cause...the effect, We Be.. With His own hand He makes waves in the Water. With His own hand He makes waves in the Water. From pure sound, hence comes The Son, and The Daughter.

Mortal eyes refuse to perceive these. Yet, accept your own and yourself you will be. Resurrection is constantly.

Protect
The Temple
with Your Life.

(The Search Procedure)

Divine Protection. You don't let just any person come into the Sacred Mosque. You put guards at the door. They must conform to your peace before they enter. Protect your Mind. Protect your Dome.

Each person is like a thought, and idea (or pattern of thinking) clothed in flesh. That is all that people are. You don't just let any idea or thought come into your head unchecked or unsearched. You search that thought or person to make sure that they will not disturb your peace, but rather <u>add</u> to your peace.

But we as gullable Black People let any kind of thought into the temple (our Mind). All the whiteman got to do, is put "one" Black Rap star on T.V. with a cigarette hanging out of his mouth, and in 30-60 days every little fool is trying to blow smoke. You just accept whatever is given you, without searching it first to see if it will cause havoc in the temple. And so the enemy crept in, bringing his mischief and death, while you slept.

Listen. You are to guard The Temple with your life, because The Temple is Your Life. The Temple is the sacred place of instruction, inspiration, and refuge from the ills of outside society. Such the same is your Mind. Now, what do you think will happen to you, if you just let any intruder (thought), enter and desecrate your temple? Negatively influencing your mind with just any type of thinking?

The condition of Your Mind creates the condition of Your Life...constantly. Think about that long and hard. The healthiness of Your Mind is determined by the thoughts and ideas you allow or disallow into Your Mind. Well, each idea and thought that approaches your temple, must be thoroughly analyzed, because each thought (or person) makes up the body of your congregation or collective Mind. Your Mind is made up of a congregation of thoughts and ideas that form the one overall thought pattern, attitude (spirit), and direction of the temple itself. All of this determines the condition of your life. This is why you must protect the temple with your life, because the temple gives you your life.

In this society, your enemy is constantly sending foreign agents (disruptive ideas and temptations) to destroy the peace and order of your temple (mind). At every turn there is something trying to persuade you to do "something evil", or in other words "something to hurt your own well being".

Yet, all that we are saying here is to protect yourself against such mental assault. Don't be so naive to receive just anything into your mind. Be discerning, discriminating, and analytical of every thought that seeks to enter your eyes, your ears, therefore your mind. Take charge and control of your own mind. "You" regulate it's affairs.

Where is the Mosque? Where is the Mosque?

Take off your shoes, for the ground where you stand is Holy! Where is the Mosque? Where is the Mosque? The Mosque? The "Holy Land" is wherever the "Holy Man", stands! Take off your shoes, for the ground where you stand is Holy!

So, he says "What is the Purpose?". What is the purpose of a Mosque, a Temple, a Church? A Mosque, Temple, or Church, is supposed to be in the business of putting itself out of business! Huh? Talk to a Blackman! True "healers", have a driving-passion to "heal", so that they are no longer needed as a "healer" amidst the people. He said, The Mosque is in the business of putting itself out of business. Interesting.

But, where is the true Mosque, anyway? Not necessarily the ones built of stone, spoken about in the previous paragraph, but where is the "true mosque"? You, me, and we...we enter these temples, these mosques, these churches in a careful reverence and respect, not truly knowing where the true mosque, temple, or church is. He said to take off your shoes, for the ground where you stand is Holy. We had better listen to that.

Still, what is the purpose of a temple in this world? The purpose of a spiritual temple in this wicked world is to give persons a place of refuge, respite, reflection, and residence, away from the corruptness of the outside world. The temple is the place where you come to commune with God. "Commune" does not mean to just sit there crying and the like. "Commune" means to "communicate" with The Master Intelligence from on high. You are at the temple to make an appeal to your Guiding Father; and/or to receive instruction from your Guiding Father. You go to the temple to conversate, when the noise of the outside world is trying to interfere with, and disconnect your connection. The temple is your telephone (tele-pathic-phone). Now did you come to conversate?

When you enter the temple, what are you really trying to enter? We need to see this thing? When you enter the temple, you are seeking to enter your Head. Okay. Entering, and expanding your consciousness is your goal. Listen. The Temple is Your Head. The soft palates on either side of your head are called "temples" themselves. The Temple is Your Head.

The Temple is representative of Your Head. When you enter the temple, you find the men sitting on one side, as the women sit on the other. Your Left Brain Rational Masculine energy sits on one side of your head, while Your Right Brain Intuitive Feminine energy sits on the other side of your head. Your Head is The Temple. In the forward middle of the two halves stands a "speaker" that The God transmits his messages to and through, to get to you. In the forehead your conscience talks to you. Now who do you have standing on your podium/forehead speaking messages to both your brains? Is it God or devil? Place yourself in the right temple. Where is the Temple? Take off your shoes, for the ground where you stand is Holy!

When you are allowed to enter The Temple, you are coming from the outside...somewhere else. You are coming in from out of a strange land amongst strange people with strange ways. You want to see The Father for His Guidance, for you found nothing but trouble out in that world. So, you make an appeal at the door to be let into the Temple. Then you humble yourself and willingly offer your person, your heart to be searched. You are searched by The Father, to insure that there is nothing in your heart of evil intent, verifying that you are only coming to seek His peace. Then The Father allows you to enter The Temple and He sits you down, that He may talk with you.

Humbly you say "Father...please just let me in." You make a sincere lettered appeal on paper, writing to Him. And if your handwriting is found pleasing to him (if what you seek to produce from your hands, will be reflective of what He produces from His) you may enter The Temple. And He celebrates the return of His prodigal Son, His prodigal daughter. Any Father is pleased to see his own seed enter into peace. Peace, here-after so much pain.

I said The Temple is Your Brains! God is in the King-Dome, where else should the King be? God is in You, in The Temple. In You! In You! In You! Buuuuuuuuuut Waiiiiiiiit!!! You never could find God IN YOU, if you have been living all of your life outside of YOURSELF! Outside of your True Self! Outside of YOUR Nature! Outside of YOUR Way!

Yes, but you didn't walk out. You have been cast-out of The Temple, cast out of your ways, your religion, your name, your history! Cast out of your Mind! Cast out of your temples. Every doorway was locking you out of the temple. Your eyes, your ears, your style of thinking...blind, deaf, and dumb. Cast out. Think about that.

I once heard some wise people say "you will never find

your heart in a Temple, until you find a Temple in your heart". Getting into The Temple, means getting a grant of entrance into your own Heart. We are gradually given a ring of keys, to different doors in The Temple, as we grow. He said, getting into the Temple means getting into Yourself. These keys, bits of knowledge and wisdom, stimulates the thoughts that will unlock different aspects unto your own self, that you may learn the Knowledge of Yourself, God, and the devil (in other words knowledge of yourself).

Yes, know thyself. You have entered the Kemetic University to study the arts and sciences of The Universe. A University (Universe-city) is a "state" of civilization that is based on the knowledge found in the way that this Universe is founded by it's Creator. Hence, a city up in the sky amidst the Greatness of the Sun, Moon, & Stars, hoovering high above the civilization of this earthly plane...up where The Temple is to take your intelligence...amidst the stars or amidst the greatest of The Greatest. This is spiritual language. The Temple is erected to explode you our into the deep regions of your own Mind; the inverted Universe...an an in-version of everything that you see mirrored out there.

Come back to Yourself. Come back home to Your Temple. Come back home to your Right Mind. Come back Home to He that dwells in the central midst of You! The Heavens await you! Mr. Muhammad's Mosques number into the Millions and beyond. You got temples walking around you everyday, and don't know it. The floor of your Temple is The Earth itself...as the Heavenly Sky is it's Dome.

Now, where is the Mosque? Where is the Mosque? Take off your shoes; for the ground where you stand is Holy!

Inside of Peace.

Beware of those who seek to "clone" God, but can not!

(Cleansing The Temple!)

Hypocrites. Please change your heart before the day comes that "the righteous" will have to bring swift justice upon you in a way you never imagined. It is the most peaceful skies, that can produce the most horrifying storms.

Believe it or not, The God knows what you hide and what you manifest. You think that you are undercover, but really God's mercy is your only cover from death. Out of His sympathy for your ignorance, he gives you time to change your deceitful ways.   Mercy is extended, but count the days. You are perceived.

Beware of those who seek to clone God, but can not. The only way that we will be able to tell our "friends" from your "foes", is to study them <u>inwardly</u>, not just <u>outwardly</u>.   A righteous label and exterior appearance is not sufficient. Don't fall prey to today's modern tricknology. Many come to God, but only a few come for the right reasons. What are their true underlying motives? What are you here for...really?

But know that this is not just a test for the hypocrites, more than it is a test for the "True" and "Living"! What does it mean to be the "True" and "Living God"? This is about "us". This is not about them, this is about "you"! This is about The "Righteous"! We wouldn't waste ink and paper to talk about the hypocrites. The ill-motivated at heart, are not even worth the breath of your words. This is about "The Righteous". This is "your" test.

Wicked ones may attempt to wear your garments and speak your words, but they can not clone God. It is impossible. It is impossible when God is really "True" and "Living". I repeat... it is impossible when God is really "True" and "Living". But the question to The righteous hearts is, "Are you True to your heart, and Alive in your expression"? Devils could not clone you if you were.

Understand this. Twisted weeds can not exist amidst "Flowers in Bloom". "Flowers in Bloom" is the fruit of being "True and Living". Weeds are weeds, all looking alike until some birth a flower to crown their tops, boldly defining their existence, their distinction! Once clearly defined, the gardener can easily pluck the weed away, assured it's not a flower just rising in the ranks.

When your heart is "True", and your spirit is "Living", your crown explodes into bloom by nature. By the Light of the Sun, you bio-chemically respond. Stage by stage the stems rise and rise to the appointed day when the truth of all will be known.

The Honorable Elijah Muhammad, has taught that on the day of Resurrection, we would grow into a new creation...a creation of beauty...no more ugliness we would have. He teaches that your "thought" will actually reconstruct your face. This is going on now.

Well, when else is the day of resurrection but now? What is the condition of our "thought", and how does it project on our physical being? Are we a garden of flowers, or a lot of weeds? See, it is easy for "twisted weeds" to come infiltrate and hide amidst us, if we <u>appear like the average weed ourselves</u>!

I'm not here taking out any time and mind to talk about no hypocrites hiding amongst the ranks! Please! They don't deserve that. I'm talking about "you", "me", and "us" trying to hide amongst the hypocrites! Not "weeds" hiding amidst the "flowers"! But "<u>flowers</u>" hiding amidst the "weeds"!!!!

If you be "True" and "Living God", how can dead men and women come seek to clone you? It can't be done. The righteous "playing small", undercover...amidst those little devils. The devil is thriving, because you refuse to be "God"!

So, why should God hide, sleeping amidst devils? You better raise up and be what you are! Bloom now! Bloom now! Bloom now...in the midst of Your Sun! Boldly accepting Your Own, and energetically being Yourself! The rose is in full bloom, with thorns to prick the wicked who attempt to touch! Your God called you up! No shame. The "True" and "Living" shall reign. He made you for a reason...Stand-Up!

It is time to go. These are the last days, and we now will have to separate ourselves from the weak and the wicked. God's order! His order! This must be done immediately, so that we may go on to complete this mighty work! Cleanse the Sacred Temple. Cleanse your heart "True", and fire your spirit "Living"!

Question: How do you cleanse the Temple?

Answer: You cleanse the Temple, by "boldly" Being God! Darkness can never exist in the midst of Light!

<u>**Becoming God III:**</u>
"Taking Dominion of The Kingdom of Self."

How did They make The Most Powerful Nation on Earth?

How did they make the most powerful nation on Earth? They didn't...you did. In this present world today, America is positioned as the most powerful nation on earth today with her economical wealth, therefore military might, therefore political influence around the world. But who made her that powerful?...You did. This seemingly insignificant Blackman & Woman who sit at the feet of American Society is the direct source of it all. Today, it may be hard to believe, but honest reasoning will present the actual fact.

Not to mention all of the sciences, mathematics, engineering, architectural, the technological genius and other general civilization knowledge that your original parents brought into this land, you made this place what it is. "Wealth" made this country, and "who" actually made the wealth? Not, who "capitalized" off of the wealth, but who "made" the wealth of this country?

Days upon weeks upon months upon years upon decades upon centuries upon sweat, upon blood, and upon tears, this country was built on top of "free" slave labor. Think.

Why did this particular American caucasian man so far exceed his european brothers? Why? Well, he had a possession that his brothers did not have. He had the cream of Africa in his hands. The European caucasians got the left-over treasures and resources of Africa, while America got the man who created those treasures of Africa. America got the cream.

The entrapment, buying, selling and slavery of Black Human beings was just another economic venture to this beastial man. His god, guide, and quest alone, is the lustful obtaining of inordinate wealth.

Think about America, for a moment. In the world of economics, every nation is like one big corporation, that is made up of a conglomerate of national corporations. In the world of business the largest expense of corporations is labor...or the paying of salary wages to it's employees. This is the largest expense, but any corporation could make no money at all without workers to perform the services or manufacture the goods. Right?

Well, here is this corporation called America that got her start a few years ago. And in that small margin of time she has greatly far exceeded the other countries (corporations) that had already been established for a while. How did she do it? She didn't..."you" did it.

See...if I went downtown today and stole some land, to construct and erect my corporate business tower in the midst of the other established major corporations, I would quickly far exceed them too if I did not have to pay one dime to any of my one hundred thousand employees. My laborers work for free, therefore bringing in a staggering amount of profit unimaginable. Imagine that! The gross-profit and the net-profit would be the same!

What if I had a business of employees who would normally on average earn wages of about 30 thousand dollars per year. If I have 10 thousand employees, 300 million dollars is what I would have to pay in wages alone, leaving me only a marginal net profit to grow with...which is normal.

Yet this devil thought to himself, imagine if I had straight-up slaves hard laboring for me from sun up until sun down, I wouldn't have to pay no anybody at all. At the end of his fiscal business year, he would pocket the additional 300 million dollars all to himself. He might have to murder, mutilate, and kidnap a few hundred million people in the process, but he just couldn't pass up the opportunity. And so he did. He didn't even have to pay a land-lease, because he just took the land and murdered the family who was living there.

Having a corporation called America, of which he did not have to pay his laborers any compensation for centuries, automatically and obviously made him profit more than his white brethren, and economically excel the entire world.

This is truer than the light shining from the sun. America's european brother didn't suffer though. It was just the difference between the "filthy-rich" and the "disgustingly-rich".

America and every other west european country is rich directly because of the Blackman. Europe didn't want all of them "niggras" living at home with them, so they instituted a different kind of slavery called "colonization". They just went down into Africa and took it over. They divided the land and peoples into sub-nations, satellite-countries or extension colonies of their own european Nations. Can you imagine someone breaking into your house, gathering up all of your riches, belongings, and resources...loading it up on a truck, and then taking it back to Europe and the rest of the World Market to sell for millions of dollars untold???? And they have the nerve to make "you" load the truck with "your own" stuff, as they pay you utter poverty wages. This is called "Colonization".

Instead of "kidnapping then slavery", it was "invasion then slavery". This is why your white counterparts are so rich today...because of "you" and "yours".

Yet today it is very easy to forget that fact. You just walk around seeing white people with money in their family, money in their pocket, figuring that they worked so hard for it. When the honest truth is that their fathers, robbed your fathers yesterday. So, now your little friends have a lot more wealth, status, and advantage than you do in the world. Yet today, they arrogantly tell you to stop crying, and pull yourself up by your bootstraps! Can you believe that? Well, they are right to a certain extent. Go ahead and pull yourself up by the bootstraps...and once you get those boots strapped on tight, get ready to do some boot-kickin.

The Most Powerful Nation in the World is Most Powerful because of you. You and Africa financed the wealth of Europe and America. Remember that always. If you can do it for them, you can do it for yourself.

The Changing of The Gods! pt. 2
(Military Attitude & Training Tactics)

This chapter is only for the "serious" at life. As a Blackman or Blackwoman, you may have never had a clear reason in mind to be "all that you can be" before, but now you do. Many souls may read over these writings, but there are some of you special souls who are mature enough to know the seriousness of this. You have that "real" type of heart, and have always been true to yourself in one form or another.

The ideas presented should have touched "you", because Your God has unmistakably and specifically made "you" for this particular time in the history. Your God specifically placed "you" in front of these words, in the perfect synchronicity that he inspired me to communicate them. He is Master of all this, and the time. This should be very serious to "you". All of this should talk to "your" soul.

Listen. Your God has Imagination. Listen. And out of His Imagination, He created all the Heavens above your head and this Earth beneath your feet. This He has done.

Listen. Your God has Imagination. Listen. And out of His Imagination, He has Invisioned a World for You and I. He has Imagined A Nation. This He has done.

Listen. Now, do "you" have Imagination? Can "you"

Imagine-Nation with Your God? Can "you" Imagine-Nation with Your God? Can you see it?

Listen. This chapter is only for the "serious" at life. You have to see and believe the reality of this thing. Let us look at an example. I want you to look outside your window to the East today. I want us to place our studious eyes on the entire Asian World today in the East. Have you noticed something?

Do you see how "rapidly" the Asian Nations have arisen in just a few days? Do you see how they have risen to the tops of Education, Business, Manufacturing and Technology...even becoming a Military Superpower? Have you noticed this?

Where were these Nations just a few days ago? They were nowhere to be seen, and some were even devastated by war. Can you imagine atomic bombs dropping over your head, and then just a few decades later, you are living in a thriving, prosperous society? A few decades?

Where was China, a few days ago? Where was Japan a few days ago? Where was Taiwan, a few days ago? Where was Korea, a few days ago? Where was Vietnam, a few days ago? Now where are these nations today? And how far have they come in the span of "one lifetime"? Look at the Asian nations as a whole. Their star is definitely rising.

Now, as we have looked at the Asian Nations, let us take note of the Asian peoples as a whole. As you look at some of the immigrants that have come to this country, and as you look at their people abroad, you will notice a certain similar attitude. These people seem to have a sense of mission and purpose. You do not see them caught up in a bunch of foolishness, sport, fun and play. You see them focused on objectives. Serious in face.

While whitefolk's children are off trying to bunji-jump off a damned bridge, and while Blackfolk's children are off shooting each other in the streets, where are the Asian children? Are they at home planning their futures? Are they in the Library studying physics? Are they in Medical School? Are they preparing to open another business or corporation? Where are they? They are not hanging out with you. I don't see them jumping off the bridge with the whiteboy. Where are they?

Out of all three of these peoples, who will be the most equipped to run, rule, and master the world tomorrow? You better think about it.

Now listen, listen, listen, listen, listen, listen, listen! All of that was only said to say ONE thing!!! Imagine-Nation! Imagine-Nation! Imagine-Nation! Can you see it?

If you can see the reality of the Asian Nations rising from "insignificance" into "prominence"...in just "one" lifetime; What is THE REALM OF POSSIBILITY for a Nation of your own in just "one" lifetime??? Your Life's Time??? Can you hear this??? Can you stop playing long enough to hear this??? Your life is no Play-ground! This is serious World Affairs! This is The Changing of The Gods! Your God has visited North America, to place you on THE TOP OF CIVILIZATION!!! He has IMAGINED A NATION for YOU, now can YOU get serious and sober minded enough to IMAGINE ONE WITH YOUR GOD????

Can you IMAGINE-NATION with YOUR GOD??? He has said, "Let US Imagine-Nation"! Then, "Let US make a Nation"! First, "Let US make Man!"..."Let US make Blackman & Blackwoman all over again"! Now, will you stand with HE, who has come to stand with you?

A merciful God has prepared and initiated a hand-crafted process that would rocket the Blackman & Blackwoman to the tops of the World...but surely we have been a people that perceive not. Surely.

It is "serious" that we must become. It is "focused" that we must become. It is a "military attitude" that we must develop. In the "military" you sleep, drink, and eat "war". All of your energy is focused in one direction. War is all that you think about.

Well we are in a different type of war. And we must sleep, drink, and eat Our Own Focused Objective! And what is that Focused Objective? "BECOMING GOD"!!! Becoming The Masters of our Own Destiny...The Masters of Our own Lives! Raising Our Nation to the tops of Civilization! Creating a Quality of Life for Our People to live in, for Our Children and Generations to come!!! Achievement! Achievement! Achievement! Pray, live, die, sacrifice, eat, sleep, and drink Achievement! The Destined Achievement! Imagine-Nation! Imagine-Nation! Imagine-Nation!

Military Attitude! (Focus! Tactics! Training! Purpose!) (Focus! Tactics! Training! Purpose!) Military Attitude...nothing stands in the way of your duty. You are fighting and achieving for the future of your children. If you are angry that nobody left you a future as a child, then it would be a crime for you to turn around and do the same for yours.

Military Attitude! (Focus! Tactics! Training! Purpose!)

Focus/Tactics: <u>What, where and how will you make your contribution to the development of Your Nation? In what way will you implement your point of excellence?</u>

You may not yet know what field of endeavor, you want to take your soldier's post in. So, how do you find out? How do you find your base, rank, position, mission, and orders?

Sit down in a quiet place. Write down all of the different fields of skills and interest that you may have had over the years. Make a list of 3-5 areas of endeavor.

Take this list to your local library. Ask the librarian to give you a list of all the magazines and books that have information under these subjects. Take one subject per day

Gather a group of magazines and books under the subject, and spread them out on a table. Take a few hours to sift through all the material. Browse until you find writings that interest you.

Upon each visit to the library, repeat the same process for every field of interest, until you find the subject that speaks to your own soul. Do this.

You may even have an interest of subjects that span as vastly different as:

"<u>Flower Gardening</u>"-because you live in an all-year warm climate, and you want to start a massive flower-farm of acres, in which you can sell and supply fresh-flowers to all of the nationwide florist businesses year round. Somebody has to do that...for your Nation.

"<u>Business & High Finance</u>"-because you want to raise investment capital amongst your own people, to conduct purchase/acquisitions of some of these suffering white businesses and corporations.

You may feel that, as our oppressor loses control of his businesses, you may want to step in and purchase it at low cost, replace his mis-management operation, and revitalize the business through the inventive and progressive management/marketing tactics that "you" have...maximizing profits for Black Investors. Somebody has to do that...for your Nation.

"<u>Computer Services</u>"-because you have always had a persistent obsession with computers. You may have the thought to lease a store front, in which you place six computer systems. You may want to set up a Computer Center in which there are individual computer stations that people can rent time to use them.

You may want to solicit your business to schools that can bring their children in for training sessions, because their school can not afford computers themselves. You may want to solicit your business to college students. You may want to solicit your business to other small business owners, to use your computer services to better manage their small businesses. Instead of setting up a "Laundromat", you may want to set up a "Computermat". Somebody has to do both....for your Nation.

"Food Preparation & Packaging"-because you may be talented at the "Culinary Arts"...you love to cook! You may want to make healthy frozen pizzas, or even healthy full-course dinner portions. You may have a special recipe for homemade cookies or pies. Who knows? You may have creative and more appealing ideas for packaging your particular foods.

You may look through the phone directory to see who sells food packaging equipment and food labeling materials in your area. You may want to wholesale your delectable items to large grocery store chains, East Coast, West Coast, Midwest, Southern chains. It all starts from "one" idea and initiative. Somebody has to do this...for your Nation.

"Hauling & Moving"-because you may want to purchase a fleet of trucks...trucks to haul shipments of goods and wares state to state for manufacturing companies. You may want to buy some garbage trucks and seek contracts for pick-up in new neighborhoods, dumpsters in business areas, and even contracts for recyclable items to be picked-up and hauled away to recycling plants. You may want to buy some trucks to move person's belongings from old home to new home; or even have moving trucks for them to rent. Somebody has to do that...for your Nation.

"Real Estate"-because you may want to purchase properties. (Our people need to own land!) You may want to purchase old abandoned lots in an area where parking spaces are needed, then rent out the spaces to commuters. You may want to purchase low cost housing to renovate, multiplying their worth and value...then sale or rent to multiply your profits. You may want to purchase housing and land outside the cities, to set up resort and retreat areas for your stressed-out people. You may want to set up an elaborate Bed & Breakfast get-away that host one or two couples at a time. There is a lot you can do with Real Estate Properties. Somebody has to do that for your Nation.

————————————————————————————

This goes on and on and on! There is something for everybody to do! The point is to find your area of interest, and your area of focus! Our Nation needs it all!!! Find out what you want to do. Find out what it takes to do it, and do it! Do it! Do it! There is no such thing as "obstacle"! Every soldier must complete the "obstacle course" to prove themselves worthy! Is that right? God sees "beyond problems" to solutions. Mathematics is The Art of Problem-Solving. Tactics. Maneuvers. Tactics. Maneuvers.

Do what you do to the highest capability...World Class and nothing less! World Class and nothing less.

Training: You might still be sitting in that library, and that is a good place to be. Find every book and tape-set on Self-Development, Character building, and even foreign languages. You must get prepared to properly deal with yourself, your society and the world at large.

Go to the white bookstores and find all the latest books

and tapes on character-building, time-management, entrepreneurship, etc., etc.

Then go to the Black bookstores and read absolutely everything of your culture and history, so that you will know what to do with the tactics you are learning from those caucasian writers. They got their knowledge from you and your ancestors, so go get it back.

They are passing wisdom around amongst themselves about how to maintain their dominance in the world, but they never expected "you" to walk up in "their" bookstore. Go behind enemy lines and gather intelligence.

As a matter of fact, you go in the white bookstore, make a list of all the books and authors that interest you, go to the black bookstore and tell your black bookstore to make a special order for you, so that you can give that profit money to the Black store. Tell them that knowledge has no color, you just want the goods.

Next...get up early in the morning, take the bus, the train, or drive out to the best part of town. Look around and see how people are living. Look and see what you want to build for your family, children, and people collectively. We can not let ourselves get satisfied with living any old type of way. Desire the best! You are the best! And you deserve the best! But you can never have an "insatiable desire" for the "best in life", if you've never been "exposed" to the "best in life". Get out and expose yourself to it!!! Get-up, Get-out, and Get Something for Yourself!!! For Your Family!!! Then for Your People!!!

Who are the successful people that you know? Who are the people that are going somewhere in life? Find them, make friends with them. Birds of a similar feather flock together. You go flock with them successful birds over there, instead of them birds that can't get up off the ground, and ain't even trying.

Find seminars, workshops, and classes that are going on in your city. Attend them. How do you find out about them? Call for bulletin board information at community colleges or universities. Call "different" local radio stations that may advertise and broadcast local events. Try everything...where there is a will there is always a way. Training! Training! Training!

Purpose: The purpose is to build a productive, purposeful, and prosperous life for yourself, your family, and your Nation. The purpose is to place yourself and your people on the tops of civilization. The purpose is to Build an Independent Nation. The purpose is to Escape the death of Niggativity, and Become God over your life destiny and direction!!! That is the purpose.

Blackman & Blackwoman, are you letting the world pass you by? This is the Changing of The Gods. Are you preparing to take your post??? A Nation needs <u>all</u> facets. Master your area, and await further orders.

Mind Control

(Mental Advertisement)
"Hold your Mind in Your Hands."

Mind control...practically. No, I'm not getting ready to take you out into some mystical mystery teachings on Mind Control. This is not the time for that.

One day we are going to talk about how to "meditate", "levitate", and "gravitate"...but as for right now I want somebody to show me how to "demonstrate"! Okay? We will get to all of that other technique, later. First things, first. May I have the "basics" first, please? ("Base"-ics), you know?

I say all of that because, while we are off burning candles and chanting hymns trying to "mystically" get control our minds, our enemy has "realistically" gained control of our minds and everybody else's on the planet! I think we had better get some kind of clue.

This man has taken over your world! Get serious today. What is the method of <u>his</u> "Mind Control"? He ain't burning no "incense", he burning "you". So, what is <u>his</u> method of "Mind Control"? His method is simple. "Mental Advertisement". What? "Mental Advertisement". Yes.

Not only does he mentally advertise his products, goods, and services to your conscious mind, but he advertises "his ideals" and "his lifestyle" around the world; powerfully persuading the entire world's population to buy into them. Oh, yes. He makes a powerful appeal to your lower nature, appetites, and desires. Temptation is his advertisement. How else did you think that Lucifer would get the whole world to follow after him? Your Bible is no storybook. This is real life.

Mind-Control, thought-control, opinion-control, decision-control, action-control...all via the science of Mental Advertisement. Powerful. Phenomenal. Can you believe it?

Well, rest assured that the science of Mental Advertisement is not just only at the disposal and usage of your devil. The science of Mental Advertisement is purely available to you and I. Actually, your oppressor is not the inventor of this (as he is truly not the inventor of anything), he got this technique from studying your own ancient wisdom as you mentally went to sleep.

I mean, he uses the screen of that television like "flash-cards"...you know? He keeps flashing and flashing and flashing these images with sound, and the next thing you know, you are unknowingly imitating what you have heard and seen...more and more and more. It is really something.

Well actually, it is really quite simple though. It is mental conditioning. When an athlete wants to train and condition a muscle, he repeats a certain exercise over and over. Thus, eventually the strength and movement of the exercise, unconsciously becomes second nature to that person.

When a student wants to learn and condition his or her mind, they will repetitively review their subject over and over. Thus, eventually the knowledge of that subject, unconsciously becomes second nature to that person.

So, the question is...what is happening to our minds as we constantly sit a front the television, soaking in these repetitive electronic flash-card images?

What is happening to our minds as we constantly sit listening to these repetitive electronic flash-card hypnotic sounds? Think about it.

Don't eat of the Mental-Swine. Be Discriminating of the sounds, sights, and words that go into your system. If you See No Evil, Hear No Evil, and Speak No Evil; you have a better chance to Be No Evil. You better hold your mind in your hands. If you don't, somebody else will.

See, even a large measure of this negative-hypnosis is due to your own hands. It is interesting to note that we also unconsciously use this Mental Advertisement upon ourselves everyday. We do this with our own mouths as we repeat negative statements into our conscious mind, reinforcing the negativity that is already there. Just go out into the public and listen to us (blackfolks) talk to each other. I mean, every other word is a curse word; and every statement is a negative one. These people hate each other, God.

Have you ever listened to the voice of your conscience, or your inner-conversation? You ever notice how "niggative" it is? It is pretty foul. And this sewage pours into our minds constantly, daily. Don't you know that "thought" travels in the bloodstream? It is no wonder we are so sick. God? Yet, we now want to get a hold of this thing, and begin to use Mental Advertisement to a positive effect in our lives. What do we want to do?

"We want to get a hold of this thing, and begin to use Mental Advertisement to a positive effect in our lives."

Well, what is "Mental Advertisement"? Advertisement uses the Science of Impressions repetitively. How many times a day do we think or say something negative about ourselves (or about someone who is like us, which is still ourselves)? We say negative things around the clock, constantly reinforcing the style of thinking that our enemy has implanted in us. But, how do we take his negative commercials off the airwaves of our minds, and replace them with some of our own? How do we hold our own minds, in our own hands?

Methods to use in recapturing Your Mind?

The method is simple. The method is the same. He takes forms of media to flash "sex, money, murder, greed, and immorality" into mind. He does this constantly from the moment you awaken, throughout your day, until you sleep at night. How often does he flash his mental advertisements, in the home and out in the streets?

To combat this onslaught, we must meet this force with an equal, opposite, and greater force of The Positiveness. The Positiveness, is that which encourages and inspires you toward "the goodness" and "the Godness". (Peace of your mind, Productivity of your hand, Power of your divine, Purity of your heart, and a Praiseworthy legacy). This is the goal.

"Implant" positive programs into your head. "Implant" positive music into your head. "Implant" positive affirmations (wise sayings) into your head over and over and over and over, then over and over. Take books, and take tapes, and use them like flashcards. There is a war going on, for the capture of your mind. And, two things can not exist in the same place at the same time. Put one in, and push one out.

As you constantly pour this affirming-positivity into your system, you will find yourself growing with an immunity to the negative environments around you...an emanating resilience. Yes, you will. Patiently and persistently, you will see.

And even the words of your own mouth, must be freshened. The language of your speech, may have been stale and sourly negative. But I'm telling you, your "own words" resonate around your "own brain", more than they do anyone else. The bone of your skull, carries that vibration like echoes, deep into your fiber. You cursing somebody else, and end up cursing yourself.

A "curse" is not just in a word; a "curse" is in the vibratory energy that <u>spits</u> the word. That means the voice, and the intent of that voice. <u>There</u>, is the actual "curse". *(For more insight, read the chapter entitled 'Idle-Chatter' in the book "12-Lessons to restore the Goddess Blackwoman".)*

Everytime you casually make a negative statement to yourself or someone else. Stop it...and re-state your statement positively. Break the habit, and say it over. Correct your "inner thoughts" and the corresponding "outer statements". With the same power that you poisoned yourself, you can also "heal" yourself. The Voice is Powerful. In every beginning, there will always be the word. We all must change.

You are what you mentally eat. So, eat to live. A steady diet of books, tapes, affirmations, correct inner and outer speech, proper attitude, etc. Repetitively, over and over and over constantly. Maybe that is why Mr. Elijah Muhammad asked us to say prayers 5-7 times a day, in his book "Message to The Blackman"? Prayer. Meditation. Affirmation. Mental Advertisement. Hmmm...let's see.

Ummm...he said we should say something like, *"Surely I have turned myself being upright to Him whom originated the Heavens and the Earth, and I am not of the polytheists. Surely my prayer, and my sacrifice, and my life and my death are all for Allah the Lord of the Worlds; no associate has He, and of this am I commanded. And I am of those who submit. Amin."* So, if I said a prayer like this five times per day, am I "praying" or is this an affirming "mental advertisement"; or is it "one in the same"? Interesting.

In essence, I would be saying; "Assuredly, I am seeking and striving to be a righteous reflection of The Creator, and I am not of the unguided ones. For my entire life existence is for the purposes, the plans, the will, and the upliftment of The God; and

His Principles, that govern this Universe. There is no valid authority greater than this, and of this I am sternly obedient. And by this oath, I live my life."

Listen to that. Isn't that something? Imagine how much greater our lives would be, if we constantly spoke to ourselves in "that" manner. Our inner conversation would be totally different. Mental Advertisement, that's all. Interesting. Interesting.

The Human Garbage-Pail.

(Bio-logical Warfare)

As our blood becomes thick and sandy; "Warfare against your biological, will afflict your psychological." Body and mind, is "bio"- "logical".

What are we putting into our mouths? What is that? Did you know that Chemical and Biological Warfare is being waged? Did you know that you are chewing on the actual ammunition? Did you know that you were ingesting the time-bombs that have been launched at you? Did you know that you are biting-the-bullet that has been shot at you?

Well, unfortunately, that is what happens when the enemy (people that hate you), control your food-supply. He doesn't have to drop chemicals over your head, he just encapsulates it in the food you eat. Twenty-years later, cancer cells blowin-up all in your body.

As was discussed in "From Niggas to Gods Pt. 1", we saw that this so-called "Soul-food" is actually "Slave-food". And, as a result, many of us have resolved to no-longer defoul our bodies with the poisons of the pork flesh, nor the parasitic worms thereof. This is very good. This is very good. But, why is it that we are still dying? Good question. Let us grow on. Pork was just the begininning of our problems.

Modern "Slave-Food" is served for the "Modern Slaves", at the "Modern Fast-Food Restaurant". "Death to Go", but please come again.

Yet, what we want to see today is that, "Slave-food" (classic & modern) is not only a torment to the body, it is more so a torment to your "Soul". Think.

Do we know who and what we are? How often do we really remember? We are intelligence in the form of energy, called "mind". "Mind" exercises through, and emanates itself around the earthly encasement called "body". When "mind" chooses to function and implement it's will on this earthly plane(t), it uses "body" as it's tool to do so.

"Body" is a bio-suit, made up of earthly elements. It is a housing, a vehicle of expression, and a covering to what you are.

Yet, the point here is this. Not only is "body" a "covering" to what you are, "body" is literally a "lens" to what everything else is.

Your Body is the lens through which the intelligence of your energy, perceives reality on this plane. All of this is via sensory perception. And your sensory perception is heightened or lessened to the degree that your body lets it be.

Yes, and if you limit the healthiness of your body, you will definitely limit the healthiness of your mind, therefore your vision. Their "potential" and "development" travels hand and hand. God still stands on two legs. Dualities rule the Universe. Some of our ancestors called it the Ma'atic Balance.

As long as your energy is in your body, you are subjected to its' limits; the limits you place on it. Spirit + Matter still equals Life. You are only supposed to die, when your spirit wears out your body, not the other way around.

A lot of our diets, are the equivalent to dumping dirty mud on our brains; packing on the wastes. The processed chemicals, the dead-animal carcasses create toxicity in all the organs; leaving the body clogged as a toxic waste dump. This shuts down the function and potential of the Mind. Leaving the intellect in a heavy-stooper. Killing the light of the soul.

It all adds up. The condition of your body, "will" effect the condition of your mind, therefore the quality of your life performance. Bio-logical warfare.

As our blood becomes thick and sandy...It would be in our good interest, to defend against this cooperative assault. You volunteer for the destruction everyday with your own teeth. But, you can stop. You can stop today.

There is information on the proper holistic nutrition of the Blackman & Blackwoman available, abundantly. Seek it out.

The Master &
The Student.

(The Journey of This Life)

The Journey of This Life is much like the relationship between The Master & The Student (of Martial Arts). Complex problems are placed before you; Seemingly impossible obstacle courses are laid before you; and the very Master of whom you beseech for help will slam you down to the ground by way of your weaknesses, until your weaknesses become strengths.

Spiritual Arts and Martial Arts, work much the same. One is Mastery of Mind, the other Mastery of Body...in the control and use of it.

The most prized students are assaulted the most, as they advance on the path. The Master will put the prized student on the path, and then will send the others to knock him off. Cruel it seems, but necessary for the conditioning of the student towards Mastery. For what is a Master, who has had to master nothing to proclaim his mastery? He is no Master at all.

Your Spiritual Obstacle Course is Life itself. While on the path, he sends some to inflict wounds, and he sends some to ad-minister to your wounds, while you must learn to know the difference between the two; lest you receive your enemies and beat-up your helpers. This is most often the case. Other times he will send no one at all but desolation, which can be a wound within itself; leaving only yourself to assault you, and yourself to heal you.

He sends test after trial after test after trial. And if you are fortunate, what you are left with is lesson. After mastering each level, you advance to the next elevated place. At each doorway you are given a different color belt or sash to tie your garment. Pretty soon, none can touch your garment. You start from a white-belt on through stages until you achieve a black-belt. You start from the absence of color on to the manifestation of all color at one time. At each stage, the color of your tie gets darker and darker, as you master each realm of life; with the last colors being contained in the next color to be achieved.

This signifies the unfoldment of Knowledge of Self. The young student first stood with an absence of knowledge to tie his garment, now he stands with all knowledge. The student was a Master all of the time. Yet, life had to give him that knowledge of Self. He struggled and searched all this time, only to obtain Himself. And his treasure is greater than he ever imagined.

Real Blackmen Cry.

(Humility precedes all Growth, all change.)

Real Blackmen cry. If you can look at the condition of self, your people, and this world...and not cry, something is wrong with you. The strongest man alive, would be the first one to cry. The saviour, wept. The saviour, weeps.

Humanity is immersed in pain. Each individual soul in a solitary desolate ache, quietly suffering unto its' self...trying to live the lie, the facade, the game. But, that soul is far from rest, far from peace. If that soul were truly honest unto itself, it would cry. It would just give in, it would just cry.

Little does the world know, the key to it's salvation. Little does the world know...that all God-Allah is waiting on to save us, is for the world to cry...just give-in and cry. Allah comes in when all else fails. And when the world falls helplessly to it's knees, it is only then that we are open for the guidance and reality of God. Why? Because "humility" now exists, where hard "arrogance" once stood and thrived.

Allah comes in when all else fails. Hard-hearts? He can not help you, until you perpetrate your total destruction. Only then will a "hard-heart", sincerely call out His name. Hard-hearts. God can only help you, when you give-in and give-up helplessly. If you don't give in, He will punk you eventually. It is a shame that a man has to be "humiliated", when he very simply could have just "decided" to humble his own self, to truth. You ran up against God, and broke yourself. Give in to His Guidance, His Way. Only then can "He" show you how to do what you need to do in this life.

He is called "The Best Knower". But "we" think we know better. We have one-gram of intelligence, and six-tons of arrogant foolishness, but we think we know better about how to live life, than "He" who created life; and created "you" in the midst of it. This is why we die. This is why we hurt.

We don't want to give up our little thinking power, to unify with The All-Seeing Power. Man could have sight, if only he gave up his eyes.

We refuse "His" guidance, and then curse Him for our misfortune. No, you are not obedient. Arrogance is so blinding, it makes a man pour "acid" in his own wounds. It makes a man "attack" his own healer, his own saviour. Little do we reflect. Little do we actually know.

You can not be saved until you posture yourself, savable. You are not savable until you have been humbled and stilled...then the healer can heal. The surgeon can work, on a body at rest. Humility puts pride to sleep. And it is this false pride, that defeats and deceives mortal man. But the massive strength of "honesty", makes man cry. He may cry for days connected.

And when the waters flow, he releases the pain of years. Years unspoken. The strength of honesty pours through his soul, washes over his heart, and drains down his tired eyes. It takes a strong Blackman to cry. It takes an honest soul to die...to die unto it's pride. Allah can only come in, when you admit that your own hands, have failed you.

The entire world must cry, in order to live. To cry, is to

repent. To cry, is to cleanse. To cry, is to admit. To cry is to confess. The world must cry.

All that is left, is shame...humility...surrender. There is Principle, in humility. There is Character, in humility. And, in this, He forgives all. He is merciful to this. He is beneficent, to an honest soul.

This has always been about love. Love from Him, to you. The whole thing. Just love. His whole purpose for coming, is to love "you", if you give Him a way into your hard-heart. He will change your life, if you let Him...if you let Him...if you let Him! Damn,...if you get yourself out of the way and let Him! Sit down somewhere! Cry! Cry! Cry...with your little proud hardened-heart! Break-down and cry, and admit that you already "broke-down"! That is the only way he can build you up into a greater creation! Do you understand that???

Resurrection can only come to those who have the courage to lie still and die! Die to your old-form! Let go! Let go! Cry! Cry! And then willingly die. Die, to that old "nigga" you! And be born into a new "God-you" that you never knew! He will exalt you unto the mastery of Himself, if you but shut-up and hold still. He doesn't owe you nothing, but he will give to you anyway, if you let Him.

You must die. You must cry. And you will live all over again...a new creation. Cry Blackman, cry.

God Crushed to The Earth, Shall Rise Again.

(Buoyancy of Heart.)

This is a message to the righteous and pure at heart. If you know that is not you, and you do, then go on. Go.

Dear righteous, and the pure at heart:

During our time here, we may fall amongst devils; (...devils, as the ones who are adding to their guilt, by reading this). We may fall amongst thieves, we may fall amongst liars. But, I want you to personally know, that in your heart is a built-in mechanism to deliver you from the evil of those around you. I want you to know that your heart itself, is your life-preserver.

This is your day. This is your day, and there are changes going on. The "mind energy", "mind clarity" and "power to rule" is being transferred today. That power is being transferred from the wicked at heart, to the righteous at heart. It is being transferred by the dawning presence of a Mastermind, who is master of requital, ushering the new day forward. It takes time, for the Sun to rise, but this "is" your day. It belongs to you. Claim it. Know it, and claim it.

The time of the rule of the wicked is expired, and their energy is gradually being confiscated, their abilities frustrated. Yet, as devils descend from power, and as you ascend, you may fall among their hands unknowingly. They will sometimes see your growing power budding it's glow, as you do not see anything at all. And, Light attracts pests.

Since he is an anti-christ by nature (a killer of God's people), he or she can't help themselves. Their entire presence is to murder your growing energy. These, will see you ascending, and they will pounce on you (consciously or unconsciously), wanting what you have...wanting what they are now being justly starved of, as the Master of Requital dries-up power in their bellies.

You are indeed growing children of God, still hidden in the womb; and these are abortionists in the worse sense. They seek not your flesh, but rather to kill your mind, your spirit. Give them not access to the alchemy of your brains.

In our fetal-stages though, we are sometimes seemingly helpless to these would-be abortionists...not yet strong or developed enough to defend. But rest your weariness, we have a Defender. Rest your weariness.

Budding Child of God, they seek you...but they can never have you. You can never die, I want you to know. Your nature exonerates you to their ill aggress.

Budding Child of God, you may fall amongst them. And they may fall heavy on you...but don't despair. Rest your weariness. These spirit killers and mind snuffers, may take your young heart into their manipulative hands. They may attack you and pull you down to the depths of the sea. Down, down, down, down, down, deep-down to the bottom earth of the ocean. Length by length, you may lose consciousness, totally blacking out at the sea floor. But, rest. Rest, in your helplessness.

As you lay, pinned under the weight of the criminal, know that they have only drowned themselves. There is a difference between "unconsciousness" and "total-death". When you are made to appear dead, they will try to swim on to their next victim. But, their attempt will be in vain. Others of you, may have been strong enough to fight but not victor; while some may have been strong enough to victor at the very end. But once, the criminal is defeated; and it's weight is cast off of you, you will rise. You Will Rise.

Although you lay cut, bruised, bloodied, and unconscious at the oceans's floor you will rise.

The heart in your chest will float you, just as the hardened-rock-heart of the wicked will surely sink them dead in the water. Dead. Dead. Dead. Justly, dead. It would have been better for them, if they would had just left you alone.

They can not imitate, nor decimate. They will reach their fate, in this end. Burning at the bottom of the sea.

Rest your weariness. Your body will rise. As the heart of stone is heavy, your heart of light, IS, LIGHT...as a feather...tumbling, floatin on air. Budding Child of God, your heart has the buoyancy of a million ships...never sinks, never dies. Temporary storms, but never dies.

Your only hope is your heart; it is the heart of your Father. You are just another angel unaware. You don't know you yet, but rest your weariness. Rest your arms and hold still. Let it float you to the top. And when you reach the surface, you will breathe again. Beaten and torn, but you will breathe again...the victor in the end...you will breathe again.

Don't doubt it. Know that you are the righteous. And never speak of (you) the Righteous as being dead; for the contents of God are Eternal. Eternal.

God Crushed to the Earth shall rise again! "Your weaknesses have now become your strengths". God Crushed to

the Earth shall Rise Again, and Again, and Again, and Again!!!
Congratulations...you are the Victorious. You are the victorious.

> Peace.
> I love You, as I love myself.
> You are the true soldier...the
> righteous at heart.

It is Sin to feel sorry for The Wicked.

(The Execution of Judgement.)

A day fast coming. A day fast coming. A day already here. Allah is The Justest of Judges. Who are we to anguish, at the punishment of the unjust, the wrongdoers? This is another message to the Righteous.

To The Righteous and Pure at Heart:

Many days and nights we have prayed, calling out for and end to our pain, an end to our suffering. Our request was heard and accepted. But, when our call is answered, are we ready for the remedy?

The day of Judgement is otherwise known as The day of Separation. Not, only will there be a separation of ways and lifestyles, but there will ultimately be a separation of people. This not only means a separation of Nations, but this separation process may start right in your home.

When you call out for an ending to your pain, He will root-out "the source" of your pain. And, the source of your pain may be someone you "think" you love, or rather someone you "want" to love.

When you cry out to God to destroy evil in your life, God

will not be swinging at "spirits". God will be swinging at "people". "People" who are the embodiment of that evil presence in your life, will be "hit" hard.

And as most swine, devils, demons, and the like...they will "squeal and cry" out to you, attempting to pull on your naive mercy. They want to lure you closer; that you may unlock the flaming-pit that God has justly cast them into.

Foolishly, all too often, we let them free. And they burn us all over again and again and again and again. Is that true?

Listen now. I know that it is painful to a righteous heart to see other people suffering! I know! But when the wicked burn for their wickedness, let them Burn!!! You have to hold your ground! Let the dead be dead, until "He" chooses to lift them up! If He chooses at all! Let those who have killed the spirit of so many, now taste their own torment.

I know you have the heart of a saviour, but if you have not the intelligent-will to save your "own" heart, then you are just as dead as the dead! To intercede on behalf of the wicked is disobedience to God. To intercede on behalf of the wicked is disobedience to God. Once they have heard the truth and the way, and "they choose" to turn their hearts hard against it, let them fall in the heaviness of their own foulness. Let them hit the ground hard. "He" guides whom "He" pleases.

I said, "He" guides whom "He" pleases. Some of these people that you are trying to save, you don't know who they are. You don't know what they keep hidden in their hearts, boiling up under their chests! But The Supreme Mind knows! He knows the "liar" from the "truthful". You walk with devils everyday, unknowingly. And, five years later, you find out what God knew all the time. So, when He snatches one down from your presence, don't question it. Let God be God, and go on. Go on.

You don't know what kind of pain these people would have brought into your life, and don't need to know. But, when you pray for protection against evil, let his security force work. When you pray to be delivered from evil, let Him deliver you. And let Him deliver your Enemies to the fire, whomever they may be. Do not interfere, lest you hasten your own destruction.

Do you arrogantly think you know better than He? Huh? You think you know best, don't you? You say with your mouth that "He is the best Knower", but you keep putting your own thinking above "His". I know she is your mother, he is your father, she is your sister, he is your brother, he is your husband, and she is your wife. But, this is your life! And if you love another, greater than you love yourself, you are outside the way of God.

In fact God angrily hates this type of behavior, because you have put a God besides He. Polytheism. He will destroy your forged God. And He will destroy "you", if you have something to say about it. He is The Justest of Judges.

On the day of Judgement, families will not be determined by genetics. Families will be gathered together by a kindred of mind, heart, spirit, and soul. You must be of Your Father, and they must be of theirs.

Only the wicked hurt to see the wicked hurt! Not, because they care, but because they know that they are next in line. So, what are you so bothered for, to see the punishment of their evil? Huh? You just "did not want to believe" that they were evil, I know. I know. But, all the believing that you did for them, did not stop them one bit from all the hell-raising they did. Now, did it? Call a spade a spade, a devil a devil, a destructor a destructor. You can not be partial lovers of the truth. The truth is full circle. The truth is the truth. Blatant.

Why would you want to ignore their behavior? Huh? What if God ignored your behavior? Huh? You are affirmed the righteous, only because of your righteous deeds. So, if God would ignore your righteous deeds, as you want Him to ignore their wicked deeds....you might be killed along with them. Then you would say that God was unjust to you...right? God would be unjust for not differentiating between "you" and "them", right? But, if you don't differentiate yourself, why should He?

If you want Him to see you for "your righteous conduct", shut-up; and let Him <u>also see them</u> for "their wicked conduct". Just, shut your mouth, turn-around, walk away, and stay away.

It is a sin to feel sorry for the wicked, when they justly burn.

> To Heaven with The Righteous,
> and to hell with the wicked.

Introduction to:

The God-Father.

(A Reality in Your Midst)

Divine Protection. As the reality of the devil becomes more and more apparent to you, you will know that you need a Mighty God. Not a formless spirit, but a Man/Mind in whom the spirit dwells. Let His reality be known to you.

Divine Protection. A killer sits on the sidelines watching the children play.; Allah God, The Killer. The totality of this devil "you" can not handle. So, who will? I have been saying over and over that you are Gods and Goddesses but "children" of The Most High...The God Father...The Father God.

Let the wars begin. Who is in control of the Planet? Answer. Now, who "thinks" that they are in control of the Planet? Answer. Who is planning a destruction for the righteous? Answer. Now, who has planned a destruction for the ones who plan destruction against the righteous? Answer.

There is a fight, a battle, a war going on. I am just trying to persuade us to get on the right side, because I know who will be killed in the end.

The God Father has put a "hit" out on your enemy...and this the enemy knows. Stock markets crash, lightening bolts flash, a storm constantly rages, disasters all across the headline pages, but who has ordered this wrath? Who is caught in the crosshairs of the path?

We are familiarized with the might and power of the god

of this world, your devil. He has been allowed to master all that we see. His power is evident. But has this little god mastered "The Master", the reality that we are not tuned-up enough to see? Such has not been allowed. Yet as we study the powers of this little god, we can get an idea of the powers of The Big God, The Master, The God Father.

As we lay mentally asleep during our cycle, did we place a guard at the door? Did we put the whole 100% of our people to sleep, or did we leave a hidden 5% to keep watch on the planet as we rest. As this young child took stewardship over the globe, did we leave at least a few of us awake to make sure that his devilishment didn't totally destroy the world? Good Questions. God Questions.

I said "If this little god can put war planes in the sky, what can The Big God do?".

I said "If this little god can control the brains of your mind, what can The Big God do?"

I said "If this little god can make weather conditions in his little controlled environments, what can The Big God do?"

Do you know your God Father? He is 95% more God-Power than the best of your little grafted gods of temporary purposes. What he has, he was given by Your Own Kind for an appointed time.

There is a Reality in Your Midst. The God Father. His planes must be dreadful, 95% more crafted. Is there a God of Power in there somewhere? Have we seen the arm of God? Has he flexed the power of his mind to be evident to his child?

The little god is a powerful god, yes...wickedly so. He is more powerful than most of us can remember. We see a man who has blasted his mechanical structures out into space, placing giant satellites appearing to revolve in an orbit around the earth. His science allowed him to command his mechanical structure to rotate on an axis. Yes, he is a powerful man.

Yet, where is the Man who blasted that other satellite out into space that revolves in an orbit around the earth?...that giant satelite called "moon"? What Man made this powerful construction so strong that it magnetically pulls on the waters of Earth, waters of Man, waters of Woman? Whose mechanical structure is this? What Man is God-Father?

This little god is a powerful god, yes...wickedly so. He is more powerful than most of us can remember. We see a man who has filled the air with radio waves of electric, sending intelligible messages from component to component. Sound and pictures condensed, travel through the air at his will to be perceived by another mind on the other side of the planet. Even nowadays he sends his messages fiber-optically through directed light! Yes, he is a powerful man.

Yet, where is the Man who originated radio-waves in the air, on frequencies that only the trained mind can attune to? Who is The Man who can take His brain/mind, and send out an intelligible communicative transmission to another brain/mind clear of outside mortal-man-made components? Who is He? Who is The One who sends Revelation from on High? And how does He do it? If you, or a prophet, or a prophetess, has received a transmission of picture and sound in your mind as you sleep, who sent it? And how did He send it? You call it dream or vision. Some of you call it up from your own mind, and some visions are sent to you from another Mind, that you do not see? Some receive waking-dreams, while most can only receive visions during sleep as their disbelief rests. Can God transmit sound and pictures through "Optic-Light"? What Man is God-Father?

This little god is a powerful god, yes...wickedly so. He is more powerful than most of us can remember. You have seen him at war times. You have seen him take his giant military planes, pack them full of tanks, trucks, jeeps, helicopters, living quarters, generators, mass food supplies, weapons, ammunitions, and troops and troops of men and women...all of this to set up a city-like base on a foreign land to prepare for battle.

So, I'm asking you can another Man...The Man...Can another Man design, and create a massive Plane that carries a city in the sky??? Can an entire city hover 40 miles into the sky? Is it scientifically and mechanically possible for the mind of a Man who has harnessed 100% of His Brain Power to create such a Plane? That is what I want to know from you? Answer me? What are you standing on...a plane(t)? I said what Man is God-Father? You believe in this little god, but can you perceivably conceive of one bigger?

Who has The Power? God has The Power? Who is God? I said, what Man is God-Father? You had better find Him, and hold him close. Attach your mind to His mind, like a baby on a nipple. He is your only chance at survival.

Understanding will be
opened to the Faithful,
the studious.

Elijah Muhammad Is a Scientist You don't Understand.

(Master of Cause & Effect)

It is no secret here, that what I am sharing is inspired by the teachings of The Honorable Elijah Muhammad. That is no secret. You remember the last chapter of "From Niggas to Gods Pt. 1" as being about him, and it was entitled "The Messenger Came, but did we Get The Message?". Yes, the Messenger came, but did we get the Message? Did we understand? That is the question. Do we ever understand? Whenever a messenger comes do we ever get the message? That is the question.

The Jesus of 2000 years ago came, and some of us still can't hear what the man was actually saying. The Muhammad of 1400 years ago came, and some us still can't hear what the man was actually saying. Thousands of years to seek understanding, but a rebellious soul is still a rebellious soul...making it's own self deaf to wisdom.

It seems as if some of our ears just are not calibrated to

hear such spiritual things? Two persons looking at the same thing, one person sees one thing, the other person is determined to see another. One man sees from above, the other man is looking from beneath. One man sees the interior, the other only the exterior. It all depends upon where your eye is on the vertical plane, on top of your vertebrae, or beneath it. Is our heart clean enough to see through it's lens clearly? Or is it obstructed by the niggardliness of our own thinking?

Yes, the Messenger came, but did we get the Message? I'm not talking about the Messenger to the peoples of Palestine, or the Messenger to the peoples of Arabia, or the Messenger to the peoples of Japan, India, China, or even Quetzucuoatl in Mexico. No, not them.

I'm talking about the one who came with a strange message to YOU...a message to the Blackman...a message to the Blackman and Blackwoman in America. The one who had to have the courage to stand up and deliver a "strange" message to the fearful self-hating black peoples in this land. Did you receive "your" strange message, from "your" messenger?

The word "strange" describes that which is different from the normal or usual. Time and time and time again it is the same scenario. As, whenever a Messenger first comes to a people, he and his message are always seen as "strange". Yet, this "strangeness" is a very good thing. "Strange" is good. This is because...why would God send you a messenger to teach you of the same "familiar" things that you were already comfortably doing and thinking? What kind of sense would that make? You wouldn't need a Messenger then. God comes to "reform" you, and to bring you that which is currently "strange" to you. But arrogance and prejudice, prevents us from seeing this.

Logic should tell us that, in order to produce a different kind of "behavior" amongst people, you have to start with producing a different kind of "thinking" amongst people, which starts with a different kind of "teaching amongst the people, which comes from a different kind of "teacher" amongst the people. Different means that which is "strange", unusual.

God is trying to <u>change</u> your condition, not <u>reinforce</u> what you already are. Get the point. So, of course your Messenger is going to be "<u>strange</u>" to you.

If you want to stay a slave, then you keep drinking in the "same", slave teachings. If you want to be a free Man or Woman, then you begin to drink in, a type of drink that is "strange" to the slave...an unusual drink that is causing other Men and Women to drop their mental chains of slavery...a drink that is strange to the taste.

We say, "but I just don't agree with everything he says". Of course you don't! Sometimes we get real silly in our heads...thinking that, at first, we are supposed to "agree" with everything that a teacher is teaching us. How silly we are. If we already "agreed" with everything a teacher is trying to teach us, then what need would we have for a teacher? If we already thought like the teacher thinks, then we would be the teacher ourselves! A teacher's job is to acquaint a student to a knowledge, that was formerly <u>unknown</u>, <u>foreign</u>, and <u>strange</u> to that student. Is that right? I said, is that right?

Of course you disagree, but the real question should be "do you understand that which you think you disagree with?". Here we are...ain't got a bit of sense, but always jumping up talking about what we disagree with. Blackfolks.

But as soon as somebody tries to give us some sense...hastily, prematurely, and arrogantly we judge that which we have not even attempted to understand in the least. This type of attitude is the requirement for failure over and over again...producing no growth, no change, no understanding. <u>Isn't this how all of the Messengers of God were first treated, when</u>

they came to help their own people?

Just think about this. Mocked, scorned, ridiculed, rejected, and misunderstood...he came to his own, and his own received him not. But he stood up anyway; trying to serve a people that did not want to be served. Yes, the messenger came, but did we get the message?

He stood up in the 1930's preaching about the fall of America. Stop, and imagine that time...being a blackman preaching about the fall of America? And here we are today with America falling-in all around us. No one could have imagined that to be a possibility in 1934, but look around today.

It's strange within itself, how no one wants to take a look at <u>what</u> the man was saying, at <u>when</u> he was saying it, at <u>why</u> he was saying it, at <u>how</u> he was saying it, and <u>to whom</u> he was actually saying it. He knew that Blackfolks didn't have the sense enough to heed his word yet; he was talking to the face of Your Slavemaster. The wise know this. You just don't know how many white people wished that Elijah Muhammad was a whiteman, so that they could follow him. Whitefolks got sense, it is just us that don't know any better. If Elijah Muhammad was a whiteman, he would have been the second-coming of Christ, Moses, Muhammad, Abraham, and Buddha! But, since he is a blackman...since he is a blackman...well, you know the rest. It is sickening.

He foretold the days that we are living in right now, years before now. But nobody wants to acknowledge that. Strange? He wrote his books "Message to The Blackman", "The Fall of America", "Our Saviour Has Arrived", "How to Eat to Live I & II", and his teachings become more relevant as each year passes. But it is as if we are trying to do every and anything, but acknowledge his teachings. Strange, isn't it?

There is no Human Being who does not know the truth

when he or she hears it. Yet, we all choose one of three reactions to it. We will either excitedly accept it, act like we didn't hear anything at all, or vehemently refuse it! But all three reactions are because we know it is truth, in our hearts. If it wasn't the truth, we wouldn't be so passionately offended, defensive, and hostile. If it wasn't truth, we just would not care at all. But since we know it is truth in our hearts, we bring a strong fight up against that which we feel warrants a strong fight; attacking what we fear. It is really a deep and abiding honor and respect. Contenders only seek to contend against that which they perceive to be champion.

Human behavior is strange. Personally, I remember...as I began to learn more about the plight of our people, and evolve in conciousness, I met many people. I met many people from different segments of our community, conscious and not. And in every circle, I met so many people whose whole existence it seemed, was to prove Elijah Muhammad wrong. I mean, I have actually met people whose entire religious theology is "I disagree with Elijah Muhammad". Strange, but it's true. That is pretty sad.

I wondered to myself, why do so many people hate this man so? Why are people running from this man so? Who is this man? The irony is that, it was all of these different person's hate for him and his teachings, that caused me to take a deeper look and interest. That deeper look caused me to find something that everyone was trying to keep me from finding. I found the truth. God, I didn't know truth was such a crime. Nor, did I know that truth was so hated. I guess I gave people too much credit, thinking they were more honest than they actually were. Pretty naive, I was. I guess I just didn't want to believe that so many people were so bent, for whatever reasons. This is a sad world, we are living in...you know?

Anyway, with all of that said, I am just trying to

encourage us to take another look at the instructions, principles, and teachings that Elijah Muhammad. His writings, lectures, and legacy are pretty well preserved for our study, if we are so inclined. I encourage us to critically think and reason with what he has said, instead of being intellectual cowards, afraid to think and reason...afraid we may lose what we thought we already knew. The day you refuse to increase your understanding of life, is the day you choose to mentally die. Fear does that, but you don't have to be afraid. This is yours.

I truly think he has something very positive to offer us; a guidance for the unguided. Try taking another look, deeper, inquisitively, and free from all learned prejudices and slander. See, what you come up with for yourself. You may be surprised. Yes, "The Messenger came, but did we get The Message?" Well, do we ever?

Holy Quran (Chapter 2-verse 87)

87 "And We indeed gave Moses the Book and We sent messengers after him one after another; and We gave Jesus, son of Mary, clear arguments and strengthened him with the Holy Spirit. Is it then that whenever there came to you a messenger with what your souls desired not, you were arrogant? And some you gave the lie to and others you would slay."

May the Light of Understanding be with you Always.

The Love of
The Flag
of Islam

(The Black Family)

Have you seen the Flag of Islam? Sun, Moon, and Star. Man, Woman, and Child. Such is a sign for those who are mindful.

The Woman rests securely, in the warm glowing Light of Her Man, as she cradles the star gently nestled unto her embrace, nursing the strength that will transform it's starlight into the fullness of Sunlight at maturity.

Sun embracing Crescent Moon, and Crescent Moon embraces Star. Man embracing Woman, as Woman embraces child, who will grow to embrace them all again. One takes care of the other in a continuous cycle, of Universe. The Flag of the Universe.

The Flag of the Universe, represents the Love of the Black Family. Sun, Moon, and Stars. Embrace to embrace to embrace. In each other we are made secure. There is no mystery god. We are the real components of that love, Our God. There, is the loving togetherness of one another resting securely. Black Family puts the pieces of God together again. Our Flag is rising...rising again.

A Blackman's Prayer

(The Opening...into new life.)

In The Name of Allah,
The Truly Beneficent, The Truly Merciful.
My Praises be to Allah, The Lord of The Worlds.

The Beneficent, Merciful, Master of This Day of Judgement.
Thee Do I Gladly Serve, and Thee Do I Beseech for Help.

Please Guide and Grow us on The Right Path.
The Path of Those upon whom is Your Favor of Success,
and not The Path of Those upon whom
is Your Wrath of Chastisement,
nor of Those who Go Astray.

Oh Allah,
Please hear my prayer in sincerity.
In Love, in Peace...let it Be.
Amen.

I Love You with all My Heart:
A Closing Word

Brother and Sister, I just wanted to say a few words here. I know that the words may have been a bit harsh, here and there. But, I pray God makes you to know that it is all love. I am concerned and deeply disheartened with the direction we have been led, as a people. I strive that you and I may find something within these words to inspire us to do better, to do right, to do excellence. You and I are so much more than what we think we are.

Hoping that you have received something here of good, I only wish you well. The messages I have expressed here...I sincerely believe them to be good for our overall well being. I do. I am not interested in encouraging you towards anything other than that which is good and wholesome for you...toward the appreciation and love of self and family. I know that this is the only thing that will make you happy and fulfilled.

Why do I want this for you? Well, because I want it for myself. I can't be totally fulfilled and happy if (you) my family is not. No, I can't sleep at night. And maybe I kind of sort of... just a little bit...maybe I might love or care for you...just a little bit. Okay? Is there anything wrong with that?

You know, we are all kind of interconnected. That's what they say. Underneath all of this everyday madness that we live here, we care about one another. Yes, you do. I mean, you get on my nerves, and you make me absolutely sick at times but you know...I care. Yeah, I gots love for you. Just a little bit now. Okay?

Well, I don't know...maybe I care a whole lot. I suppose. I just realized that I have put aside my own dreams and aspirations in life, to contribute to the needs of my peers. I've just realized that I have made a sacrifice of some of the best years of my young life. I wasn't paying attention. But, if I had it to do all over again, I don't think I would have done it too much different. Maybe this here is my dreams and aspirations...to inspire a better life amongst us. But, there is so much more work to do.

These resurrection processes can be painful...to the "ressurector" and the "ressurectee". They both are you. But this is what it takes for us to live again. So, submit yourself to the cleansing process. There is light on the other side of this situation, like you have never known.

Some of us were born so painfully deep down into the graves of death, we don't even know that there is a such thing called life. So, for those of us who were born up a little bit further, it is up to us to be a shining example to those who travel behind us...letting them know that there is indeed the possibility of life and light ahead. Keep looking. Keep walking. Somebody in front of me please grab my hand, as I grab the hand of the one behind me. We are going to make it through this thing. Allright? Allright. Much love.

Sincerely,
Mr. Akil
Striving to Civilize Self & People

G r a t i t u d e :

• First Thanks be to The Supreme, from whom all blessings flow.

• Peace to "<u>all</u>" the Righteous, striving in His way. You know who you are.

• All love to the whole Hip-Hop Nation...East to the West and All in between.

> *"Progressions can't be made, if we separate forever."*
> Q-Tip *(September 1991)*

• Eternal Respect to The Two Million Man Marchers. "You shook the world, Blackman!!!" This is just the beginning!

• And thanks to "you", the reader especially...for having the courage to seek a higher way for yourself. Unfortunately, you are rare in this world. But, you are a very valuable type of person. Every improvement you strive to make in your life, will be an improvement to the life of us all. Thank "you". And thank "you" for your heart. Stay striving. We have "survived", now let us "succeed".

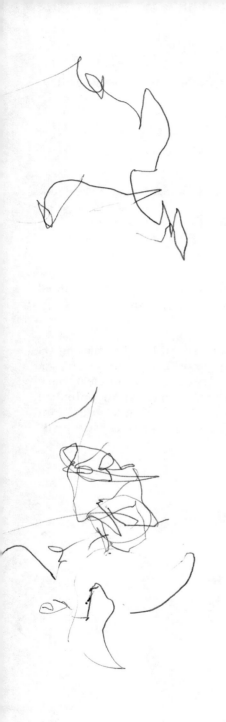